Nan E. Johnson

RURAL
HEALTH CARE

RURAL HEALTH CARE

Innovation in a Changing Environment

EDITED BY LaVonne A. Straub
and Norman Walzer

FOREWORD BY Robert T. Van Hook

PRAEGER

Westport, Connecticut
London

Library of Congress Cataloging-in-Publication Data

Rural health care : innovation in a changing environment / edited by
  LaVonne A. Straub and Norman Walzer. Foreword by Robert T.
  Van Hook
      p.   cm.
   Includes bibliographical references and index.
   ISBN 0–275–94315–1 (alk. paper)
   1. Rural health services. I. Straub, LaVonne. II. Walzer,
Norman.
   [DNLM: 1. Hospitals, Rural—United States. 2. Rural Health—
trends—United States. WA 390 R9483]
   RA771.R88   1992
   362.1′0425—dc20
   DNLM/DLC
   for Library of Congress   92–11921

British Library Cataloguing in Publication Data is available.

Library of Congress Catalog Card Number: 92–11921
ISBN: 0–275–94315–1

First published in 1992

Praeger Publishers, 88 Post Road West, Westport, CT 06881
An imprint of Greenwood Publishing Group, Inc.

Printed in the United States of America

The paper used in this book complies with the Permanent
Paper Standard issued by the National Information Standards
Organization (Z39.48—1984).

10 9 8 7 6 5 4 3 2 1

Contents

Tables

Foreword

"May you live in interesting times," states an old Arabic curse. Without question the 1980s were interesting times for rural health care. It was an era of unprecedented change. In fact, change became the constant in the rural health care equation. The changes in the 1980s involved a radical reordering of nearly every part of the system: financing, technology, patient utilization, and providers' practice and supplies.

The 1980s marked the end of cost-based reimbursement for discrete services, and the implementation of a payment system based on prospective pricing for bundled hospital services. In 1983, Medicare implemented its Prospective Payment System (PPS), which was based on the "law of large numbers," i.e., a hospital with enough cases, over time, will have costs that will approximate payments. Many rural hospitals did not have large numbers and hence lost money on their major source of payment.

Medical technology has become increasingly expensive and complex. During the 1980s, much of the new technology was financially beyond the reach of rural hospitals strapped with fixed price reimbursement and declining patient volume. Many rural hospitals were unable to finance large capital expenditures, often not even necessary equipment replacement or facility renovations were possible. This made it difficult for them to compete in the acute care marketplace because rural patients have the same, often misguided demands for high technology care as their urban neighbors.

Both payment systems changes and technology changes contributed to a precipitous decline in rural hospital admissions during the 1980s. Perhaps the most important factor, however, was the shift in medical practice patterns away from inpatient care to outpatient services. Doctors quit hospitalizing for "social" causes, such as keeping Grandma in the hospital because she didn't have transportation home. Also, the increasing specialization of medicine and the centralization of technology attracted patients from rural communities to urban specialty centers. Declines in utilization began even before the advent of PPS, but were accelerated in the mid–1980s as the payment system impact was felt.

The general economies of rural communities also experienced difficulty during the 1980s. The "farm crisis" of the early 1980s was followed by the "rural economic crisis" of the middle part of the decade, and it is increasingly apparent that the economic problems of rural communities are not a "crisis" at all, but a chronic and continued reshaping of the way business is conducted in this country. Economic problems brought more unemployment and underemployment, resulting in more uncompensated care for rural providers as the numbers of uninsured patients increased. Declining rural business also resulted in a less-than-adequate tax base in many communities, making decisions about tax support for rural health care more difficult.

The 1980s also brought continuing shortages of health professionals including nursing, medicine, and nearly all varieties of therapists, proving once again the bankruptcy of trickle-down distributive theories. Physician-to-population ratios in rural areas continue to be much lower than in urban communities, especially for primary-care physicians. Because of the small numbers of health professionals in most rural communities, small changes in those numbers can mean the difference between an adequate supply and a serious shortage.

The immediate reactions to these changes have been both dramatic and erratic. During the 1980s, more than 250 rural hospitals closed, and the trend line was markedly up during the last half of the decade. Some of the closings were justified, but the essential issues, including which hospitals will close, who will make the closure decisions, and, what services will be left in the community after closure of the hospital, are being resolved by a patently imperfect health-care market.

Another, more positive, response to these problems is that rural hospitals have increasingly linked with other rural hospitals or with urban hospitals, to obtain specialty services and technology for their communities. Voluntary networks and consortia are present throughout the country, and they represent an increasing, though often irrational, move toward regionalization of services. A few of these networking activities have been supported by private foundations like the Robert Wood Johnson Foundation's Hospital-Based Rural Health Care Program, but most are home-grown responses to regional needs.

In response to the shortages of health professionals, rural communities have used employee-wanted posters, bounties, and other innovative recruitment methods. But rural communities often find they are swimming upstream against the powerful currents of payment system incentives, increasing specialization in health professionals' education, and changing life-style requirements of the professionals themselves.

Many rural communities, often spurred by the financial distress of their rural hospitals, have embarked upon communitywide health planning efforts. These activities too have sometimes been supported by private foundations, such as the W. K. Kellogg Foundation and the Northwest Area Foundation. This has demonstrated that nonhealth sectors can be legitimately and profitably involved in tailoring health services to the needs of the community.

"Interesting times" may be either a blessing or a curse, and for rural health care the 1980s certainly brought both, depending on where you were, your facility's characteristics, your ability to anticipate and adapt, and the relative well-being of your community. Long-term adaptation to the unprecedented changes that occurred in the 1980s will require a fundamental reordering of our thinking about rural health services, a paradigm shift. We need to rethink the fundamentals of rural health care in a systematic way, from the bottom up. Rural America can become a laboratory for an increasingly sensitive, caring system of community-based care, in contrast to the emphasis on overspecialized, high technology-dependent, fragmented care in metropolitan areas.

Actually, the paradigm shift is already occurring, and it is up to rural communities to recognize it. Otherwise rural health care may make the same devastating mistake as made by Swiss watchmakers in the 1960s. Prior to that time, the Swiss were the premier makers of watches in the world, with about 60 percent of the watch market. In the mid–1960s, technicians in a Swiss laboratory came up with a new kind of watch, a battery-powered digital watch. When the engineers presented their discovery to their employers, they were turned away because the watch did not have the usual mainspring, analog face, and moving parts. "How could it possibly be a watch without a mainspring?" the company's management said. The following year, the technicians took the new watch to an international watch exposition where the idea was seized upon by Texas Instruments in the United States and by Seiko in Japan. The rest is history. Today, the Swiss have less than 20 percent of the world watch market, which is dominated by digital watches from Japan.

We are beginning to see the reaction to a paradigm shift in the provision of rural health care. The new paradigm involves a shift from emphasis on "curing" models to "caring" models. It involves the analysis of rural health problems in a community context rather than in an institutional context. For example, we are moving from concern about the rural hospital, to thinking of the hospital as the community health center, to concern about community health systems, which include rural hospitals. The new rural emphasis in the area of the health professions is on generalists rather than specialists, on integrative rather than reductionist approaches to care. It is possible to foresee a rural paradigm that may more closely resemble a nursing model than a medical model. That is not to say that medicine will disappear, but it will be seen as a component in a larger, more pervasive system of interlocked service, from home-based prenatal care outreach to hospice.

Many of the articles in this volume contain evidence of this paradigm shift. Alternative rural hospital models, changing medical education methods, new means of telecommunications, and shifting public policy at the state and federal level are some of the topics explored here. Obviously, not every rural community is aware of these responses. Most rural communities, for example, are dealing with the changing health-care environment in traditional ways by trying to emulate high-tech, specialty-driven urban systems, or by taxing themselves in support of the status quo. However, if rural health is not to go the way of Swiss watches, we will need vision to develop and accept a new paradigm and leadership to get the job done.

Changes as radical as those suggested in this volume will require great leaps of faith for rural communities, health-care providers, and policymakers. George Bernard Shaw wrote in *Man and Superman*, "The reasonable man adapts himself to the world; the unreasonable one persists in trying to adapt the world to himself. Therefore, all progress depends on the unreasonable man." Rural health needs to be "unreasonable." We need to step outside the facility or provider-driven models to search for new solutions.

Finally, rural people are a minority in this country. Rural America is increasingly disadvantaged in many ways, but we are not disenfranchised. Without a vigorous advocacy voice, rural needs tend to be forgotten by public policymakers. Their neglect is not malicious; policymakers simply forget about the special needs and opportunities in rural America. Rural residents must strive for a community-based system of health care that meets the changing needs of rural people, rather than for downsized versions of urban models of medical care. Even though rural people are a minority, we should be encouraged by Margaret Mead who wrote, "Never doubt that a small group of thoughtful citizens can change the world; indeed, it is the only thing that ever has."

Robert T. Van Hook

Preface

Rural areas, across the country, did not fare well in the 1980s with economic stagnation and population outmigration commonplace in many states. This trend is part of a long-term economic transformation, which has adversely affected the rural environment. Shrinking tax bases and fiscal resources are placing considerable pressure on state and local public officials to maintain many services to which residents have become accustomed. The alternative to not maintaining basic services is to foster an even larger decline in population because of a growing disparity in quality of life between rural and more urban communities.

Health care is one of the most essential services sought by rural residents. The delivery of services has been undergoing significant changes in response to advances in medicine, cost considerations, and competition for personnel. Transportation methods have improved markedly, encouraging rural residents to seek more specialized care in large urban centers. Rural health providers are treating a higher percentage of patients whose reimbursements do not always cover costs. All of these factors have negatively affected rural health-care institutions.

The key to a successful future is to adapt local health-care institutions and delivery systems to the economic and demographic changes that have occurred, and many local areas are actively engaged in these practices. In many ways, this is an exciting era, because new technology permits substantive changes in the quality of care and in ways of serving rural residents. This book contains a selection of articles concerning trends in access to health care in rural areas and attempts to adapt to these trends through innovation.

Many persons have contributed to the preparation of this volume. The authors of various chapters were willing to work with us to tailor their presentations in such a way as to make a useful collection. Bob Kustra, lieutenant governor of the State of Illinois, provided financial support for the preparation of the papers included. Louis DiFonso, Governor's Rural Affairs Council, State of Illinois, provided insights and suggestions at various stages of the project. Nancy Baird had responsibility for preparing the manuscript for publication and was assisted by Nancy Burns. Many others assisted at various stages, and their efforts should be recognized. As usual, the editors assume responsibility for the contents of the volume.

Introduction

The 1990s is shaping up as the decade of health care—the decade in which significant departures from accepted wisdom will be debated by health-care decision makers. The 1980s brought a recognition that health-care costs were out of control, and access to the highest quality of care was not satisfactory in some areas. Many strategies, including mandated cost restraints, cost shifting, and foundation-funded community programs, have been tried and found unsuccessful in resolving the access/cost dilemma. The relatively radical idea, by traditional norms, of a national health insurance plan is now being openly proposed. At this stage, it is far from clear how all the special health interests will be served as the decade progresses; one of those interests is rural health care.

A significant result of the health-care turmoil in the 1980s is the growing attention paid to rural health care. There is a recognition that policy changes to improve the health-care system, coupled with economic and demographic movements in rural America, have left large pockets of health-care deficits. Concerned providers, community leaders, legislators, and advocates of diverse approaches promote the cause of better health-care access for those outside urban America. Their efforts have been successful in that federal and state legislators are working to ensure that residents in these areas are not without access to care.

Guaranteeing access is not an easy task, when there are many opposing forces, some of which come through the same legislative bodies. For years, the reimbursement system and medical research focus have produced economic disincentives for medical and health professionals to locate in rural areas. Advances in medical technology have sharpened the distinction between urban and rural care. Advances in communication technology have not been coordinated with medical technology and applied to rural areas, although doing so would help offset the exodus of both practitioners and patients. A persistent, narrow focus on traditional forms of care has not benefited rural areas because the population and economies cannot always support them, and innovative and creative alternatives have been slow in developing.

PURPOSE OF THE BOOK

This book presents a collection of papers, focusing on innovative approaches to alleviate the "rural health crisis." The common use of the term "crisis" indicates the severity of the problem. Innovation indicates new and different approaches; however, it is recognized that these must accommodate and work within the existing system. The chapters in this book examine the flexibility within that system and present ways in which access to health care for rural residents can be retained during this transition period, between the flux of the 1980s and what is yet to come in the 1990s.

Optimism regarding resolution of the crisis in the 1990s is founded in the substantial effort being devoted to the problem. The rural health-care funding agenda for existing programs and new initiatives fared well in recent Congressional action. For example, the National Health Service Corps was revitalized and has received increased funding. This legislation addresses one of the major access problems—too few primary-care physicians and health-care professionals in rural practice.

Hospitals should also benefit from a phasing out, by Congress, of the urban-rural differential for Medicare hospital reimbursement, as well as from a significant increase in funding for the rural transition grant program. More funds were also authorized for Community Health Centers and Migrant Health Centers, which play a significant role in providing primary care in underserved areas. Mental health, farm safety, and emergency services legislation include special rural components. In recognition of the importance of encouraging more state-level activity, state offices of rural health will be promoted through matching federal dollars (Gibbens 1991). Appropriations for a variety of research and demonstration projects, with a rural focus, were also passed. It is difficult to overstate the importance of this thrust because it indicates that solutions to rural problems require dedicated efforts.

Discouragement arises from the reality of restrained budgets at both the federal and state levels. Health-care programs are in competition with other service programs for limited dollars. The 1990s opened with as many as 30 states experiencing acute budgetary problems. Defensive budget management, occurring within states, may limit implementation of needed, creative solutions aimed at resolving access problems. One budget response has been for states to postpone paying vendors, including those providing health-care services to clients reimbursed through state aid. Both rural and urban providers of services have been forced to absorb the costs and deal with postponement of state reimbursements, which typically are anywhere from 50 to 70 percent of costs. In many rural communities, hospitals, physicians, pharmacies, and other providers of health care are forced to refuse clients, sue the state, shift the costs to other payers, or absorb the losses.

It is time for solutions to health-care delivery and finance. Some solutions must come from community leaders who feel the impact of federal and state budget problems. Local health care is not independent of larger government rules and revenues, and more flexibility in local control is being encouraged. Rural communities will be rewarded for taking creative, nontraditional approaches in providing and funding health-care services.

Timing is especially critical in rural areas, because once the existing health delivery structure is completely eroded, it will be nearly impossible to retrieve it. Solutions must build on and modify the parts of the system that work. A sobering and ironic fact is that, within the most heavily funded health-care system in the world, access to medical care for the most fundamental of human experiences, childbirth, is a significant problem. Several states have vast areas without obstetrical services, and rural areas are especially disadvantaged. For example, in Illinois, a 1991 report by the auditor general showed nearly half of the counties with no practicing obstetrician, and 40 counties (of 102) lacked a hospital with a maternity ward (Cronson 1991). This is in spite of the fact that Illinois has a high rate of obstetricians per population overall, and is the third highest producer of physicians in the country through its medical education programs.

Critical solutions must be found and local officials must be encouraged to be innovative. The pursuit of new strategies in rural areas has been inhibited by a lack of awareness of options, and by the absence of professional staff with the background necessary to develop innovative strategies (Cigler 1991). The topics in this book provide guidance and encouragement for those actively involved with the problem, especially at the local level.

TOPICS COVERED

Subsequent chapters focus on the demand for and supply of health-care services in rural areas, with the underlying idea that excess demand leads to concerns about health status and excess supply is inefficient. Balancing rural health demand and supply in the 1990s requires innovative approaches, and even though these are influenced and directed by federal and state policies, ultimately local communities determine the outcomes.

Discussions throughout the book emphasize local community actions. Which demographic characteristics determine the demand and need for health care? How can community officials use local resources effectively to finance services? What are creative ways in which rural communities can attract and retain health-care personnel? What can local communities learn from demonstration projects, and how can they take advantage of technology specific to their needs? The topics present strategies that rural communities might consider in shaping their health-care system for the 1990s. The range of topics covered is broad due to the diversity among rural communities and in recognition of the fact that there is no one solution or model for all needs. The changing health-care environment will be more receptive to innovative approaches.

Demand for Rural Health Care. The first section of this book discusses the demand for rural health care from the perspectives of financing and access or utilization. In recognition of the importance of public financing to rural care, Straub & Walzer present national data to examine the effects of fiscal federalism in the 1980s. The main focus is, to what extent, and how, local communities are picking up the slack in funding health-care services under growing federal and state budget constraints. The shift from federal to state and local is masked by dollar amounts that appear to be generous. Nevertheless, the payments in constant dollars have not increased as rapidly, and federal funding comes attached with mandates for additional services.

Demographic shifts have been dramatic in rural areas, increasing the share of people with special needs, while decreasing the share of residents with higher incomes, better educations, and better health. The changed composition of the rural population affects both the need for services and the ability to finance these services locally. Hicks examines these changes and their impact on rural care, and offers suggestions for refining the delivery system to accommodate the demographic realities.

Supply of Rural Health Care—Facility Inputs. The issues involved in supplying rural health care are addressed from the perspectives of facilities and personnel. In his chapter on facilities, Damasauskas proposes that retention of the rural hospital must fit into an innovative framework. Acute care needs cannot all be met elsewhere; rather, retention of the traditional facility should be considered, even if subsidies are required. Rural hospital efficiency can be improved through a variety of creative arrangements and linkages. The heavy prior investment in hospital facilities should be considered in finding creative solutions to rural health problems.

McNeely reviews efforts to develop alternative rural health delivery models and examines the diversity of these nontraditional models. He discusses the successes and limitations of models used in Colorado, Montana, Florida, and California and offers suggestions as to the application of these models in other states.

Bauer uses an economics perspective to describe ways in which an adequate supply of care can continue in small communities threatened with hospital closure. Economic and clinical arguments for conversion of the traditional hospital to a primary-care institution are provided. A basic model for a primary-care hospital is also included. Bauer's view is that resources should not be wasted. He proposes that innovative thinking will result in the best use of scarce resources for the provision of effective and efficient health care.

Supply of Health Care—Labor Inputs. The provision of high quality local health care requires trained personnel. However, recruiting and retaining personnel have been major obstacles in rural areas. Fickenscher, as a physician and educator, analyzes the role of medical education programs, and describes how the focus and philosophy of these programs affect rural areas. The societal responsibility of academic medicine, which should insure that rural residents have equitable access to high quality medical care, is considered. This chapter confirms a growing suspicion, by rural advocates, that medical education programs have not supported the retention and recruitment of physicians into rural practice. Suggestions for changing the focus or orientation of these programs are provided.

The importance and the role of nursing inputs are discussed by Weis. Heavy dependence on nurses in rural delivery programs is threatened by imbalances in the national nurse market. Rural communities can be more effective in using midlevel practitioners and in attracting and retaining nurses. Developing creative ways to stimulate and retain nurses is the challenge for rural communities as they adjust to a changing health-care environment. The author suggests that understanding the characteristics of rural nursing is critical to insuring an adequate nurse supply.

Technology to Optimize Provision of Rural Services. Technology has been a boom and bust for rural areas. On one hand, technology offers opportunities for rural institutions to link with urban counterparts and to upgrade quality of services. On the other hand, the cost of technology has been seen as prohibitive for small rural hospitals and has made them less competitive in terms of available services. Nevertheless, technology can be a key in preserving rural health care. Innovative uses of communications and medical informatics technology—technologies that expand access to medical information—are presented. Although much of the technology is basic and currently exists, its application has been sorely lacking in rural health care. Cordes & Straub claim that technology is not simply the key to preserving a limited rural care program; rather it should be used to guide the entire system through a paradigm shift. The technology already exists and is affordable; therefore, the innovation focus is on the leadership required for full implementation into health-care delivery. A collaborative network that benefits both rural and urban providers, as well as rural residents, can be linked through technology.

Thorp & Cordes illustrate several ways in which medical informatics can alleviate many of the negative aspects of isolation in rural practice. Examples illustrate the potential for technology to change the rural practice environment. The importance of government policies in expanding the rural communications infrastructure is noted.

With the loss of traditional services, the role of emergency medical services to remote rural areas is becoming more critical. Demands on providers of rural emergency services are stringent, and technological additions to the system are welcome. Anderson provides several examples of areas which have taken advantage of specialized technology to improve efficiency and access to emergency care. He points out numerous benefits from this technology and ways in which stress can be reduced and time saved for personnel.

Linkages. The final segment of the book links state and federal policies with the sociology of the rural environment. Kovner & Kiel present insight into various innovative state policies for sustaining and improving rural health systems. Demonstration projects funded by a Robert Wood Johnson Foundation program are discussed. The resulting strategies can be used by rural health-care planners as a model.

Patton presents the federal perspective on financing to alert rural areas to changes in policies which affect delivery and financing. A summary of federal legislation is provided, along with insight into the process of its development. The significance of rural health, in overall federal financing, is a factor in successful pursuit of innovative strategies for rural areas.

The book closes with a chapter by Hassinger & Hobbs to show how rural health care fits into the context of rural sociology overall. The authors point out that rural society is not monolithic and rural communities differ widely in characteristics. The diversity of the environment and its uniqueness are explored. It is proposed that the success of innovative programs will depend, in part, on the extent to which they are developed with appreciation of the composition of these communities.

This book contains features not found elsewhere in a single source and should be of interest to several audiences. First, health-care professionals and providers concerned with improving access to care in rural areas will gain insight from the discussions. The chapters focus on innovative approaches, in many areas, to stimulate thinking among administrators and providers of health care.

A second group who will gain from the material is state and local public officials responsible for insuring the delivery of quality health care under increasingly difficult conditions. Local elected officials must stay abreast on a range of issues, and this book will assist them in the task.

Others who will find the material current and stimulating are teachers of health-care policy and administration at the university and college levels. This group includes political scientists, economists, sociologists, public administrators, and health-care faculty. The book's design allows for chapters to be used individually as supplemental or reference material.

CONCLUSION

The changing environments of health-care delivery, rural economies, technology, government fiscal policies, and demographics will present an interesting and challenging decade for rural health care. In a comprehensive summary of state and local taxes and issues, it was noted that health-care costs will be the number one problem for state budgets in the 1990s (Mahar 1990). These costs are also a primary concern to the federal sector, private enterprise, and local communities. There will be little margin for error when rural communities make decisions about effective and efficient provision of health-care services.

The chapters in this book are intended to provide some guidance and reassurance to those responsible for these decisions, by stimulating creative thinking about the problems and about solutions. Shaping rural health care will be one of the most important considerations for rural areas in the decade of the 1990s.

PART I

The Demand for Rural Health Care

1. Financing the Demand for Rural Health Care

LaVonne A. Straub and Norman Walzer

Financing traditional health services, especially in rural areas, has become increasingly difficult in recent years for several reasons. First, the rural population base increased very slowly, or even declined in many states during the 1980s. Nonmetro counties, nationwide, increased 3.3 percent in population, compared with an increase of 10.1 percent in metro counties (Mazie 1990). This contrasts sharply with the trend of the 1970s when nonmetro population increased 14.4 percent compared with a 10.5 increase in metro areas.

Second, government reimbursement rates for major providers of care have been lower in rural areas than in urban areas, a discrepancy that has persisted even though costs of providing comparable services have not justified the differences. Costs of health-care personnel have grown, due in part to the increasing competition that has resulted from shortages in many occupations. Rural areas must offer comparable wage and benefit packages in order to recruit and retain qualified professionals. Although the differential rates have been addressed by Congress and should improve in the 1990s, damage has already been done. Lower reimbursements, combined with the fact that rural hospitals and medical providers treat a disproportionate share of uninsured and underinsured patients, have placed significant pressures on rural institutions (Mick & Morlock 1990).

Third, advances in medical technology have changed treatment procedures, and have created a shift from inpatient to outpatient care. This has eroded the financial stability of the many rural institutions that have not altered fixed costs to accommodate this change. Many rural areas, unable to offer modern facilities, are disadvantaged in recruiting medical personnel without substantial subsidies to upgrade facilities.

Fourth, the demand for health-care services has continued to expand in rural areas. Elderly and low income populations demand services beyond basic primary care. In recognition of the multiple needs, government mandates for local provision of services have increased, and these mandates further pressure the limited pool of funding for health care. In the overall scheme, the pattern of expanding program needs and constrained budgets presents a severe problem. In addition, the need to finance health-care programs competes with the financing of other important social services, which are also experiencing demand and cost pressures.

It is clear that the population, economics, and financing trends of the 1980s changed the viability of rural health and hospital services substantially. These services are financed through many arrangements, involving multiple, private, and public revenue sources. Private financing continues to evoke protests over increases, but the more severe problems are occurring in the public sector.

The public sources of revenue for services differ by region, and change with shifts in government programs, as well as with taxpayer attitudes and abilities. In general, federal fiscalism during the 1980s placed more of the burden of financing on state and local governments. Within health-care financing, providing care to those lacking adequate insurance has emerged as a major, unresolved problem. For several reasons, the previous cost-shifting method of paying for indigent care no longer works. As the federal and state governments reduce their relative support, more of the burden is being carried by local resources, such as property taxes and charges for services. Continuation of this trend, in light of lagging local fiscal capabilities in rural areas, may bring even more significant changes in methods of finance and arrangements for providing services.

This chapter examines several major topics of local health care and hospital financing. An overriding theme is evaluating how rural communities cope with the need to provide health services under changing conditions. The first section reviews arrangements through which health-care services in rural areas currently are financed. Second, national expenditure patterns for local hospital and health services illustrate how funding for these services, in constant dollars, changed during the 1980s. Next, financing patterns and trends are presented, with special attention to the role of federal and state governments. Finally, new options for financing the demand for health services in rural areas are presented.

RURAL AREA HEALTH-CARE FINANCING

The demand for rural medical and health-care services is satisfied through a variety of private and public arrangements. The specific institutional structure for providing services depends on historical patterns, and on the structure of reimbursement, as much as on conscious planning efforts.

Institutional arrangements often do not keep pace with population shifts or economic changes, and some have become inefficient or obsolete. These forms, however, have evolved in direct consequence of financing methods. To the extent that they provide a level of service that satisfies residents, and as long as alternative forms are not readily supported through reimbursement, change will continue to be slow.

Health services and hospitals are organized and financed in most states through a variety of ownership forms, ranging from private entities to counties, municipalities, and single function districts. Typically, every community has several local agencies, each responsible for a portion of health-care services, and financed independently with separate revenue sources. The potential for duplication of services and the lack of coordination among agencies have long been problems in efficiently providing rural care.

Within states, wide differences exist in governmental responsibility for health services and hospital finance. Table 1.1 shows the distribution of local expenditures among governing units in 1982 and 1987.[1] The most common arrangement has counties bearing the largest share of burden, with an average of 48.3 percent in 1982. The exception to this arrangement is in the Northeast, where counties, on average, have responsibility for only 17.4 percent of the total health and hospital expenditures. The low spending by counties in this region is because city governments in New England states provide many services financed by counties in other regions. In the Northeast in 1987, city governments had responsibility for 47.4 percent of the hospital and health spending. Counties in Massachusetts, Maine, and New Hampshire provided less than 10 percent of the expenditures, and in three of the states, counties financed no health-related expenditures at all in 1987.

Nationally, city governments represent between one fourth and one third of public expenditures for hospitals and health. The exceptions are in the Northeast, as discussed before, and in the West, where cities represented only 21.5 percent in 1987. Within states, however, substantial differences exist. For instance, city governments in Hawaii assume full responsibility in health-related expenditure, while cities in 10 states in the Western region have less than 15 percent responsibility.

Special districts, often created for a single purpose, such as for hospitals or specific health services, are relatively important providers of services, especially in rural areas in many states. Thirty-one states reported health and hospital expenditures by special districts, but in five states they represented less than 1 percent. In states such as Georgia (89.4 percent) and Washington (68.7 percent), special districts are especially important. Special districts are most important in the West, where they represented an average of 22.1 percent of expenditures in 1987.

Florida, Georgia, and Washington are especially interesting because of the high proportion of services provided by special districts. Special districts

Table 1.1

Percent Distribution Health and Hospital Expenditures by Types of Local Government, 1982 and 1987

State	1982					1987				
	Local	Counties	Municipalities	Townships	Special Districts	Local	Counties	Municipalities	Townships	Special Districts
NATIONAL										
Average	*100.0*	*48.3*	*31.4*	*5.2*	*14.6*	*100.0*	*47.8*	*30.8*	*5.1*	*16.3*
WEST										
Alaska	100.0	28.0	72.0	-	-	100.0	21.3	78.7	-	-
Arizona	100.0	90.1	2.1	-	7.7	100.0	92.5	0.5	-	7.0
California	100.0	62.9	5.8	-	31.3	100.0	62.2	8.1	-	29.7
Colorado	100.0	34.7	41.0	-	24.3	100.0	21.7	48.1	-	30.2
Hawaii	100.0	-	100.0	-	-	100.0	-	100.0	-	-
Idaho	100.0	75.3	1.6	-	23.0	100.0	67.8	1.4	-	30.8
Montana	100.0	58.7	7.9	-	33.1	100.0	62.5	4.9	-	32.6
Nevada	100.0	94.3	5.7	-	0.1	100.0	87.3	12.6	-	0.1
New Mexico	100.0	49.7	50.3	-	-	100.0	88.3	6.9	-	4.8
Oregon	100.0	52.4	7.3	-	40.3	100.0	46.4	11.1	-	42.5
Utah	100.0	97.2	1.2	-	1.6	100.0	95.0	2.5	-	2.5
Washington	100.0	30.4	1.5	-	68.1	100.0	28.1	3.2	-	68.7
Wyoming	100.0	88.8	3.0	-	8.2	100.0	59.9	1.3	-	38.8
Average	*100.0*	*58.7*	*23.0*	*-*	*18.3*	*100.0*	*56.4*	*21.5*	*-*	*22.1*
MIDWEST										
Illinois	100.0	48.6	26.5	0.4	24.4	100.0	52.7	24.1	0.6	22.6
Indiana	100.0	78.4	19.7	-	1.9	100.0	78.8	21.2	-	-
Iowa	100.0	71.3	28.7	-	-	100.0	69.2	30.8	-	-
Kansas	100.0	53.1	31.3	-	15.7	100.0	60.4	25.3	-	14.3
Michigan	100.0	51.7	32.5	0.1	15.8	100.0	56.5	27.6	0.1	15.8
Minnesota	100.0	41.0	36.2	-	22.8	100.0	48.8	22.3	0.1	28.8
Missouri	100.0	42.9	40.3	-	16.8	100.0	46.4	32.2	-	21.4
Nebraska	100.0	46.5	15.6	-	37.8	100.0	28.9	15.2	-	55.9
North Dakota	100.0	58.3	41.7	-	-	100.0	57.0	42.2	-	0.8
Ohio	100.0	79.5	15.3	-	5.2	100.0	81.8	12.8	-	5.4
South Dakota	100.0	46.4	53.6	-	-	100.0	36.1	63.9	-	-
Wisconsin	100.0	94.0	5.6	0.3	-	100.0	88.3	10.7	1.0	-
Average	*100.0*	*59.3*	*28.9*	*0.1*	*11.7*	*100.0*	*58.8*	*27.4*	*0.1*	*13.7*

NORTHEAST										
Connecticut	100.0	-	71.1	28.9	-	100.0	-	64.7	35.3	-
Maine	100.0	1.4	85.4	12.5	-	100.0	1.4	50.3	8.1	40.2
Massachusetts	100.0	9.8	74.6	15.6	-	100.0	9.4	75.3	15.2	-
New Hampshire	100.0	5.1	35.9	59.0	-	100.0	4.7	39.2	56.2	-
New Jersey	100.0	69.0	26.1	4.9	-	100.0	66.3	28.6	5.1	-
New York	100.0	27.9	71.2	0.9	-	100.0	26.3	72.4	1.1	0.1
Pennsylvania	100.0	43.2	23.5	0.5	32.8	100.0	65.4	33.5	0.5	0.7
Rhode Island	100.0	-	37.5	62.5	-	100.0	-	36.0	64.0	-
Vermont	100.0	-	18.8	81.3	-	100.0	-	26.5	73.5	-
Average	*100.0*	*17.4*	*49.3*	*29.6*	*3.6*	*100.0*	*19.3*	*47.4*	*28.8*	*4.6*
SOUTH										
Alabama	100.0	10.2	40.8	-	48.9	100.0	10.5	26.9	-	62.6
Arkansas	100.0	86.8	13.2	-	-	100.0	85.9	14.1	-	-
DC	100.0	-	100.0	-	-	100.0	-	100.0	-	-
Delaware	100.0	40.0	40.0	-	-	100.0	-	100.0	-	-
Florida	100.0	40.4	7.0	-	52.6	100.0	38.1	8.7	-	53.2
Georgia	100.0	11.9	0.3	-	87.8	100.0	9.0	1.6	-	89.4
Kentucky	100.0	49.7	42.2	-	8.1	100.0	56.1	36.4	-	7.5
Louisiana	100.0	90.4	9.6	-	-	100.0	84.9	15.1	-	-
Maryland	100.0	55.3	44.7	-	-	100.0	67.4	32.6	-	-
Mississippi	100.0	84.4	15.5	-	0.1	100.0	81.4	18.5	-	0.1
North Carolina	100.0	62.9	5.9	-	31.3	100.0	64.9	2.2	-	32.9
Oklahoma	100.0	39.9	60.1	-	-	100.0	29.2	70.8	-	-
South Carolina	100.0	94.5	0.3	-	5.3	100.0	91.1	0.2	-	8.7
Tennessee	100.0	70.1	29.9	-	-	100.0	81.6	18.4	-	-
Texas	100.0	51.7	16.5	-	31.8	100.0	55.8	15.1	-	29.1
Virginia	100.0	27.6	27.2	-	45.1	100.0	26.5	20.9	-	52.6
West Virginia	100.0	18.8	58.6	-	22.5	100.0	42.8	57.2	-	-
Average	*100.0*	*49.1*	*30.1*	-	*19.6*	*100.0*	*48.5*	*31.7*	-	*19.8*

Source: U.S. Bureau of the Census 1982, 1987.

7

replace both cities and counties as major service providers in these states. In Florida, many public hospitals that had no taxing authority were taken over by private organizations in the late 1970s and early 1980s. A combination of factors was identified as important in this shift. These include the expense of the public sector retirement program, coupled with conservative management approaches, which caused local officials to be reluctant to raise sufficient revenues to keep the hospitals financially feasible. Many local hospital districts in these states overlay others within the state. For example, a county may contain many separate and autonomous districts, or one district may overlap several counties. These districts were created largely by historical circumstances, and by need, such as the need to care for the growing indigent population.

Georgia's experience is somewhat similar to Florida's in that hospital authorities were created to serve many areas during the Hill-Burton expansion period. The hospitals rely heavily on patient revenues, and in some instances smaller hospitals that could no longer remain viable were sold to private companies. It is not completely clear why the hospital authority route was selected instead of providing services through general purpose governments, such as counties. Apparently, the financing arrangements were determined by historical precedent as much as by any other factors. Response to a single purpose, rather than ongoing need, influences the longevity of districts.

In Missouri, hospital districts are used mainly for building construction, and as this purpose is completed, districts may be eliminated. Between 1982 and 1987, for instance, the number of health districts decreased 21.1 percent, and hospital districts declined 21.7 percent (U.S. Bureau of the Census 1983b and 1988a). In some states, where substantial percentage changes in number of districts are reported, the number is sufficiently small that large percentage changes are misleading.

Both institutional arrangements, through which health and hospital services are provided, and size of the population served, are important for several reasons. First, the population served must be sufficiently large to support the services financially; this is especially relevant to hospitals in rural regions with population declines. When occupancy rates are low, fixed costs per patient may be excessive, and must be paid by a small number of patients, or else large subsidies are required.

Second, each form of government has access to different types of revenue sources, and, therefore, varying abilities to raise revenues. Cities, towns, and counties typically can access a broader range of revenues than special districts, which depend heavily on user charges or property taxes. Thus, the ability to finance services depends on institutional arrangements through which services are provided.

A significant shift in the provision of health-care services occurred during the 1980s with an erosion in the use of hospital-based, inpatient care. Between 1980 and 1988 approximately 400 hospitals closed; 200 of those were in rural communities (U.S. General Accounting Office 1991). A variety of clinics and community health centers, public health agencies, and individual provider offices replaced some of the services. Many replacement agencies are direct recipients of federal grant funds, enabling them to provide primary care and basic health services, including mental health.

The nonhospital-based providers serve an important role in rural health care by increasing access, especially in more remote areas. The public funding is basically of several forms; one is through direct reimbursement of fees for services provided (such as Medicare and Medicaid); another is through grant funds for programs provided by these agencies; a third is through local and state tax revenues. Government funds used as economic incentives for professionals to locate in rural sites are yet another revenue source.

The institutional arrangements governing these revenues frequently have limiting features, which offset some of the benefits. For example, a federal act authorizing establishment of special rural health clinics was passed in 1977 (Social Security Act, amendment, P.L. 95–210). This act includes a favorable reimbursement structure, requires use of midlevel practitioners, and helps underserved areas. However, changes in the complex rules governing eligibility have discouraged clinics from developing their potential. In general, the administration, paperwork, and staffing demands required by Medicare often cause compliance difficulties for small rural facilities (U.S. Congress, Office of Technology Assessment, 1990).

Other segments of rural health care that are highly dependent upon public sources of funding are mental health services, long-term care, home health care, and emergency medical services. Federal funds for mental health are distributed through block grants to the states, and services are provided largely through Community Mental Health Centers. Long-term care is heavily funded through Medicaid and therefore through state and federal dollars. Funding arrangements for emergency medical services (EMS) range from local voluntary units, to public-funded fire districts and local hospitals, to private units. Special taxing districts to fund emergency services are also used in some states. As funding and delivery arrangements filter down to state and local governments, they diversify and decrease in consistency. Therefore, overall evaluation of the financing structure of these services is difficult.

The ability to understand hospital and health-care finance in rural areas is also limited by lack of detailed systematic data broken down by type of government. General purpose governments—counties, cities, and townships—spend funds collected from many sources. Although one can obtain detailed spending information for health and hospitals, it is difficult to determine the source of revenues for a particular expenditure category. Thus, county health expenditures, as an example, may be financed from property taxes, sales taxes, user fees, and an assortment of other revenues.

Some governments maintain an enterprise fund for special services like hospitals. These funds function much like a business, with revenues and expenditures closely matching. The parent government, however, may subsidize the service when it is not self-supporting, or may charge the service fund for general administration. When an enterprise fund is maintained within a general purpose government, it is easier to determine financing patterns and trends.

Tracing revenues and expenditures is much easier for health and hospital districts. These governmental units have a single purpose, so all revenues or expenditures are for either health or hospital services. In subsequent discussions, general purpose and single function governments are examined separately.

FINANCING TRENDS: SINGLE FUNCTION DISTRICTS

Earlier in this chapter, differences among states, regarding the financing of services, were noted. In certain instances, special districts provide a majority of expenditures, whereas in others such districts are relatively insignificant or even nonexistent. Within these special districts, the relative importance of revenue sources changed during the 1980s. These changes are summarized in Table 1.2.

In 1982, health districts collected an average of $444,000 in general revenues, and by 1987 the revenues had grown to $683,000, an increase of 53.8 percent in current dollars. In constant dollars, however, the increase was only 9.5 percent. The overall growth differed in metro compared with nonmetro areas. Current dollar growth was 82.5 percent in metro areas and only 7.1 percent in nonmetro areas. In constant dollars, the nonmetro areas experienced a 22 percent decline, whereas the metro growth was 29.8 percent. The obvious explanation for these differences is slow population growth and economic stagnation in rural areas during the 1980s.

Services provided by health districts are financed mainly from own-source general revenues—property taxes, charges, and miscellaneous collections. Dependence on these revenues, relative to intergovernmental transfers, increased substantially during the 1980s. Overall, these sources provided 87 percent of the total revenues collected by health districts by 1987, compared with 80 percent in 1982.

In 1982, charges and fees for services represented the largest single component of local revenues (36.3 percent), and property taxes were second (24.1 percent). The miscellaneous revenues category made up 18.7 percent. By 1987, however, the pattern had changed, with charges representing only 15.2 percent, property taxes representing 25.5 percent, and

Table 1.2

Sources of Revenues and Percentage Distribution, Health Districts, 1982 and 1987

Sources of Revenue		Nonmetro			Metro			Nationwide		
		1982 (n=264)	1987 (n=293)	Pct. Chg. 82-87	1982 (n=176)	1987 (n=191)	Pct. Chg. 82-87	1982 (n=441)	1987 (n=485)	Pct. Chg. 82-87
		($000)			($000)			($000)		
General Revenue	(Nominal $)	$240	$257	7.1	$697	$1,272	82.5	$444	$683	53.8
	(Real $)	240	187	-22.1	697	905	29.8	444	683	9.5
	(%)	(100.0)	(100.0)		(100.0)	(100.0)		(100.0)	(100.0)	
Intergovernmental		54	56	3.7	131	126	-3.8	89	88	-1.1
		54	40	-25.9	131	90	-31.3	89	63	-29.2
		(22.5)	(21.8)		(18.8)	(9.9)		(20.0)	(12.9)	
Federal		11	8	-27.3	28	41	46.4	20	23	15.0
		11	6	-45.5	28	29	3.6	20	16	-20.0
		(4.6)	(3.1)		(4.0)	(3.2)		(4.5)	(3.4)	
State		35	41	17.1	63	58	-7.9	50	51	2.0
		35	29	-17.1	63	41	-34.9	50	36	-28.0
		(14.6)	(16.0)		(9.0)	(4.6)		(11.3)	(7.5)	
Local		7	8	14.3	39	26	-33.3	20	15	-25.0
		7	6	-14.3	39	18	-53.8	20	11	-45.0
		(2.9)	(3.1)		(5.6)	(2.0)		(4.5)	(2.2)	
Gen. Rev. from Own Sources		187	201	7.5	566	1,146	102.5	355	594	67.3
		187	143	-23.5	566	815	44.0	355	422	18.9
		(77.9)	(78.2)		(81.2)	(90.1)		(80.0)	(87.0)	
Property Taxes		54	75	38.9	168	302	79.8	107	174	62.6
		54	53	-1.9	168	215	28.0	107	124	15.9
		(22.5)	(29.2)		(24.1)	(23.7)		(24.1)	(25.5)	
Charges		120	117	-2.5	205	82	-60.0	161	104	-35.4
		120	83	-30.8	205	58	-71.7	161	74	-54.0
		(50.0)	(45.5)		(29.4)	(6.4)		(36.3)	(15.2)	
Misc. Revenues		13	9	-30.8	184	642	248.9	83	260	213.3
		13	6	-53.8	184	457	148.4	83	185	122.9
		(5.4)	(3.5)		(26.4)	(50.5)		(18.7)	(38.1)	

CPI for medical care: 1982=100.0, 1987=140.6

Source: U.S. Department of Commerce 1982, 1987.

miscellaneous revenues representing 38.1 percent. The miscellaneous revenues include interest on savings accounts, donations, sale of equipment, and other related activities. Charges make up a much larger segment of own-source revenues in rural areas than in metro areas. Although charges declined somewhat in both rural and metro areas during the 1980s, by 1987 they still accounted for 45.5 percent in rural areas. Property taxes were stable in relative importance as a source of health district funding overall, but increased from 22.5 percent to 29.2 percent in nonmetro areas.

Clearly, local revenues have grown in importance in funding health services, but substantial changes have occurred in intergovernmental revenues also. Between 1982 and 1987, state funding for health districts increased 2 percent overall in current dollars, and declined 28 percent in constant dollars. Nonmetro health districts received a larger share of state transfers than those in metro areas, but this pattern was reversed for federal transfers. Federal assistance declined from 4.5 percent of general revenues in 1982 to 3.4 percent in 1987. In nonmetro districts, the decline was much more dramatic, down 27 percent in current dollars or 45.5 percent in real dollars. Dependence on aid from other local governments declined from 4.5 percent of revenues to 2.2 percent during the 1980s for all districts.

Hospital districts fit a generally similar pattern, with charges representing a significant share of the total revenues in both rural area hospital and health districts. Service charges are a much larger share of total revenues in nonmetro hospital districts (Table 1.3). Overall, charges declined slightly in importance in the 1980s, with property taxes and miscellaneous revenues making up the difference, but all the decline was in rural areas, with the distribution remaining stable in metro areas. The importance here is that federal and state funds are heavily imbedded in charges through Medicare and Medicaid reimbursement. In the funding of nonmetro hospital districts, the general revenues from own-sources, exclusive of charges, depend more on property taxes and less on miscellaneous revenues than is true overall.

TRENDS: FEDERAL FINANCING OF RURAL SERVICES

Because the demand for rural hospital and health-care services depends heavily on public financing, the status of this funding during the 1980s and changes in its status during the 1990s will have significant consequences for determining how well demand for services is met. Approximately 44 percent of state spending for rural health care comes from federal revenues (U.S. Congress, Office of Technology Assessment 1990). Federal contributions flowing through the Medicare and Medicaid programs are a significant share of financing the demand for care, and especially for care provided by hospitals and long-term care facilities. On average, rural hospitals rely on Medicare for nearly 41 percent of patient revenues. In fact, this source accounts for at least half of patient-care revenues in 30 percent of rural hospitals (Reczynski 1987).

The reduced access to rural hospitals has increased demand for services in other primary-care facilities. Federal funding of community and migrant health centers for primary-care services and other related health-care resource programs has been instrumental in influencing the level of care in rural areas. The share of public reimbursement, relative to private payment, used by community and migrant centers has increased to the point where federal funds represent almost half of the total revenues (U.S. Congress, Office of Technology Assessment 1990).

Congressional Research Service Study. At issue is the extent of changes in federal funding for health-care programs during the 1980s, and state and local replacement of funding losses to rural communities. A Congressional Research Service (CRS) report on appropriations for health programs during the 1980s addresses this issue by tracking program-specific funding (Klebe 1990).

The CRS report summarizes appropriations for 49 separate health programs administered by various agencies in the Department of Health and

Table 1.3

Sources of Revenues and Percentage Distribution, Hospital Districts, 1982 and 1987

Sources of Revenue		Nonmetro			Metro			Nationwide		
		1982 (n=548)	1987 (n=527)	Pct. Chg. 82-87	1982 (n=265)	1987 (n=239)	Pct. Chg. 82-87	1982 (n=817)	1987 (n=771)	Pct. Chg. 82-87
		($000)			($000)			($000)		
General Revenue	(Nominal $)	$2,946	$4,539	54.1	$14,271	$24,741	73.4	$6,693	$10,868	62.4
	(Real $)	2,946	3,228	9.6	14,271	17,596	23.3	6,693	7,730	15.5
	(%)	(100.0)	(100.0)		(100.0)	(100.0)		(100.0)	(100.0)	
Intergovernmental		59	186	215.2	1,009	718	-28.8	367	349	-4.9
		59	132	123.7	1,009	511	-49.4	367	248	-32.4
		(2.0)	(4.1)		(7.1)	(2.9)		(5.5)	(3.2)	
Federal		30	110	266.7	293	112	-61.8	115	110	-4.3
		30	78	160.0	293	80	-72.7	115	78	-32.2
		(1.0)	(2.4)		(2.1)	(0.5)		(1.7)	(1.0)	
State		19	42	121.1	323	236	-26.9	117	102	-12.8
		19	30	57.9	323	168	-48.0	117	73	-37.6
		(0.6)	(0.9)		(2.3)	(1.0)		(1.7)	(0.9)	
Local		10	34	240.0	392	370	-5.6	134	138	3.0
		10	24	140.0	392	263	-3.9	134	98	-26.9
		(0.3)	(0.7)		(2.7)	(1.5)		(2.0)	(1.3)	
Gen. Rev. from Own Sources		2,887	4,354	50.8	13,263	24,023	81.1	6,326	10,519	66.3
		2,887	3,097	7.3	13,263	17,086	28.8	6,326	7,482	18.3
		(98.0)	(95.9)		(92.9)	(97.1)		(94.5)	(96.8)	
Property Taxes		91	174	91.2	280	621	121.8	152	312	105.3
		91	124	36.3	280	442	57.9	152	222	46.1
		(3.1)	(3.8)		(2.0)	(2.5)		(2.3)	(2.9)	
Charges		2,671	3,942	47.6	11,956	20,664	72.8	5,727	9,192	60.5
		2,671	2,804	5.0	11,956	14,697	22.9	5,727	6,538	14.2
		(90.7)	(86.8)		(83.8)	(83.5)		(85.6)	(84.6)	
Misc. Revenues		125	238	90.4	1,027	2,738	166.6	448	1,014	126.3
		125	169	35.2	1,027	1,947	89.6	448	721	60.9
		(4.2)	(5.2)		(7.2)	(11.1)		(6.7)	(9.3)	

CPI for medical care: 1982=100.0, 1987=140.6

Source: U.S. Department of Commerce 1982, 1987.

Human Services. The analysis does not distinguish between rural and urban funding, but, because many of the programs target rural areas, the overall analysis reflects funding changes for rural communities. By design, most of the programs are structured to assure basic medical-care services to those who cannot pay, and for communities designated as medically underserved, or for populations with special needs, such as migrant farmworkers and the Native American population. Thus, target groups for these programs comprise a large share of the rural population.

According to the CRS summary, most programs experienced funding reductions between 1980 and 1982, but appropriations then increased in subsequent years, to the point where many programs equaled or exceeded the funding levels prior to the 1982 cuts. However, in most cases, the gains did not match inflation.

Two programs, especially important in meeting health needs of rural residents, are Community Health Centers (CHCs) and Migrant Health Centers (MHCs). In FY1980, appropriations for the CHC program were

$320 million. With the exception of a reduction to $281 million in 1982, funds increased annually, with the FY1990 appropriation at $427 million. Funding for the MHC program during this time went from $39.7 million to $47.4 million.

Block grant programs are also important funding sources for rural health care. The CRS reports that the maternal and child health block grant funding grew from $438.8 million to $553.6 million between FY1980 and FY1990. At the same time, the total Preventive Health Block Grant program (under Centers for Disease Control) appropriations decreased from $169.9 million to $83 million. Total block grants for alcohol, drug abuse, and mental health administration increased from $606 million to $1,192.8 million, the largest gainer among the block grant programs. Research programs in mental health, drug and alcohol abuse, and other prevention programs, such as immunization, also experienced growing appropriations during this period. These expenditures reflect the growing concern over these problems, which emerged with the early 1980s farm crisis.

Similar increases occurred in appropriations critical to rural areas for a number of programs, including those targeted for health professions education and public health administration. In the absence of this support for health professionals, personnel shortages in rural areas would be even more severe than at the present time. The overall picture for the 1980s is one of dollar growth in the federal support of these programs. Consequently, federal financing of rural health demand, as reflected by this growth, appears to have been solid in the 1980s. When assessed in real terms, however, this conclusion does not hold true.

Institute Phone Survey of States. An additional perspective comes from an Illinois Institute for Rural Affairs telephone sampling of several state public health offices, regarding changes in federal funding status (Illinois Institute for Rural Affairs 1991). Because of the variety of programs and agencies involved, as well as the diversity among states, aggregate numbers are difficult to compile. Most responses demonstrated that the relative stability of federal dollars for programs has been affected by two important qualifying factors.

One is that the costs of providing the same level of services have increased significantly, thereby decreasing real funding capability. Second, several states report marked growth in program demands; thus, funds are being continually stretched. The federal government has asked states to do more, provide more programs and services, and serve more people with health dollars. Underfunded federally mandated health programs require state and local agencies to seek funds from other sources. These agencies have been strained by growth in the number of people eligible for program services, especially in rural areas facing economic hardship.

The situation of declining federal funds (in constant dollars) and expanded service demands is not confined to rural areas, but is shared by those in urban areas. Within each state, friction is created between geographic and population areas when financing is inadequate to cover all needs. Additional friction comes about when health-care programs must compete with other service programs for funds.

During the 1980s, the financing structure has come under increasing pressure. The prognosis for the 1990s is that the shift from federal to state responsibility will increase. For hospitals, the entire process of cost-shifting, including that to finance uncovered care, leads to uncertain budgets, and a generally undesirable financing situation (Boeder 1988). Internally, hospitals have shifted the burden onto private pay and privately insured patients. Externally, the government payers attempt to shift more of their burden to providers. Most of the reform, in providing care for the indigent, has been by states in recent years and is affecting the states differently.

TRENDS: STATE LEVEL FINANCING

The state contribution to financing health care for low income and elderly populations through Medicaid has nearly doubled in the past 15 years, when measured as a percentage of personal income, now requiring 60 cents out of every $100. The near absence of solid, private long-term care insurance is straining Medicaid as the population ages. Approximately 42 percent of rural hospitals are owned by state or local governments, compared with 15 percent of urban institutions; thus, rural hospitals depend more on public revenues for support. It is revealing that only 10 percent of rural community hospitals are investor owned or operated on a for-profit basis (Reczynski 1987).

The dependence of rural hospitals and health-care facilities on public funding makes them especially vulnerable to the ability of state financing to replace lost federal funding. The Omnibus Budget Reconciliation Act of 1990 includes a $3.22 billion reduction in Medicare spending for FY1991 and a $34.11 billion reduction over the next five fiscal years (Fassbach 1990). If the reduction in federal funding is not replaced with state funds, a portion of the demand for health services in rural areas will go unmet.

General information on this important question of replacement funds was provided through a 1988 survey by the Office of Technology Assessment (U.S. Congress, Office of Technology Assessment, 1990). Information was collected from all states regarding the extent to which they were accepting greater responsibility for maintaining rural health services. It is not surprising that state responses varied widely. One general finding was that more rural states have a relatively higher share of state funds dedicated to rural health care than federal funds. Of the 33 states reporting financing information for both 1987 and 1989, 25 had some increases in budgets for rural health care between these years, while 8 had reduced this budget category. The range of rural health activities among the states is broad, with recruitment and retention of health-care providers the most common, reported by 38 states. Although a majority of states provided financial assistance to local areas, this typically was not direct financing of care.

State expansion or reform of Medicaid programs was frequently cited in the survey as a current activity in addressing rural health care (U.S. Congress, Office of Technology Assessment, 1990). It was also listed for several states as an important future activity. In Illinois, the state hospital association is pressuring the state legislature to reform the Medicaid payment system. The association claims that inadequate reimbursement results in the state's hospitals subsidizing more than $600 million dollars of uncompensated care annually (Illinois Hospital Association 1991).

The significant demand shifts for health-care services and the inadequacy of private funding have burdened public financing. A painful example is the recent addition to the demands on health-care financing at all levels, arising from costs associated with treatment and care of AIDS patients. According to Health Care Financing Administration figures, AIDS patients may cost the United States as much as $50 billion during the 1990s, about 5 percent of the Medicaid budget (Pascal et al. 1989). Nationwide, Medicaid pays approximately 23 percent of health costs associated with AIDS; in some states, it represents 10 to 15 percent of the Medicaid budget. Even so, many public hospitals are forced to pay a share of treatment costs because patients have no insurance, and Medicaid only reimburses a fraction of the treatment costs.

At this point, it is difficult to estimate the exact impact of AIDS spending on rural health care. Funding from all public sources is expanding as the problem grows. Federal appropriations for AIDS treatment went from zero in FY1980 to $1.6 billion in FY1990 (Klebe 1990). One source estimates that state spending allocations had reached a total of $229 million to AIDS-related activities from general revenues by FY1988. These figures are exclusive of the state Medicaid funds, matched with federal dollars, dedicated to the problem (Rowe & Ryan 1988). This state-only funding represents a willingness by states to commit resources to the problem.

In an environment of constrained budgets, the fact that federal and state dollars are appropriated at an increasing rate for this single problem (some from general revenues) implies that other areas of health care may experience reduced spending. Revenues that would have gone to rural health-care programs may be diverted to prevention and treatment of AIDS. Rural areas will, of course, be required to target a portion of their own resources as well. The availability of testing methods for HIV infection has made proactive control efforts more viable, and increased the demand for public health departments everywhere to address the epidemic. Therefore, even in areas with low incidence, testing must be available, and services must be provided to diagnosed victims. Statistics on state expenditures for AIDS, through 1987, show a wide variation among states. Even states with small caseloads report expenditures dedicated to preventing the spread of the disease to epidemic levels found elsewhere. Some of these states with small caseloads are very rural, including Montana, New Mexico, Alaska, and Maine (Rowe & Ryan 1988).

States with sizable rural populations receive a double hit under funding conditions. The industrial structure typically is comprised of smaller firms offering fewer benefits, especially costly health-care coverage. The percentage of employment-related private coverage is lower in nonmetropolitan areas (57.4 compared to 67.4 percent for all metro areas, with the exception of the 20 largest areas), and the percent with no coverage is also greater in rural areas (17.4 percent compared with 14.7 percent) (U.S. Congress, Office of Technology Assessment, 1990). As the number of uninsured has increased, rural hospitals have provided more uncompensated care, including bad debt and charity. According to the American Hospital Association, small or rural hospitals serve a larger volume of uncovered patients because the rate of poverty is higher in rural areas, and there is less likelihood of employer-provided coverage (Reczynski & Denmark 1988). For rural hospitals, charity care and bad debt costs grew from $0.7 billion in 1981 to $1.2 billion in 1985. At the same time, the ability of rural governments to cover these costs through subsidies or tax appropriations has been weakened by an erosion of state and county tax bases, and reductions in federal revenue-sharing funds.

For specific rural hospitals, the financial scenario limits their potential to enter the debt market. On average, the extensive accounts receivable (more than 72 days for rural hospitals in 1988) and sparse revenues do not present a favorable liquidity picture for borrowing, yet the hospital industry is becoming more dependent on debt financing to cover expenditures (Mick & Morlock 1990).

The uncertainty of hospital budgets has motivated these facilities and their trade associations to pressure governments into seeking other methods of funding uncompensated care. Expansion of the Medicaid program to broaden eligibility and expanded private-sector coverage of workers and dependents are popular considerations. Federal expansion of Medicaid is unlikely under current budget deficit conditions, and, in the absence of a Congressional mandate requiring employer-provided health care, this is unlikely to be the source on a national basis. Employers faced with higher minimum wage payments and increased competition are not willing to take on the additional and growing labor costs associated with providing health-care coverage. Some states have considered making employer-provided coverage more attractive by eliminating or reducing the mandated general required benefits in employer packages. However, the fact remains that, in the current period, many rural hospitals face decreasing or negative patient-care operating margins.

FINANCING LOCAL RURAL HEALTH SERVICES

While federal and state lawmakers ponder and grope for solutions, rural communities should not wait. Rural leaders and advocates must continue to search for creative ways to fund services through other sources, and creative ways to use existing funds and resources efficiently. Unfortunately, the compounding problems of eroding economies and greater demand for all social services make this task difficult.

Some of the difficulties were outlined in conclusions from a 1989 state-wide survey of Pennsylvania local rural officials (Cigler 1991). The governments of small rural towns and counties are slower to adopt innovative options in meeting their fiscal challenges because they lack awareness of potential approaches. This is partly because these governments do not have paid professional staff with training and time to devote to searching out and initiating new strategies. Consequently, the fiscal challenges, such as insuring the delivery of health care, are more acute and these governments rely mainly on traditional solutions.

The survey reported by Cigler (1991) found that raising existing taxes was the most prevalent rural response, and there was limited use of nontraditional revenue-raising strategies. However, among options for reducing costs of providing services, innovative (more nontraditional) approaches are becoming more popular. These include (1) joint-service provisions with other governments, (2) contracting with private sector vendors, (3) increased volunteerism, and (4) purchasing services from another government. One conclusion is that states should provide technical assistance and staff to local governments—an important part of the solution.

Several creative grassroots strategies designed to meet local health-care financing needs were described recently by Landers (1991). The strategy in one rural community was to establish a task force, followed by an imaginative fund-raising scheme to save the local hospital. In another region, several small towns cosponsored medical education for a local physician's assistant (PA). Residents in the communities formed a contract with the PA and paid medical school tuition in exchange for commitment of at least eight years of practice in the communities. This is an interesting approach, and one that contrasts with traditional forms of physician recruitment. Another town, facing loss of ambulance service, raised money to purchase an ambulance, and 50 residents completed emergency medical technician training to form a volunteer corps.

CONCLUSIONS

It is clear that community decision making can be effective in avoiding erosion of local health care. Important in this community model is a prioritized definition of residents' health-care needs. It is interesting, and somewhat ironic, that this resembles a pre–1950s model when local communities relied far more on their own definition of need than on that developed by state and federal officials. When federal and state government funds began entering rural communities, the initiative shifted, and the designation of need was established elsewhere. In many small towns there is a reawakening of the inclination to take charge. Although there remains a heavy dependence on outside public funds, there is also recognition that retention of local control is not only important but desirable.

The limited capability to finance health-care services to meet expectations is a challenge for rural leaders. It is necessary to explore a range of possibilities, such as creative uses of local taxing capability and user fees, and to assess existing resources. In some states, mutually beneficial agreements may be formed for increased use of VA hospitals by rural residents. Innovative demonstration programs have been funded, and rural areas should examine these carefully to determine those that might apply and that could be supported locally.

Innovative strategies in the delivery of services have the potential to provide rural residents with quality services at reasonable costs. However, such strategies may require modifications to rules and regulations governing delivery of services, as well as to the attitudes of those seeking care. For example, statutory changes may be necessary for implementing a clinic staffed by midlevel practitioners. Financial reimbursement and regulatory constraints, limiting the flexibility of rural communities to provide health care for their needs, should be carefully reviewed. If the costs of these requirements far exceed benefits, active programs for change should be promoted. Most important is that solutions must be found locally. The federal or state governments can help stabilize funding but the changing local market for health care often requires significant alterations in the local delivery system. Local leaders will become more accountable for outcomes; for some, this may represent a challenge, for others concern.

NOTE

1. The years 1982 and 1987 were chosen to show results of important changes through the decade. These years represent differences in economic conditions and, importantly, rural area adaptations to Medicare's prospective payment system of hospital reimbursement.

2. Access and Utilization: Special Populations—Special Needs

Lanis L. Hicks

A basic transformation is occurring in the social, demographic, economic, and political structure of rural communities. This transformation is bringing about changes in types of industries, trade patterns, social and family patterns, and human service needs in rural communities (Hersh & Van Hook 1989). However, these changes are not homogeneous across communities, and solutions designed to meet the new problems must recognize the economic, cultural, and regional diversity in rural communities.

This chapter reviews the unique features of access to care for rural residents. Statistical data on utilization of services demonstrate the inequitable access to health services in rural areas. Finally, factors influencing the demand for health care by special populations are discussed, along with suggestions for improving access.

OVERVIEW OF AVAILABILITY AND ACCESSIBILITY

Geographic differences in availability and utilization of health-care services create concerns about the physical health status of populations in the various areas (Andersen et al. 1983, Berk, Bernstein & Taylor 1983, Gabel, Cohen, & Fink 1989). If health status indicators were similar across areas, the issues surrounding inequitable distribution of and access to health care would be less critical. However, as nearly all of the indicators in Tables 2.1 and 2.2 illustrate, the health status of rural residents is significantly lower than that of metro residents. Even by their own perceptions of health status, 12.1 percent of the rural population considered their health to be fair or poor in 1988, compared to 9.3 percent of the metropolitan population (U.S. Department of Health and Human Services 1989).

Table 2.1
Respondents Self-Reported Assessment of Health Status, Metropolitan and Rural Areas, 1988

Respondent Assessed Health Status	Metro Pct.	Rural Pct.
Excellent health	40.4	34.6
Very good health	27.8	27.9
Good health	22.5	25.4
Fair health	6.9	8.3
Poor health	2.4	3.8

Source: U.S. Department of Health and Human Services 1989.

The National Health Interview Survey, a continuing nationwide interview conducted weekly, examines a probability sample of approximately 80,000 households (210,000 persons) among the civilian, noninstitutionalized population (Tables 2.1 and 2.2). This survey gathers information about health conditions and other characteristics of the population. The self-reported data from household members are based on what the person knows and is willing to discuss. Although the interviewers are highly trained and the questionnaire is designed to minimize the effects of differences in reported health events among respondents, some sampling error may occur (U.S. Department of Health and Human Services 1989). These potential limitations must be recognized in interpreting the results of the survey.

Even though the metropolitan residents experienced a slightly higher rate of episodes of acute conditions, the rural population experienced a substantially greater number of restricted activity days, and a somewhat higher number of bed days associated with episodes of acute conditions. Also, the number of days lost from work due to acute conditions was greater among the rural population than among metropolitan residents. Rural residents also reported greater amounts of activity limitations with chronic conditions than did the metropolitan population. For example, 22.8 percent of the rural population reported limitations associated with their major activities due to chronic conditions, while only 17.7 percent of the metropolitan population reported such limitations (U.S. Department of Health and Human Services 1989a). Accidents resulting in injury also occur more often in rural areas than in metropolitan areas, and the restrictions resulting from those accidents are substantially greater in rural areas.

Part of this differential in the impact of acute, injury, and chronic conditions may reflect differences in the types of work performed by the two

Table 2.2
Selected Health Status Indicators Metropolitan and Rural Areas, 1988

Indicators	Metro Rate[1]	Rural Rate[1]
Incidence of Acute Condition		
Infective and parasitic diseases	21.8	24.2
Respiratory conditions	87.7	84.2
Common cold	29.5	25.0
Influenza	42.5	44.1
Digestive system conditions	6.0	7.3
Injuries	24.1	26.0
Other acute conditions	11.3	9.6
All acute conditions	175.5	174.6
Restricted Activity with Acute		
All restricted activity days	689.5	733.8
Bed days	302.1	308.9
Work-loss days per 100 employed	309.5	318.4
School-loss days per 100 (5 - 17)	412.7	384.4
Episodes of Persons Injured		
All types of injury	23.4	25.8
All restricted activity days	245.4	273.2
Bed days	70.1	81.0
	Percent Responded	
Activity Limitations with Chronic		
With no activity limitation	87.0	83.7
With activity limitation	13.0	16.3
With limitation in major activity	8.9	11.4
Unable to carry on major activity	3.8	4.7
Limited in amount/kind of major	5.0	6.7
Limited but not in major activity	4.1	4.9

[1] Number per 100 persons

Source: U.S. Department of Health and Human Services 1989.

groups, with illness having a greater impact on individuals performing manual labor (May 1978). As reflected in the injury rate among rural residents, many of their occupations such as mining, lumbering, and farming are hazardous. Without adequate access to health-care services, these injuries may lead to significant disabilities or even fatalities (Moscovice &

Rosenblatt 1985a). Also, pesticides and other chemicals used in these occupations may contribute to the greater occurrence of chronic illnesses among rural residents, resulting in increased need for health-care services (Wakefield 1990). These differential impacts, however, may also reflect severity of illnesses resulting from delayed access to medical care by the population in rural areas (Andersen 1968). Table 2.3 shows differences in utilization of health-care services between metropolitan and rural populations.

Access to health care reflects not only availability of health-care services, but also the extent to which entrance into the system is reachable, obtainable, and affordable (Parker 1974). Since access to health-care services is extremely difficult to evaluate directly, actual utilization of these services is often used as a proxy (Sheps & Bachar 1981). Actual utilization can be viewed as evidence that access has been achieved (Fiedler 1981). Actual utilization not only reflects the availability and accessibility of services, but also the social and cultural characteristics of the population, because of the effect these have on an individual's expectations and willingness to contact the health-care system for a specific medical condition (Andersen et al. 1983, Banahan & Sharpe 1982, Berk, Bernstein, & Taylor 1983). As Rosenblatt and Moscovice (1982, p. 6) noted, "Rural dwellers are inherently more conservative, unbending, and independent, living in a social setting where role constraints are more rigid." An example of the implications for health care is the conclusion that the self-reliance and determination of farmers to put the needs of their farms first causes them to use physicians less often than any other group (Ingersoll 1989).

In 1988, the residents of rural areas had 5.1 physician contacts per person compared to 5.5 contacts per person among the metropolitan population. Also, 77.2 percent of the population in metropolitan areas had at least one contact with a physician, compared to 75.1 percent of the rural population. These differences in utilization are further exacerbated by the larger proportion of elderly in the rural population than in urban areas. In 1988, elderly persons had 8.7 physician contacts per person, compared to 5.4 contacts by the general population (U.S. Department of Health and Human Services 1989). While the differences in these aggregate measures of utilization are not large, they do indicate the existence of a gap between metropolitan and rural populations' access to health-care services, assuming that utilization is a valid proxy for access.

However, the rural population uses hospital services more than the metropolitan population. Roughly 10 percent of the population in rural areas had at least one hospital episode in 1988, compared to 7.8 percent of the metropolitan population. In addition, the rural population using hospitals had more multiple admissions than metropolitan residents, as reflected in the number of discharges per 100 persons in the two areas: 13.9 discharges per 100 persons in rural areas, and 10.5 discharges per 100 persons in

Table 2.3
Selected Utilization Indicators, Metropolitan and Rural Areas, 1988

Health Care Utilization	Metro	Rural
Physician contacts per person per year[1]	5.5	5.1
Percent persons with one contact or more in past year[1]	77.2	75.1
Percent persons with one hospital episode or more in past year[1]	7.8	9.6
Hospital days per person hospitalized in past year[1]	7.9	8.1
Discharges per 100 persons per year[1]	10.5	13.9
Average length of stay per discharge in days[1]	6.4	5.8
Percent of population without a regular source of care (1986)[2]	18.6	15.3

Source: [1]U.S. Department of Health and Human Services, October 1989; [2]Robert Wood
Johnson Foundation, 1987.

metropolitan areas. Once admitted, however, the rural population had a shorter average length of stay, 5.8 days, compared with 6.4 days.

Much of the differential in hospital-care utilization may reflect the older age structure of the rural population. In 1986, individuals aged 65 and over represented 14 percent of the rural population and only 11 percent of metropolitan residents (Reczynski 1987). Individuals of age 65 and over used 211 days of hospital care per 100 persons, compared to 65 days of hospital care by the general population (U.S. Department of Health and Human Services 1989). If hospital-use rates are controlled for age differences between the two populations, then the differential in utilization narrows substantially.

Furthermore, lack of ambulatory-care services may contribute to higher hospitalization rates, if people delay seeking care until they are more severely ill. Also, physicians may hospitalize patients more frequently because it is more convenient and more time efficient for physicians in areas with few ambulatory services available (Kleinman & Wilson 1977). Because consumers gain entrance to much of the health-care system through physicians, their presence in an area is an obvious component of medical service availability. As a result of this gatekeeper role, a deficiency in the supply of physicians affects the availability of other health-care services (Dettelback 1988, Moscovice & Rosenblatt 1985a). As the data in Table 2.4 illustrate, wide discrepancies exist in the availability of physicians between rural and metropolitan areas.

In 1986, metropolitan areas contained 76.7 percent of the population and 85.5 percent of all physicians (M.D.s and D.O.s). This left 14.5 percent of the physicians to serve 23.3 percent of the population (U.S. Bureau of the Census 1989a). Within rural areas, there were also significant differentials in the availability of physicians. While the RAND studies (Newhouse et al. 1982a, Newhouse et al. 1982b, Williams et al. 1983) reported that almost all towns of 2,500 people or more had at least one physician, Langwell et al. (1985) found that only 21 percent of nonmetropolitan counties under 10,000 could attract even one additional young physician between 1975 and 1979.

The most severe availability problems still arise in small, remote communities. A study by Kindig & Movassaghi (1989) found that physician availability in counties with populations under 10,000 was only about one third of the United States average. Further, the rate of growth in physicians per population was much lower in these counties than in other rural counties or in metropolitan areas. As physicians consider a practice location, they tend to select a community where other practitioners and health-care resources already exist, rather than an isolated, remote community without the presence of supporting colleagues (DeFriese & Ricketts 1989). The ability to attract physicians to rural areas has been shown to be strongly related to the rural origin of the targeted physician. If the physician is originally from a rural area, there is a greater likelihood of selecting a rural setting to establish a practice than if the physician is originally from an urban setting (Bruce 1985). In 1981, 129 rural counties had no active physicians; by 1985, with an overall increase of approximately 72,000 active physicians, 125 rural counties still had no active physician (U.S. Department of Health and Human Services 1988).

A potential contributor to this distribution problem is the medical education process. Physicians are trained in highly sophisticated medical facilities with easy access to modern technology. In addition, the attitude is instilled during their education that without this technical equipment, they are providing substandard medical care. Because most rural facilities do not have many of the sophisticated technologies, a deeply ingrained feeling is fostered that excellent care cannot be provided in these settings, reducing physicians' willingness to locate in these areas (Bishirjian 1989).

Another potential contributor to the inequities in physician distribution is the increasing specialization of medicine. Rural providers must be generalists, capable of handling a broad range of problems. However, fewer

Table 2.4
Distribution of Nonfederal MD Physicians, Metropolitan and Rural Areas, 1986*

Physician	Total Number	Total Ratio MD/100,000	Metro Number	Metro Ratio MD/100,000	Rural Number	Rural Ratio MD/100,000
Total	544,308	225.5	478,343	258.2	65,965	117.5
Patient Care	444,705	184.2	389,993	210.5	54,712	97.5
Office	325,757	134.9	278,389	150.3	47,368	84.4
GP/FP	53,622	22.2	37,684	20.3	15,938	28.4
Medical	99,239	41.1	88,813	47.9	10,426	18.6
Surgery	93,679	38.8	80,975	43.7	12,704	22.6
Other	79,217	32.8	70,917	38.3	8,300	14.8
Hospital	118,948	49.3	111,604	60.2	7,344	13.1
Other Activites	39,107	16.2	37,307	20.1	1,800	3.2
Inactive	46,835	19.4	38,934	21.0	7,901	14.1
Unclassed	13,661	5.7	12,109	6.5	1,552	2.8

*There were also 25,479 active Doctors of Osteopathy in 1986. Of these, 16,816 were located in rural areas and 8,663 were located in metropolitan areas.

Sources: Roback et al. 1987, and American Osteopathic Association 1988.

and fewer physicians are selecting general and family practice, thereby reducing the number available for rural service. In 1987, only 11 percent of all nonfederal active physicians were in general or family practice (U.S. Department of Health and Human Services 1990a).

In the past, some of the deficiencies in physician availability were relieved by certified nurse practitioners, nurse midwives, and physician assistants in rural underserved areas. In recent years, however, these practitioners have begun to concentrate in urban areas, and their location patterns now resemble those of physicians (U.S. Department of Health and Human Services 1988).

MEDICALLY UNDERSERVED RURAL AREAS

A clear definition of what constitutes adequate amounts and kinds of medical services is a key factor in determining equity of access to health services. Although a single definition of medically underserved has not evolved, most definitions are based on a ratio of population to provider, and many incorporate high infant mortality rates, high poverty rates, and high elderly population rates in designating needy areas (*Federal Register* 1991). Although ratios do not incorporate qualitative determinants of a population's access to health care, they do provide a rough estimate of the availability of services in an area.

Other factors that influence the need and demand for medical services are included, in an attempt to identify differentials in health status and other conditions that exacerbate problems with health-care access. In 1986, there were 1,949 federally designated primary-care shortage areas in the United States. Of these, 1,304 (66.9 percent) were in rural areas. However, the designated shortage areas located in metropolitan areas contained 53 percent of the population residing in shortage areas (U.S. Department of Health and Human Services 1988a).

Residing in a designated medically underserved area, however, has not been found to have a significant impact on the utilization of health-care services (Kleinman & Wilson 1977, Chiu, Aday, & Andersen 1981, Berk, Bernstein, & Taylor 1983, Palm & Booton 1984). These various studies show that, although residents of underserved areas encounter more inconvenience in traveling to obtain health services, their utilization of health care is not significantly lower than comparable populations in nonunderserved areas. Apparently, residents leave the local community to receive needed health care, rather than forgo necessary health services. Factors other than residing in an underserved area, such as income, health status, and insurance coverage, shed much more light on health services utilization patterns among individuals (Chiu, Aday, & Andersen 1981).

Table 2.5
Specific Barriers to Access, Metropolitan and Rural Areas

Characteristics	Metro	Rural
Families below poverty level (1985)[1]		
Percent of total families	10.3	14.7
Percent of black families	27.1	36.6
Percent of hispanic families	24.9	32.7
Percent of white families	7.9	12.7
Unemployment rate (1985)[2]	6.8	8.0
Economic underemployment rate (1982)	12.3	18.1
Health insurance coverage (1986)[3]		
Population under age 65		
Percent with private insurance	76.8	72.7
Percent with public assistance	4.6	4.8
Percent with Medicare	1.1	1.4
Percent with no insurance	14.5	18.2
Education (1980)[2]		
Median years completed	11.6	10.9
High school dropout rate	15.0	16.9
Percent with college education	12.8	9.2
Federal expenditures per capita for		
human resource programs (1980)[4]		
Total expenditures	$ 86	$ 51
Health services	14	7
Social services	4	2
Training and employment	47	18

Sources: [1]U.S. Bureau of the Census 1986; [2]Cordes 1989; [3]U.S. Department of Health and Human Services, 1987; [4] U.S. Department of Agriculture, 1984

SPECIFIC BARRIERS TO ACCESS

The characteristics of rural life necessitate the presence of accessible, high quality health care. However, some of the same factors that create a need for health care also create barriers. As Table 2.5 demonstrates, many characteristics of the population living in rural areas differ from those of urban populations. Many of these characteristics reflect increased barriers to accessing health-care services for the rural population.

Low income individuals have poorer health status than high income individuals, and also lack the personal resources necessary to access much of the health-care system (Rowland & Lyons 1989). The residents in rural areas are poorer than their metropolitan counterparts; 14.7 percent of rural families were living below the poverty level in 1985, compared to 10.3 percent of metropolitan families (U.S. Bureau of the Census 1986), and 18.3 percent of rural individuals were living in poverty in 1987, compared to 12.7 percent of metropolitan individuals (American Hospital Association 1989). In addition, of individuals less than age 65 living in rural areas, 18.4 percent were without health insurance in 1986 compared to 14.5 percent in metro areas (U.S. Department of Health and Human Services 1987).

Part of the difference in poverty level and insurance is attributable to employment patterns. Traditionally, rural areas have not had large, unionized manufacturing firms, which offer high wages and extensive fringe benefit packages (Rowland & Lyons 1989). As the economy of the United States matures, employment opportunities will increasingly occur in metropolitan areas since most new businesses and new jobs arise in service industries. Service industries tend to be labor intensive and highly specialized, requiring concentrated and densely populated areas in order to secure sufficient demand for the services (Cordes 1989).

Reversing earlier trends, where unemployment was greater in metropolitan areas, the unemployment rate in rural areas in 1985 was 8.0, compared to 6.8 in metropolitan areas. In addition, the economic underemployment rate was 18.1 percent in rural areas and only 12.3 percent in metropolitan areas (Cordes 1989). Underemployment refers to individuals working in jobs for which they are unsuited because of their qualifications. Their employment in jobs that do not use the training or expertise they possess indicates that their compensation (pay plus benefits) is less than it would be otherwise. Underemployment also refers to working fewer hours per week or fewer weeks per year than desired, again resulting in lower compensation.

These characteristics imply a greater need for public assistance in rural areas; however, in reality, metropolitan areas receive a greater share of public resources per person than do rural areas. As in many other cases, resources are needed to attract federal programs, and many rural areas do not have sufficient resources or talent to compete successfully for federal dollars. In 1980, federal per capita expenditures for human resource programs in rural areas were only 59 percent of expenditures in metropolitan areas. Federal per capita expenditures for health services in metropolitan areas were twice as high as in rural areas (U.S. Department of Agriculture 1984). One of the main public income assistance programs is Aid to Families with Dependent Children (AFDC). This program is often limited to single-parent families, and single-parent households are less likely to occur in rural areas than in urban areas (Deavers & Brown 1984).

Currently, metropolitan community health centers receive over 60 percent of available federal dollars, despite the fact that rural areas contain more than half of the targeted population (Wakefield 1990). This discrepancy in public assistance further exacerbates the rural/metropolitan inequities in accessing health-care services, especially because many of these federally sponsored programs are also financed with state matching funds. Also, simply being designated as metropolitan increases an area's eligibility for some federal programs and the level of revenues received for similar programs, such as Medicare reimbursement.

The problems faced by rural populations in accessing health-care services include lack of financial resources, inadequate number of providers, excessive distances to providers and corresponding transportation problems, and substandard living and hazardous working environments. The rural population, in general, experiences more of these problems and barriers than their metropolitan counterparts. Moreover, certain subgroups of the rural population, including the elderly, poor, and chronically ill, experience even greater problems accessing the system.

SPECIAL GROUPS ENCOUNTERING ACCESS PROBLEMS

Age and income are two major determinants of the health status of the population. The data on these (Tables 2.6 and 2.7) are not disaggregated by place of residence, but nonetheless inferences can be made about the implications of the data for rural populations based on information presented earlier in the chapter. As the age of the population increases, the proportion of the population reporting excellent health status declines, from 53.9 percent of those under age 5 to only 16.3 percent of those 65 and over. Conversely, as the age of the population increases, the proportion of the population reporting poor health status increases from less than 1 percent to almost 10 percent.

A factor possibly contributing to this perception of poor health status is the substantially greater number of restricted days of activities reported by the elderly, because of chronic conditions. Individuals 65 and older had 22.4 days of restricted activity due to chronic conditions, compared to only 1.5 days for individuals under 18 years of age. The existence of these chronic conditions among the elderly increases the number of times they need to contact a physician. In 1988, the elderly had 8.7 physician contacts compared to 5.4 contacts among the total population. The elderly also had 26.1 hospital discharges per 100 persons, compared to 11.2 for the total population. Although the elderly experience fewer acute episodes of illness than do other age groups, they more often seek medical attention for these episodes than do other age groups, except for the very young (under 5 years of age).

In 1988, a disproportionate number of the elderly lived in rural areas, and the rural population is continuing to age at a faster rate than the

Table 2.6
Health Status Indicators by Age, 1988

Indicator	Less than 5	5-17	18-24	25-44	45-64	More than 65
Number acute episode per person	3.6	2.5	1.7	1.6	1.1	1.1
Percent acute episode medically attended	83.2	55.0	54.5	59.9	62.5	70.9
Restricted days acute episode	10.0	7.2	7.1	6.4	5.8	8.2
Bed days acute episode	4.9	3.4	3.0	2.6	2.4	3.4
Restricted days chronic conditions	0.7	1.7	2.3	5.9	13.2	22.4
Bed days chronic conditions	0.4	0.6	0.9	2.1	5.5	11.0
Physician contacts per person	7.0	3.4	3.8	5.1	6.1	8.7
Percent seeing physician during year	93.2	75.7	72.3	71.9	76.1	85.0
Hospital discharges per 100 persons	7.8	3.8	10.6	9.9	13.4	26.1
Average length of stay	6.7	5.1	4.3	4.8	7.0	8.0
Self-Reported health status						
Excellent	53.9	52.5	43.9	41.0	28.2	16.3
Very good	26.2	26.6	30.7	31.0	26.5	21.5
Good	16.4	18.2	21.2	21.8	28.2	32.8
Fair	2.8	2.4	3.7	5.0	11.6	19.9
Poor	0.6	0.3	0.4	1.3	5.4	9.5

Source: U.S. Department of Health and Human Services 1989.

metropolitan population. Although rural area residents accounted for 22.7 percent of the total population, these rural areas accounted for 25.8 percent of the total elderly population. As discussed earlier, the elderly utilize health-care services much more frequently than do younger populations. Much of this increased utilization is necessitated by the existence of more chronic health problems among the elderly. As a consequence, inequitable access to health care may create excessive burdens on this population, as the rural elderly have to travel significant distances more frequently to receive care for their chronic illnesses.

Lower income individuals also have poorer health status than do higher income individuals. In 1988, only 25.8 percent of individuals with incomes under $10,000 reported their health status as excellent, compared to 49.7

Table 2.7
Health Status Indicators by Income, 1988 (in thousands of dollars)

Indicator	Less than $10	$10-19	$20-34	More than $35	Total
Number acute episode per person	2.0	1.7	1.7	1.8	1.8
Percent acute episode medically attended	64.8	59.5	61.5	64.7	62.8
Restricted days acute episode	10.0	7.8	6.5	5.8	7.0
Bed days acute episode	4.7	3.5	2.7	2.4	3.0
Restricted days chronic conditions	16.6	10.0	5.8	3.9	7.7
Bed days chronic conditions	7.5	4.4	2.2	1.4	3.3
Physician contacts per person	6.6	5.6	5.2	5.3	5.4
Percent seeing physician during year	78.0	74.9	76.3	78.9	76.7
Hospital discharges per 100 persons	18.7	13.4	10.1	7.7	11.2
Average length of stay	6.9	6.3	5.8	5.4	6.3
Self-Reported health status					
Excellent	25.8	31.3	39.9	49.7	39.1
Very good	23.1	27.0	30.2	28.4	27.8
Good	28.9	27.5	22.6	17.9	23.2
Fair	14.6	10.4	5.7	3.2	7.2
Poor	7.5	3.9	1.7	0.8	2.7

Source: U.S. Department of Health and Human Services 1989.

percent of individuals with incomes of $35,000 and above. Also, 7.5 percent of individuals at the low income level reported their health status as poor, compared to less than 1 percent of the upper income individuals.

In 1988, individuals with incomes of less than $10,000 contacted a physician 6.6 times, compared to 5.3 contacts by persons with incomes of $35,000 and over. The difference in the utilization of hospital care was even more pronounced: low income individuals had 18.7 discharges per 100 persons compared to 7.7 discharges per 100 persons in the high income category. Low income individuals also had more days of restricted activity due to chronic conditions than did high income individuals, 16.6 versus 3.9, respectively. All of these are indications that lower income individuals have more health problems, which necessitate increased access to health-care services.

In 1988, 14.7 percent of rural families had incomes below the poverty level, compared to only 10.3 percent of metropolitan families. As a result of the disproportionate distribution in 1988, rural families reported 30.2 percent of all families with incomes below the poverty level.

Although, in general, low income individuals utilize more health services than do high income individuals, the ability to finance these services varies substantially between rural and metropolitan populations. This may, therefore, cause aggregate data to camouflage significant variations between these two populations. Health-care services are generally paid either privately through personal income and private insurance, or by public assistance through public insurance and charity. Costs of expensive services, such as hospital care, for low income people, have often been handled through cost-shifting to private payers. As mentioned above, a higher proportion of individuals below the poverty level live in rural areas than in metropolitan areas. In addition, the rural population is less likely to have private insurance than the urban population (U.S. Department of Health and Human Services 1987) and the availability of public assistance, including Medicaid, in rural areas is much lower than in metropolitan areas (Butler 1988, Wakefield 1990).

The lack of financial resources, especially the lack of insurance coverage (private or public), has been shown to impact negatively on the utilization of health services (Butler 1988). Low income urban residents have better access to public insurance coverage than do their rural counterparts, increasing their ability to access the system. Combining the lack of financial resources with the physical barriers (distance, lack of providers, inadequate transportation) faced by the rural population further reduces their ease of access to the health-care system.

In the future, access to services may become even more limited for low income rural residents. Hospitals and other providers experience increasing difficulties shifting the costs of uncompensated care to other payers, thereby limiting their ability to continue providing care, below cost, to medically indigent people. Also, as the number of people who are uninsured or underinsured continues to rise in rural areas, increasing the number of people at risk of becoming medically indigent, these areas will become more unattractive to new practitioners. As access to health care becomes more difficult, rural residents will face both immediate and long-term declines in health status. Consequently, as access declines, need for access will increase.

INNOVATIVE WAYS TO INCREASE ACCESS

Traditionally, access to health-care services has been evaluated in terms of distance to a provider and waiting time. Realized access has been measured in terms of actual utilization of services. Increasingly, access is being considered in terms of the integration of services, using such measures as continuity, appropriateness, and quality (Freeman, Blendon, & Aiken 1987, Bauer & Weis 1989). In addition, access to health care is now measured in terms of access to information. Computers and other telemetry systems connect physician offices to major medical centers, increasing the information available to providers and to consumers in more remote areas. Many rural consumers gain direct access to health information through medical channels on home satellite systems. Expectations of rural consumers about potential health-care services are becoming more similar to their in metropolitan counterparts (Bishirjian 1989). Access to health care is thus redefined in terms of access to services or even access to medical information, rather than access to facilities (Winkenwerder & Ball 1988, MacStravic 1989).

A key to developing successful solutions to rural access problems is understanding their diversity. Efforts to define equity of access and to develop solutions; with a single measure or strategy, will have to give way to multivariate measures. Recognition of rural diversity must be incorporated in the solutions to allow for different delivery mechanisms, with the capability to meet specific local medical needs. In some areas, geographic distance and spatial isolation are major problems; in others, persistent poverty deprives residents of access to services and has a negative impact on health status. Because medical problems vary among rural areas, the mix of services needed to meet these problems also varies. In determining the appropriate mix of services for a local area, input from local community members and leaders regarding perceptions, expectations, needs, and commitments to support the services is crucial. It would be counterproductive to develop a service mix that ignores the willingness and ability of the local population to support the mix of services identified. A study of rural consumers' willingness to travel for care found that a significant factor in this increased travel was a negative attitude about local services (Straub & Walzer 1990). Rural providers must continually seek input from local residents regarding their perceptions of quality.

As strategies and policies are undertaken to improve the rural population's access to health services, the problems must be considered in terms of new perspectives and innovations. The traditional health system, even if it were viable, would not be effective in responding to many of the needs it currently faces. Intervention strategies to improve access to health services in rural areas must be specifically designed to address rural conditions; they must not simply continue to emphasize small-scale mimicry of urban programs (Coward 1987, Freeman, Blendon, & Aiken 1987, Cordes 1989).

Viable solutions to rural access problems cannot be designed and implemented strictly from the federal perspective, but continued outside subsidies (both financial and human resource) will be necessary for many sparsely populated and economically depressed rural areas (Joint Rural Task Force 1989). Along with these subsidies, however, leadership and involvement indigenous to the local area must occur. Without a local cadre of concerned, creative, dedicated, and motivated community leaders, momentum to effect the desired changes in rural communities cannot be achieved (Cochran & Ericson 1989, Rosenberg 1989). Rural leaders must take the initiative in adapting to the changing environment of their community, by evaluating the health-care needs of their local constituency and by designing systems that are responsive to those needs. The federal and state governments must also be flexible in designing their assistance programs for rural areas, to enable those areas to maximize benefits.

PART II

The Supply of Rural Health Care—Facility Inputs

3. The Case for Keeping the Rural Hospital

Ron Damasauskas

The survival of rural hospitals is paramount to the continued availability of health-care services in rural areas. Can health care in rural areas be delivered outside the hospital setting? Of course it can. But the need to maintain a broad spectrum of care and to insure its availability to residents in rural areas requires a centralized focus of services. The rural hospital can provide that center.

Rural hospitals have faced extraordinary obstacles over the past decade. The issues of changing demographics, a declining economy, manpower shortages, financial shortfalls, and overall difficulties in providing access are not new among the difficulties facing rural hospitals. These problems are disturbing, however, in that they persist and hold the potential to impact negatively on rural health care on a long-term basis. Furthermore, the approaches taken toward resolving these problems are often disadvantageous for small or rural hospitals. Instead of seeking to build on what currently exists within the environment in order to provide needed health-care services to rural inhabitants, the trend is toward new and innovative approaches. These approaches are designed primarily for delivery of modified and abbreviated care in the rural environment, and usually incorporate a shift of extensive care to urban areas.

The basis for this approach is founded in the concept of regionalization. In the past several years, proponents of regionalization have advocated this approach to help minimize or decrease the proliferation of new technologies. The underlying assumption is that by controlling the level of technology, it is possible to reduce the overall cost of health care, while at the same time developing more coherent mechanisms for providing services. However, the concept of regionalization has not been wholly embraced. In part, this may be due to a realization that the gains to larger hospitals, such as from referral networks, are not partially returned to offset costs to rural hospitals (Bateman 1991). It is instructive to evaluate the rural health-care system within the context of its rejection of the regionalization approach.

This chapter briefly evaluates the rural environment and uses this setting to examine the options available in providing rural care, arguing that the rural hospital is effective as a centralized focus of service. Implications for this practical approach are offered, suggesting that innovation does not require abandonment of the traditional form of rural services.

THE RURAL ENVIRONMENT

In order to assess the position of rural hospitals and the provision of care to rural inhabitants, it is necessary first to explore the environment within which these facilities operate. Several dynamic factors influence the position of these institutions, including population shifts, declining rural economies, manpower and financial shortages, capital and infrastructure issues, and an abiding desire to provide access for all who need care.

In its broadest sense, the aging of the population is a potential time bomb in rural America. The elderly account for 36 percent of total health-care costs, but comprise only 12 percent of the population in the United States (U.S. Congress, Senate, 1988). Furthermore, those 65 and over comprise 13 percent of the population in nonmetro areas, as opposed to only 10.7 percent of the population in metro areas (U.S. Congress, Office of Technology Assessment, 1990).

Projections indicate that by the year 2030 approximately 20–25 percent of the United States population will be older than 65 years of age. Furthermore, nearly 1 in 4 of those 65 and over will be over age 85. This is significant in terms of its potential impact on the need for health care. In 1987, those 75 and over used health care at a rate 4 times greater than did those between the ages of 45 and 64. Similarly, those 75 and over used health-care services twice as frequently as did those between the ages of 65 and 74 (U.S. Congress, Senate, 1988).

Several other health-care concerns also prevail in rural areas. There is a relatively higher rate of chronic disease than in urban areas (Norton & McManus 1989). There is also a slightly higher infant mortality rate and a dramatically higher injury-related mortality rate. Finally, there is a higher proportion of hospitalization in nonmetro areas, particularly for those populations 65 and over.

Economic conditions have declined in much of rural America. Many of the causes for the vulnerability of rural economies relate to strong dependence on a single major industry. Furthermore, rural manufacturing tends to be concentrated in blue collar occupations and low wage industries;

the national shift to a service economy has exacerbated already serious rural employment shortfalls (U.S. Congress, Office of Technology Assessment, 1990). The rural unemployment rate skyrocketed during the 1980s, and when it is adjusted to account for discouraged workers and involuntary part-time workers, it is much greater than that in urban areas.

The deteriorating economic condition has affected rural hospitals in at least three ways. First, it has resulted in an increase in the percentage of uninsured and underinsured rural residents, thereby expanding demand for uncompensated care. Second, it has renewed the migration of productive rural residents to urban areas. Finally, the declining rural economies have placed additional stress on the resources of local and county governments, which, nationwide, own more than half of rural hospitals (Reczynski 1987).

Population changes and economic conditions, therefore, have a significant effect on the viability of rural hospitals. On the one hand, population changes result in greater need for resources to provide treatment to an older and more vulnerable population. On the other hand, the rural economy is substantially depleted, resulting in a greater number of rural poor and a decreased ability to provide services. Due to these changes, a growing number of Medicare and Medicaid patients are served by rural hospitals. This leads to a greater dependence on sources of government funding through both the Medicare and Medicaid programs (U.S. Congress 1988).

The hospital is the fundamental link to the health-care system for most of the poor and elderly in rural areas. However, the federal government has, by virtue of developing and supporting certain programs over the past several years, indicated that alternative sources of providing care to rural inhabitants would be beneficial. There are several questions that must be addressed to determine which is the optimal means for delivery of health care, the hospital, or an alternative facility. First, do these alternative facilities provide improved access? Second, if access is improved, does utilization result? Third, suppose access is diminished and overutilization declines; will decreased access and underutilization ultimately result in the same cost problems that prompted much of the federal government's decisions regarding rural health delivery in the first place?

RECRUITMENT OF HEALTH PROFESSIONALS

The components of the personnel shortage issue are physicians, nurses, midlevel practitioners, and allied health specialists. In each of these areas, rural hospitals have been faced with severe difficulties in recruiting and retaining personnel. This difficulty is directly linked to compensation. A comparison of average compensation levels (money earnings and benefits) for health-care professionals between metropolitan statistical areas (MSAs) and rural areas, reveals vast inequities (Illinois Hospital Association 1990).

However, this disparity is not the only factor associated with health professional recruitment difficulties in rural areas. For physicians, the economic shortfall associated with rural practice is coupled with problems of spousal preference for an urban area, the necessity of maintaining longer work hours, and seeing higher volumes of patients to meet an economic standard, as well as professional isolation, burnout, and the lack of backup equipment. These all contribute to difficulties in recruiting and retaining the level of physicians necessary to staff rural hospitals. The availability of nurses, midlevel practitioners, and allied health personnel is also affected by concerns of professional isolation, legal barriers to the development of an accepted practice, marginal financial liability, and the question of community acceptance.

In 1988, rural hospitals spent 54.3 percent of their total operating expenses on labor costs (Illinois Hospital Association 1990). Increasing salaries in hopes of mitigating the personnel shortage would result in further financial disadvantage for these institutions, especially given their heavy dependence on relatively fixed government reimbursement.

Nearby urban institutions can and do actively recruit from rural settings to fill the shortages in their own institutions, thereby creating additional pressures for rural institutions. By virtue of the higher reimbursement rates urban hospitals receive for treating Medicare patients, a larger share of patients with private insurance, and the generally better overall conditions of these institutions, they are able to offer a more attractive package. Higher salaries, improved benefits, flexibility in scheduling, better working conditions, and professional opportunities are among the advantages (American Hospital Association 1990). Furthermore, the workload in a rural setting is often extreme, especially for nurses. The cuts in staffing, undertaken to increase productivity and ensure a positive bottom line, have resulted in fewer nurses handling more cases. As a result, the stress associated with rural nursing can be substantial. In some cases, this is offset by the type of nursing practiced in rural hospitals. Many nurses find the generalist approach required in rural hospital nursing extremely attractive.

Dangerous shortages continue to persist, and vacancy rates are reported for nurses, allied health personnel, pharmacists, and dieticians. In certain rural areas of Illinois, for example, staggering shortages exist. In Northwestern Illinois in 1988, the pharmacist vacancy rate was 44.8 percent, dietitian vacancy rate 61.5 percent, and social work vacancy rate 59.5 percent (Illinois Hospital Association 1988). It is also worth noting that, although vacancy rates in certain categories are generally lower in many rural areas, even a single shortage in key areas can have a significantly negative impact. A single missing pharmacist or lab technician in a rural hospital can represent 33 to 50 percent of the total complement of those allied health professionals.

FINANCE

The financial condition of rural hospitals is precarious. A declining volume of patients has resulted in decreased ability to meet fixed costs. The shortfall of payment from Medicare and Medicaid is a principal, if not primary, culprit in this problem. Several other factors, however, have contributed to the financial condition of many rural hospitals.

First, rural hospitals have been required to allocate significant funds for increasingly expensive, technologically advanced equipment, as well as for personnel capable of operating such equipment. The need for this specialized technology results from its value in the recruitment and retention of physicians. Second, communities require that their institutions remain capable and competent in providing the most current diagnostic and therapeutic care. This issue has a clear impact on the profit margins of rural hospitals. In the first three years of Medicare's prospective pricing system, 83 percent of those hospitals with negative hospital margins were located in rural areas (American Hospital Association 1990). Furthermore, in 1988, 38 percent of all rural hospitals had negative total operating margins. Expensive technology and the personnel needed to operate that technology are difficult to maintain in an environment where operations are not profitable.

An additional factor placing stress on the finances of the rural hospital is the fact that 30 percent of rural inhabitants have no health insurance. Poverty rates tend to be higher in rural areas, with 18 percent of the rural population estimated to be living below the federal poverty level, compared to 12 percent of the urban population (Cordes 1989). Rural residents often are unable to qualify for Medicaid because they are either self-employed or are part of a two-parent family.

Finally, because of the financial hardships faced by many rural hospitals, funded depreciation has been used to offset operating losses. This practice leads to an often inescapable spiral of decline, especially for facilities of the early Hill-Burton era. The inability to replace needed capital assets can result in decreased quality of care and an unwillingness on the part of physicians to practice in the facility.

Although the problems facing rural hospitals are severe, they are not insurmountable. Many rural facilities have taken significant actions to minimize the effects of these difficulties. The next section of this chapter discusses strategies pursued by rural hospitals to circumvent these difficulties.

RURAL HOSPITAL RESPONSE

Rural hospitals have responded in a variety of innovative ways to the pressures facing them. Conversion, affiliation, diversification, downsizing, and closure have been the predominant avenues of response. Given the incentives within the government-sponsored payment systems and the review mechanisms designed to limit inpatient care, a significant proportion of rural health care has been oriented toward other forms of delivery. The question that remains to be answered with regard to these innovations is whether the rural hospital has become an anachronism within the health-care environment. In other words, is it time for rural hospitals to reorient the forms and delivery mechanisms of the care they provide in such a way that the hospital, as we now know it, ceases to exist?

Conversion. Nationwide, several rural hospitals have converted from acute-care inpatient facilities to other, more specialized forms of delivery. Preeminent among these forms is conversion to long-term care. Conversion to other forms—which reflect an orientation toward outpatient care with limited inpatient capability—include ambulatory-care centers, urgent-care centers, recovery centers, and specialized forms of inpatient facilities.

It is necessary to question whether or not needed health care, at the acute level, remains available. If a rural hospital converts services to long-term care, and the nearest facility providing acute-care services is 10 miles away, the issue of access to acute care is marginal. However, if that same facility is located 40 or 50 miles from the nearest acute-care facility, the question of access is both real and threatening.

Similar access questions can be posed with regard to ambulatory care, urgent care, and recovery care concepts. The notion of providing organized outpatient care in rural areas is appropriate. However, it is equally important to remember that a disproportionate percentage of rural inhabitants tend to be elderly and poor. If relatively immediate access to acute care is not available, do we introduce disincentives to the psychology of their treatment by further reducing their willingness to present to acute-care facilities at earlier stages in the progression of their disease?

Similarly, there are social questions that must be posed as to the accessibility of more distant acute facilities to these older and poorer rural inhabitants. Transportation represents a significant barrier. There is virtually no available public transportation in rural areas. Those elderly and poor who do not own an automobile may find a trip to a distant acute-care facility sufficiently burdensome to avoid the trip altogether. From a long-term perspective, it is also important to consider whether the conversion to alternate forms of delivery enables rural areas to maintain the necessary health-care personnel required to provide services within their community, and whether doctors still want to practice if not near an acute-care hospital?

The principal drawback to conversions is that they are often more a result of economic realities and less oriented toward the medical and social needs of the communities they had previously served. What is retained is a corporate entity, which may meet some, but not all, of the community's needs.

Affiliation. Affiliation reflects the simplest form of regionalization. The creation of multihospital systems can provide geographic dispersion across an area and result in patient flow from primary- to tertiary-care facilities all within one system. The fundamental difficulty encountered by rural hospitals with regard to the development of multihospital systems is in finding affiliation partners. For many urban facilities, the prospect of courting a rural partner is less than optimal. Many times the urban facility believes that the eventual decline or elimination of the rural facility will result in the patients eventually gravitating toward the urban hospital. Furthermore, urban facilities have often demonstrated a relative ignorance, with regard to the operations of rural hospitals, resulting in unhappy and unprofitable arrangements.

Still, the notion of service or clinical arrangements is one which has grown and prospered. Formal or informal relationships between smaller rural hospitals and larger community or tertiary facilities have resulted in clinical outreach programs that increase the level of care provided in rural areas. They also increase the economic viability of rural hospitals, through utilization of services, and they capture a patient load for the large community or tertiary facility. The need for access to a broader array of specialists has been a significant concern identified by rural residents. Services or clinical relationships meet these needs and help everyone involved. The patients win because they get the services, the rural facility wins because it is seen as being a "fuller service" facility, and the urban facility wins because it gets additional referrals. Furthermore, screening and early diagnosis will generally result in improved outcomes for patients.

The concept of affiliations or rural networks is one that bodes well for all involved, if the guidelines for the operation of these systems are designed with the intention of benefiting all parties. Furthermore, physicians who participate in the clinical or service relationships, as well as medical staffs from each of the facilities, must be willing to maintain their commitment to the program. Nevertheless, experience throughout the United States with such relationships is proving to have a positive result on the delivery and maintenance of a broad spectrum of health care in rural areas.

Diversification. Many rural facilities have attempted to maintain their acute-care base in either a full or modified form, while at the same time broadening the array of services that they provide to their communities. Long-term care, alcoholism and chemical dependency, rehabilitation, home health, and health promotion are some of the many alternate services that have been created to help supplement the operation of rural acute-care hospitals. In many cases, though, the results of diversification efforts have been marginal. The common form of long-term care and acute hospital joined in a single operation has been the most successful diversification effort. Nonetheless, many of the problems that plague the acute-care side, such as staff retention and financing, also affect long-term care provision of service and reimbursement.

Similarly, shortages in trained professionals inhibit the development of successful service delivery programs, such as alcoholism and chemical dependency, and rehabilitation. Ongoing staff shortages and physician availability make such diversification efforts adventuresome on a day-to-day basis. Home health activities have been relatively successful, as an adjunct service, in many rural facilities. However, because of the relatively small population base and extensive travel distances required, as well as low reimbursement rates, home health has been only modestly beneficial in financial terms.

Downsizing. Virtually all rural hospitals have undertaken either a full or modified downsizing. Decreasing staff and beds and increasing part-time employees have been fundamental components in the downsizing efforts. By replacing full-time staff with part-time workers, rural hospitals have managed to cut operational floor expenditures, while gaining flexibility in responding to a fluctuating census. By decreasing staff beds, they have effectively eliminated the cost of those beds. In many cases this effort has resulted in greater productivity within these institutions, but is typically a step that can be accomplished only once. There are also limits in that some fixed resources cannot be reduced by increments, and in such cases, benefits from scale economies are abandoned.

Closure. Many rural hospitals have closed. Between 1980 and 1989, 252 rural hospitals closed nationwide, and it is likely that additional closures will follow (American Hospital Association 1990). As an option, closure is the most debilitating of potential reactions for a community. The social, political, and economic ramifications of closure are substantial. The psychological impacts also weigh heavily on inhabitants of the community, both current and future. Finally, the health and welfare of local community residents are unquestionably compromised. The middle-age, relatively healthy population within those communities may already obtain needed medical care in more distant locations; however, the elderly and poor who remain in the rural community are at the greatest disadvantage. Poverty, advanced old age, lack of transportation systems, and marginal support systems all contribute to potential health disasters, which might otherwise be readily addressed, were necessary health resources available locally.

KEEPING THE HOSPITAL

The notion of maintaining a hospital threatened with closure is one that bears serious consideration for several reasons. First, in many cases, the big bills associated with construction of the facility have already been paid by the time a rural hospital is threatened with closure. Typically, these facilities do not face extraordinary debt as the result of physical plant or even technology purchases. Instead, they are threatened with shortfalls from payers, inability to attract necessary medical personnel, and relatively modest budgetary considerations that could be resolved if the will existed within the community to do so.

Keeping the hospital open ensures the continued economic, social, and medical benefit of maintaining local health-care providers. It ensures that the very young, the poor, and the elderly can receive needed medical care. The solution to maintaining the hospital is often related to tax proposals that are dismissed out of hand. A recent study compared the subsidy needed to keep a hospital open with the income that would be lost to a community if a hospital were to close (McDermott, Cornia, & Parsons 1991). Direct and indirect economic benefits accruing to the community as a result of the hospital's operation were calculated. It was determined that a 70-bed hospital, with annual costs of nearly $9 million, and a 5 percent annual operating loss, would require an annual subsidy of approximately $450,000 to maintain its operation. On the basis of the methodology employed in this study, this rural hospital would bring approximately $3.7 million per year to the local economy. In this case, a $450,000 subsidy or tax for the hospital would pay for itself many times over, as a result of the broad-based economic gains that accrue to the community from operation of that hospital.

Aside from the financial and the obvious medical benefits associated with maintaining the hospital, there are other questions that warrant consideration. Recently conducted public relations surveys provide a sense of what rural inhabitants are interested in with regard to the provision of health care (Illinois Hospital Association 1989, Illinois Farm Bureau 1989). Among the problems identified is a lack of specialists able to provide a broader array of services to rural inhabitants. Also apparent is an image problem associated with the "bigger is better" concept, and that urban hospital care is generally perceived as better than the care provided in rural facilities. This emphasizes the need for an assessment of how these desires can be fulfilled and perceptions changed in rural areas.

An issue of particular concern in this regard is the creation of smaller, nonhospital alternatives or local area clinics that have been offered as the solution to the rural health-care crisis. It is clear that these forms of providers will not be optimal in resolving the "care" questions identified in these public relations surveys. For example, if community residents do not seek care in the existing local hospital because of its size or technology level, it is not reasonable to assume that they would opt for care in a reduced service facility or clinic. Patient analysis studies have shown that many care seekers between the ages of 20 and 55 simply do not go to local community hospitals (Illinois Hospital Association 1989).

Although this is a concern, the larger problem in many rural hospitals is that those remaining, especially the elderly and the poor, typically need hospital-based care. This is true because they tend to experience a higher degree of simultaneous diseases (comorbidities) and complications associated with the medical problems they incur. As a result, what has been created is a new problem for the wrong group. Clinics and alternative hospital delivery are inappropriate for the older and poorer populations in rural areas, even though they are wholly appropriate for the relatively healthy population already seeking medical care outside their local community.

The alternative then becomes a short-term solution to a political and economic problem rather than to the real social and medical problems that exist in rural areas. The difficulties associated with alternatives reside somewhere in a distant future. Hospital problems, on the other hand, are clear. Hospitals are underfunded from both Medicare and Medicaid. They are bound by rigidly inflexible systems, required to hire and maintain endless levels of health professions. They are bound by regulations that exceed all rhyme or reason. Financial shortfalls and inflexibility are problems that we recognize in regard to hospitals, but find difficult, if not impossible, to change.

Several inferences can be drawn from this perspective. First, alternatives, either in the form of clinics or limited service hospitals do not serve the basic access and care questions for the poor and elderly, whose needs are oriented toward hospital care. Second, by espousing these alternatives, we have replaced known problems (finance and flexibility) with unknown problems. The development of these alternative forms of care are politically advantageous because they ensure some level of medical services in rural areas. However, the long-term implications of these alternatives are not yet within our grasp. When they are, the consequences may be even more formidable than the financing and flexibility issues facing our rural hospitals today. For example, would a further decline of health-care services in rural areas result in a virtual abandonment of the rural life-style? If that were the case, would the dynamics of our social structure allow for urban areas to meet the new needs and stresses created by mass migration of rural populations?

Third, health policy, developed exclusive of economic policy, will ultimately lead to a diminution of the quality of rural life. Federal attempts to resolve access and budget problems by overemphasizing alternatives to hospital care will exacerbate those problems rather than resolve them.

Finally, by emphasizing alternatives, we have given the federal government a convenient "out" when considering the resolution of budget problems facing small or rural hospitals. Instead of emphasizing adequate financing for hospitals, additional money—and, more importantly, time and energy—are being diverted away from the provision of hospital care.

The disservice to rural inhabitants is that they become the guinea pigs for a federal health-care strategy that could run the risk of damaging the overall health care of rural inhabitants for generations.

HOW TO KEEP THE RURAL HOSPITAL

In an era of cost cutting and budgetary problems, it seems almost anathema to recommend that the solution to rural health care is the reimbursement of Medicare costs to rural providers. However, that is certainly one solution. A majority of rural hospitals providing extensive amounts of Medicare services would be able to continue to provide services in a reasonable and efficient manner if their Medicare patient reimbursements covered the costs of care.

A second option is government-based subsidies. The question that needs to be addressed, through research, is whether or not there are greater costs to the federal government in implementing new forms of delivery for health care in rural areas than would be experienced if health-care services were continued in the local rural hospital. Federal subsidies have maintained various other rural services, and it would not be unreasonable or irresponsible to consider such subsidies for the provision of services in rural hospitals.

A private/public partnership, whereby subsidies from local communities could be matched by the federal government, may be a possibility. For example, a $200,000 subsidy tax in a local community could be matched at the federal level to ensure the continuation of services to Medicare, Medicaid, and uninsured clients, and all local residents. In such a way, the commitment of the local community to the value of their hospital would be demonstrated, and the subsidy from the federal government would be only 50 percent of a total subsidy.

Finally, it is clear that the concept of regionalization, particularly in the form of affiliations, ought to be an element of the changes in the rural health delivery system. If a broader array of services is to be brought to rural areas, if personnel shortages are to be addressed in coherent fashion, if rural health flexibility is to generate political support for implementation, and if technology is to play a role in the continued provision of rural health services, then formal affiliations may well need to be developed.

One consideration with regard to these affiliations is the creation of a rural affiliation adjustment for larger institutions. By meeting a certain set of criteria, the larger hospital would be eligible for an adjustment, not dissimilar to those currently paid in the direct and indirect medical education lines. So, for example, a larger facility would guarantee to provide clinics with specialists in rural areas, provide access to technology, personnel, and support resources, and perhaps provide management and even peer review options. In return, the urban institutions would receive an add-on for each bed, or some other indicator within the rural hospitals, which would evidence their support for rural health and at the same time ensure that the appropriate incentives are in place for the larger institution to maintain such a relationship.

CONCLUSION

The rural hospital cannot be all things to all people. However, the rural hospital can be the lifeline in the provision of necessary hospital services in rural communities. It is unclear exactly what form those services should take. In the changing times, within the health-care delivery arena, it is difficult to determine whether or not the highly advanced and technological services in urban teaching facilities ought to be available in rural areas.

As is the case with many issues, the ultimate question is one of commitment. Is the commitment of the local community—the doctors, nurses, and administrators, the state and local governments, and the federal government—sufficient to warrant the maintenance of the rural hospitals in their areas? Without that commitment, the ability of those institutions to survive is in danger. With commitment and an innovative approach to the hospital as a focal point of rural care, these institutions can continue to provide service.

4. Evaluating Alternative Rural Hospital Models: What Are We Learning?

George H. McNeely

The crisis facing small rural hospitals in the United States is receiving an increasing amount of attention, both on a national level and in individual states with large rural populations. Numerous factors have created this crisis for rural hospitals, including depressed rural economies, declining rural populations, shortages of rural physicians, nurses, and other health personnel, spiraling costs of new medical technologies, low rural Medicare reimbursement rates, and the aging physical plants of most rural hospitals. These factors have resulted in an increasing number of rural hospital closures, contributing to declining access to essential medical care in rural communities (U.S. Congress, Senate, 1988).

The debates over the causes and solutions to this critical situation have generated many proposed improvements and solutions to the rural hospital crisis. These proposals include a variety of recommendations for the improvement of rural health care and focus on many different aspects of the system. Among other things, recommendations have covered the following:

- licensure and certification regulations;
- reimbursement mechanisms;
- staffing requirements;
- staff training and scope of practice;
- service requirements and configuration;
- technological requirements; and
- relationships among rural hospitals.

These proposals have been extensively reviewed and debated in the literature (Moscovice 1989a, Phillips & Luehrs 1989, Rosenberg & Runde 1988, Rosenberg 1989, U.S. Congress, Senate, 1988).

Until recently, the notion that rural hospitals should meet the same standards of service and care as all other (usually larger) hospitals was widely accepted. The Hill-Burton Act ensured that most rural areas were provided with a full-service hospital, and most rural hospitals had little trouble providing the mandated level of services and care, prior to the implementation of the prospective payment system. The numerous problems that face rural hospitals today, however, have changed this situation. Over the past several years, increasing debate has focused on the possibility that small, rural hospitals may be distinct from the majority of larger urban and suburban hospitals. This perception has, in turn, caused a rethinking of the function and structure of such small rural hospitals (Hart, Rosenblatt, & Amundson 1989).

Out of these debates has come a number of attempts to develop models for a reconsidered small rural hospital that is better suited to the health-care needs of today's rural communities. Several states have initiated programs for the creation of "alternative" rural hospitals, including Colorado, Montana, Florida, and California. These state-based efforts, the Montana and Colorado models in particular, have received considerable attention in recent years (Rosenberg 1989). In addition, with the passage of the Essential Access Community Hospital (EACH) and Primary Care Hospital (PCH) legislation in late 1989, the federal government has moved into this arena as well.

The Colorado model is already in place, with five licensed facilities, and the Montana model has crossed its last obstacles to achieve implementation. As with all such hypothetical models, these two programs have come up against a significant number of difficulties in each state's attempts to convert its model into reimbursable and operational reality. At the same time, the Florida and California models are being moved into the implementation stages. In addition, several other states are interested in developing their own models, including among others Kansas, South Carolina, and Oregon. When the proposed federal EACH/PCH legislation is added to this list, it is clear that the concept of the alternative hospital model has been accepted as an important element in the solution to the crisis in rural hospitals.

At this juncture, however, it is important to review the progress of these early models in order that future models may benefit from their experiences. This chapter will discuss the progress of the most prominent existing and proposed models, their varying structures, and the hurdles that they have confronted in the implementation stages. The goal of this discussion is to raise issues and questions that may benefit both these and future models.

ANALYZING EXISTING ALTERNATIVE MODELS

The alternative model programs that have been (or are being) developed represent an effort to find solutions to the rural hospital crisis, within the broader context of current thinking on rural health care. Accepted notions concerning the effective provision of health care in rural areas are, however, constantly changing, and new research in the field continually provides additional data for analysis of the situation. Alternative hospital model planners must inevitably forge a path through a wide variety of opinions about and goals for rural health care. As with all complex and evolving situations, these goals may at times be conflicting or contradictory. A primary confusion in this situation is the conflict over the goals of the development of alternative models. In the broadest terms, of course, such models are intended to preserve access to health-care services in rural areas. The consensus often ends there.

Certain issues central to defining the structure and success of these models are discussed below; however, this discussion is by no means intended to cover all of the significant issues confronting planners of these alternatives. These issues raise questions about the effectiveness of the existing and proposed models. As a method by which to evaluate these models, questions are posed at the end of each section below. These questions can then be asked directly of the specific models that are discussed later in this chapter, in order to assist in their evaluation.

1. Defining the Purpose of Rural Hospitals

The difficulties in creating these alternative models are compounded by the variety of important roles that rural hospitals play in their communities. Rural hospital administrators and board members have long understood the fact that a rural hospital is a vital part of the economic life of rural communities (U.S. Congress, Senate, 1988, Hart, Rosenblatt, & Amundson 1989). Such hospitals are often not only the sole provider of health care in remote areas, but they also typically have the following additional pivotal roles.

- They serve as the organizational core for other health-care services in their communities, including physician recruitment and retention, the local emergency medical-care system, and provision of other social services.

- They are often among the largest employers in their communities.

- They are typically an integral part of local economic development plans, including efforts to retain major employers and to encourage additional employers to relocate to the area.

Research into the economic impact of rural hospital closures has indicated that the social and economic costs of such closures far outweigh whatever cost savings are gained through the closure (Lichty, Jesswein, & McMillan 1986, Sharpe 1987).

This broader local context suggests a strong argument for saving existing rural hospitals, at any cost, because of their strategic economic and organizational significance to rural communities. This recognition of the broader local role of the rural hospital has at times served to confuse the focus of both statewide and national efforts to preserve rural health care.

QUESTION: Are there goals for the alternative model, such as maintaining employment, other than to preserve access to health care?

2. Determining Appropriate Services

The extent of inpatient services offered by most rural hospitals is typically a result of certain notions concerning what is appropriate for hospitals to offer, rather than of actual patient demand. Little empirical analysis has been undertaken to define specifically which inpatient hospital services are actually required and utilized in specific rural areas. Such an analysis was undertaken, however, as part of the development of the California Alternative Rural Hospital, as discussed later in this chapter.

Typically, rural hospital administrators, physicians, and hospital boards have assumed that the expansion of a hospital's services will reduce patient outmigration and increase revenues for the hospital. Additionally, during the past decade, as medical technology has increased dramatically, administrators and physicians have assumed they are at a major disadvantage, in both quality of care and patient retention, if they are unable to keep up with this technological rush. Although this notion may be true in terms of the perceptions of rural residents, it has increasingly become understood that expanded technology and services are not automatically essential to the provision of appropriate health-care services.

It is also claimed that high technology services should be maintained, despite clear operational inefficiencies and high costs. The large number of rural hospital closures during the past 5 years has confirmed that it is not financially feasible for such hospitals to be "everything to everybody," nor is such a policy essential to providing high quality health care (Rosenberg & McNeely 1989).

QUESTIONS: What dictated the scope of services offered by the model (empirical research, state licensing requirements, etc.)? Are the services offered by the model flexible enough to meet the needs of diverse rural communities?

3. Control of Health-Care Resources

Further confusion is created by the fact that health care is a local product. Research undertaken as part of the development of the California Alternative Rural Hospital Model confirms the fact that inpatient services performed at rural hospitals vary widely among Western states, as well as within the 4 regions of California itself. When studying the discharges of individual hospitals, the specific inpatient services demanded are affected by numerous environmental factors that may not correspond to those in other rural communities (Rosenberg & McNeely 1989). These factors include, but are not limited to, a hospital's proximity to other hospitals, services provided at neighboring facilities, availability of physicians and other specialty services, and characteristics of patient demand.

Given the local nature of health care, it is natural to question who is most appropriate to regulate rural hospitals. The level of involvement with regional health care by the federal government is necessarily limited, as the California research indicates. State governments may also have difficulty responding to the diversity of health-care conditions within their own states. Local hospital administrators, governing boards, and physicians are inevitably most intimately involved with the provision of health services in their local communities. However, such individuals may also have valid reasons not to recommend that their local hospital provide the most cost-efficient health services.

The question that remains then is how to best encourage rural hospitals to make rational (but at times unpopular) decisions concerning delivery of cost-efficient health services, while not removing the primary responsibility for such decisions from local control.

QUESTIONS: Does the structure of the model encourage an appropriate level of local participation? Is the model flexible enough to allow communities to "tailor" the model to their needs?

4. Reimbursement

Current thinking on ways to improve the financial situation of the small, rural hospital has moved toward the creation of a new federal category of hospital. This new category would receive a higher level of reimbursement for the provision of limited, "essential access" health-care services (Rosenberg 1989). The new federal EACH and PCH program, to be discussed below, provides exactly such a category.

It remains unclear, however, whether higher reimbursement is necessary in order to ensure the continued operation of small rural hospitals, and the continued availability of health-care services for Medicare beneficiaries. How such a category should be tied in with the state-based alternative hospital models, typically in the form of a waiver from the federal Medicare conditions of participation, also remains unclear.

The proposed models deal with this issue differently; most have accepted that such a waiver should be at least considered. On the contrary, the financial projections developed as part of the creation of the California Alternative Rural Hospital Model indicate that the three demonstration hospitals could break even without a higher level of reimbursement. The California Model, as a result, specifically avoided including any provisions that would trigger the need for such a waiver.

The experience of the California Model does not, however, indicate that such a higher level of reimbursement would be undesirable. Such a new federal category may, in fact, be appropriate, but perhaps not for the reason behind the proposal, which is to preserve access to health care for Medicare beneficiaries. Rather, the category may be appropriate from the standpoint of protecting existing rural community resources, including jobs. In addition, such a category may serve primarily as an incentive for existing full-service hospitals to downsize, a change that many rural hospitals are reluctant to make.

The creation of the federal EACH/PCH program changes the terms of this debate, in that the new reimbursement mechanism for the PCH, in particular, is clearly intended as an inducement for smaller, rural hospitals to downsize. As currently planned, however, only seven states will be designated to participate in the EACH/PCH program. This means that the issues surrounding federal waivers will remain potent and confusing for the remaining states.

QUESTIONS: Has the model been structured so as to be eligible to receive all types of third-party reimbursement? If not, has this hindered the implementation of the model? If implementation has been hindered, can the model be changed to overcome this problem?

5. Relationship to Other Services

Hospitals may offer a variety of services, all of which contribute to the financial health of the facility, including outpatient clinics and long-term-care beds. The careful planning and restructuring of these services may result in substantial subsidies to the operations of the facility.

Research indicates that long-term care is a vital part of the health-care delivery system in rural areas (Reczynski 1987, Hart, Rosenblatt, & Amundson 1989, U.S. Congress, Senate, 1988). Some small rural hospitals survive solely as a result of the revenue generated by their long-term-care beds (Rosenberg & McNeely 1989). Despite these findings, the dialogue on the shape of alternative rural hospital models has not always specifically addressed the question of how such long-term-care facilities would be integrated into the models.

In addition, the legislation aimed at expanding Rural Health Clinics (Social Security Act, amendment, P.L. 95–210) is significantly underused in the struggle to retain rural health-care providers. Among the greatest benefits of the act is that it already exists and has strong Congressional and executive support. The act is also specifically targeted to Health Manpower Shortage Areas (HMSAs) and Medically Underserved Areas

(MUAs). Many, if not most, small rural hospitals in trouble are located in HMSAs or MUAs. These factors render the act an appropriate measure to assist in the support of remote rural hospitals as part of any state or federal model.

QUESTION: Can the model be easily combined with other types of programs (swing beds, Rural Health Clinics, etc.)?

In the ongoing efforts to create alternative rural hospital models, it is important to consider the models themselves, within the context of these and other broader issues, in order to ensure that they can function effectively in a complex environment. The consideration of these broader issues should not, however, cloud the primary focus of such models, which is to ensure the future of cost-efficient, and stable health-care services in rural areas. It is essential that model planners be clear in what they are attempting to achieve in the creation of their models. If other, broader considerations start to compete with this primary goal, model planners should acknowledge such considerations as being of importance and analyze their impact on the cost efficiency and stability of health-care services. Inevitably, all models will be a compromise between competing interests (local versus national, state versus federal, cost containment versus breadth of services, efficiency versus employment).

STATE-BASED MODELS

This section reviews several of the more prominent proposals for hospital transition, from acute care to an alternative form designed to serve the health-care needs of rural Americans better. Until recently, most of these proposals have been developed by individual states. Prior to the recent legislation creating the EACH/PCH program, federal involvement with rural health care over the past decade had been driven primarily by a focus on health-care cost containment. Federal policy had accepted the existing hospital system, but emphasized the need for tightening and streamlining it, instead of rethinking the entire concept. This trend, combined with the fact that health care is a local product, has meant that the development of innovative new rural models had, until recently, emerged mostly from state-based efforts.

The structures of the four models included here will be reviewed briefly. The primary focus of the discussion of these models is to apply the questions from the previous section to each model in order to determine what can be learned from their experiences.

1.   Colorado Community Clinic/Emergency Center (CCEC)

The State of Colorado implemented the Community Clinic/Emergency Center (CCEC) in 1987. The CCEC integrates primary care with a holding facility for patients who require observation. The CCEC regulations define the facility as "planned, organized, operated and maintained to provide basic community facilities and services for the diagnosis and treatment of individuals requiring outpatient service and inpatient care, including in-patient accommodations for emergency care" (6 Colo. Code Regs. § 1011–1, 1991).

The regulations for the CCEC maintain certain hospital services, in-cluding at least minimal laboratory services on site and dietary services. In other ways, the regulations approach those for a primary-care clinic, including limits on the types of surgery that can be performed, and a maximum holding period for patients of 72 hours. In addition, the CCEC is relieved of many hospital facility regulations, allowing it to maintain only the basic facilities and to share those offered by separate departments.

The CCEC has been implemented without a federal waiver to allow for Medicare and Medicaid reimbursement. Only 5 facilities have been licensed to participate under this program, including 3 in skilled nursing facilities, and 2 community health centers. It is assumed that the minimal use of the CCEC licensure category is directly related to its limitations in receiving Medicare and Medicaid reimbursements. This suggests that eligibility for Medicare and Medicaid reimbursements is an important element in at-tracting providers interested in participating in an alternative model.

The CCEC regulations provide for a reasonably wide degree of flexibility in the types of services offered, and in the ways that they are provided. This is an advantage of this model. Without a restructuring of any hospitals into CCECs, however, there has been little opportunity to test the use of the flexibility built into the CCEC regulations. If the reimbursement issue is not resolved to the advantage of hospitals, this opportunity may never arise.

The implementation of the model has, on the other hand, indicated that it offers certain advantages to other types of providers, including long-term-care facilities and primary-care clinics. Clearly the model encourages coordination of various types of uses at one site. The question then remains as to whether the primary goal of the model was to assist various types of providers or specifically to assist rural hospitals. If the goal was the latter, then the use of the model by other types of providers may be a beneficial although unexpected outcome; this may indicate that the model has other, secondary uses. This history suggests, however, that the CCEC will not serve as a successful mechanism for encouraging rural hospitals to re-structure.

2. Montana Medical Assistance Facility (MAF)

The Montana Medical Assistance Facility (MAF), as established in 1987 by the Montana Hospital Association and the Montana state legislature, was one of the first alternative models to challenge the legal and service definitions of the traditional hospital. It is defined as a health-care institution that provides inpatient care to ill or injured persons for no longer than 96 hours, combining emergency and short-term acute-care services. The MAF regulations stipulate the criteria for eligibility of hospitals, or other health-care providers (including physicians' offices and nursing homes) interested in restructuring into an MAF (Wellover 1989).

The two most significant components of the MAF are the staffing requirements and the patient time limitation, as discussed below.

- Staffing. The MAF is staffed by a midlevel practitioner, with a physician available within 20 minutes. A physician is required to visit the site at least once every 30 days. In addition, the MAF requires skilled nursing only during the regular 8-hour day shift; during the remainder of the day, a registered nurse need only be on call.

- Patient Time Limitation. The MAF may hold patients for up to 96 hours, at which point the patients must be discharged or transferred.

The MAF is the first alternative model that has sought and received funding from the Health Care Financing Administration (HCFA), as a demonstration project to explore fully the viability of such a model. MAFs are not currently eligible for Medicare or Medicaid reimbursement; this situation, if not changed, will render the MAF financially infeasible because of the high number of Medicare patients in rural areas. As a consequence, HCFA has agreed to grant, under Section 1905(a)(21) of the Social Security Act, a waiver from the Medicare conditions of participation to providers licensed as MAFs (Phillips & Luehrs 1989).

The State of Montana has sought existing providers interested in participating in the model, but it has discovered that few facilities are currently interested in participation, despite the benefits offered by the additional regulatory flexibility under the MAF. In order to find 3 facilities willing to participate, the state has considered reopening 2 closed facilities.

When our list of questions is applied to the MAF, several important issues are raised. The process of obtaining an HCFA waiver for facilities participating under the program has been cumbersome. It is not clear that a model requiring such a process is the most efficient for replication in other states. This difficulty suggests that a less cumbersome approach would be to construct an alternative model that provides the necessary regulatory flexibility, without requiring an HCFA waiver.

Despite the benefits offered by the MAF, facility administrators and board members have been reluctant to participate. It appears that the service and staffing standards would require existing hospitals to downsize to an extent considered undesirable. This suggests that the MAF may not be sufficiently flexible in its service regulations. A successful model must be adaptable to a wide variety of different rural hospitals; without this flexibility, there is little local participation in the restructuring of each hospital. This may reduce the chances of the model's success.

Nevertheless, the reduced size of the MAF (when compared to a standard rural hospital) has appealed to closed facilities. The question is then raised as to whether it is a valid public policy goal of an alternative model to reopen closed facilities. Will an alternative model, for which the planners cannot find sufficient open facilities for implementation, be a viable solution to the rural hospital crisis?

3. Florida Emergency Care Hospital (ECH)

Following Montana's lead, several other states have initiated alternative model programs based on the MAF concept. These states include Washington, Wyoming, and Florida.

Florida has passed legislation that would create a new optional hospital licensure category, the Emergency Care Hospital (ECH—not to be confused with the federal EACH). The locational eligibility criteria for the Florida ECH differ from those for the MAF, but in most other ways, the two models are similar (Fla. Stat. § 395.01465, 1989). The primary difference is the fact that ECHs retain their existing hospital licenses, thereby enabling them to offer a wider range of services than can MAFs.

The ECH does not meet the Medicare conditions of participation for several reasons; the most significant of these is the 96-hour limit on the patient's length of stay. In most other aspects, the ECH model could be implemented under state authority, without federal involvement or approval. This raises the question as to whether the 96-hour limit is an important enough element in an alternative model to undertake the burden of seeking a federal waiver. As noted, the 96-hour limit has been used in several similar models, but is generally seen as an arbitrary proxy measure, rather than a limit that has been supported by empirical analysis.

Research undertaken by the WAMI Rural Health Research Center has shown that the average length of stay in an acute-care bed in a small rural hospital (one with fewer than 25 beds) is 4.9 days, very close to the 96-hour limit (Hart, Rosenblatt, & Amundson 1989).

In addition, research undertaken as part of the development of the California Alternative Rural Hospital Model included an analysis of the percentage of rural discharges in California occurring under the 96-hour limit. The results show that approximately 85 percent of all patients are discharged within 96 hours at those facilities that had already downsized, by reducing their scope of services and concentrating on basic medical services. The research also shows that this percentage decreased to approximately 70 percent in those rural facilities that had resisted downsizing and still offered a broad range of specialized medical services (Rosenberg

& McNeely 1989). These findings appear to confirm that the limit is generally a good proxy measure, particularly for facilities that have already downsized to something similar to an MAF.

The research for the California model also suggests that the 96-hour limit may not be necessary (Rosenberg & McNeely 1989). If rational regulatory flexibility were offered, most hospitals would gradually move toward limiting services to those that do not require holding patients beyond this 96-hour time limit. Considering the experience in California, it may be assumed that the regulations for the ECH in Florida would encourage participating hospitals to maintain this limit for their own benefit, regardless of the strict 96-hour limit. These findings suggest that a new federal category or a Medicare waiver, based solely upon the requirement for a 96-hour limit on patient stay, should not be sought in Florida. The state is currently attempting to redefine the length-of-stay limitation in order to permit a less rigid proxy measure. If this is accomplished, the waiver could be avoided.

The success of the Florida ECH has yet to be tested in the implementation process. The Florida model has benefited from the experiences of the Montana MAF. The ability of participating hospitals to retain their existing licenses and to maintain a wider range of services than permitted under the MAF regulations may encourage more hospitals to restructure under the ECH program. In addition, if the need for a federal waiver for the 96-hour limit is avoided, the entire process would be streamlined.

4. California Alternative Rural Hospital Model (ARHM)

The creation of the California Alternative Rural Hospital Model (ARHM) followed a very different approach from the three models discussed above. Instead of reviewing and revising existing hospital regulations, an approach that had been tried by several other states with limited success, the creators of the ARHM focused on services. They undertook a process of hypothetically structuring the medical services demonstrated to be necessary in small rural hospitals in California. After first determining by empirical analysis which health-care services would be offered under the ARHM, they developed hypothetical service, staffing, and facility regulations.

The service regulations for the ARHM include a set of required basic services and a "menu" of optional additional services, including inpatient and outpatient surgery, obstetrics, expanded inpatient services and expanded radiology. With this structure, the ARHM enables each hospital to choose, within a relaxed regulatory climate, those services most appropriate for its market area. This bottom-up approach was necessary in a large state like California, where the health-care needs of patients may vary between communities or regions. In addition, in light of the difficulties that other states have had in encouraging hospital participation, it was important to allow hospital administrators, boards, and physicians to decide about the services provided at their facility.

The development of the ARHM included a component for studying the impact of hypothetically reconfiguring services under the ARHM regulations at three demonstration sites in California. The results of this analysis suggest that the most significant problem faced by rural hospitals is not inadequate federal reimbursement, but rather the overly stringent regulations imposed on small rural hospitals.

In addition, the California analysis indicates that, when offered a range of regulatory relief in services, staffing, and facilities, hospitals consistently chose hospital services. These hospitals were less interested in the personnel and facility flexibility. The administrators' lack of interest in staffing changes appears to be due to a variety of social and political factors, including a reluctance to reduce the level of care provided, loyalty to existing staff, and the perceived role of the hospital as a local employer. These broader considerations were discussed earlier. In addition, none of the hospitals decided to take immediate advantage of the flexibility in facility standards, because none was in a position to undertake major capital improvements.

The financial analysis undertaken in the development of the California model indicates that regulatory flexibility, with regard to services, enables hospitals to lower their fixed costs sufficiently to become more fiscally sound. Such high fixed-cost services as surgery and anesthesia are required in California, but are not utilized often enough at many small, rural hospitals to support such high costs. The hospital must, therefore, subsidize such services with revenues from other, more profitable services. If hospitals were allowed to eliminate such high fixed-cost services, they might be better able to survive.

This analysis indicates that the preferred forms of regulatory flexibility do not require a new federal category of essential access hospital. The types of flexibility that were chosen (service reduction or reconfiguration) were all in conformity with the federal conditions of participation. The types of flexibility offered under the ARHM which were not in conformity with the federal conditions of participation (staffing and facility changes) were not requested by the hospital administrators at the sites analyzed. The service reductions or reconfigurations that proved most desirable to hospital administrators are governed by state statutes, rather than by federal requirements. The results of the California analysis suggest, therefore, that it is within the power of individual states to relax their statutes sufficiently to allow rural hospitals the service flexibility necessary to become more fiscally sound.

The level of expressed interest confirms certain lessons that have been learned through the experience of earlier alternative models, and that have been incorporated into the ARHM. The ARHM does not require a federal waiver and is eligible for all types of third-party reimbursement. Empirical research indicates that the services offered should be flexible enough to adapt to many different rural locations. In addition, the "menu" approach encourages communities to participate in the restructuring process. The responses from administrators at the three demonstration sites indicate that the rural hospital's role as an employer is significant; the ARHM, therefore, has attempted to concentrate on cost savings through service reconfiguration rather than on mandated staffing changes. Finally, the ARHM permits participating hospitals to maintain rural health clinics and swing bed units, which may be used for either acute care or longer-term care patients.

FEDERAL ESSENTIAL ACCESS COMMUNITY HOSPITAL PROGRAM (EACH/PCH)

In the midst of the development of and debate over state-based alternative rural hospital models, the federal government has entered the arena with its own proposed solution to the rural health-care crisis. Enacted as part of the Omnibus Budget Reconciliation Act of 1989, the Essential Access Community Hospital Program (EACH) provides cost-based reimbursement to two tiers of rural hospitals, as well as considerable financial assistance for state health planning around the implementation of the program (U.S. Congress, House, 1989). Initially, 7 states will be able to participate in the program, as well as 15 individual facilities in states not designated under the program.

The program establishes a two-tier system of rural hospitals: Essential Access Community Hospitals (EACHs), which must have at least 75 beds, or be located more than 35 miles from any other hospital, and Primary Care Hospitals (PCHs), which must have no more than 6 inpatient beds. The legislation requires that the PCHs retain patients for no more than 72 hours, after which such patients would be transferred to the nearest EACH. In addition, the EACH would provide necessary service and technical support to the surrounding PCHs.

The reimbursement mechanisms for EACHs and PCHs would be different. EACHs would be considered to be sole community providers for reimbursement. PCHs would initially receive cost-based reimbursement; the move to a prospective payment system in 1993 is now being reconsidered.

Part of the advantage of the EACH/PCH system is that designated states would receive substantial transition planning grants, both on a statewide basis and for individual facilities or consortia, to restructure as required under the program.

This program represents a significant shift in federal policy regarding rural hospitals. As noted earlier, traditional federal policy in this area concentrated on regulating hospitals to ensure the health and safety of the public, rather than on encouraging hospitals to offer health-care services in the most cost-efficient and coordinated manner. With the introduction of the EACH/PCH legislation, the federal role has changed. The transition grants, which include an extension of the existing Rural Health Care Transition Grant Program, are intended to encourage states to review their rural health resources, and to determine how best to reorganize these resources most appropriately and cost-effectively. A primary focus of this reorganization is, naturally, the creation of EACHs and PCHs in those states. The broader public policy goals are to promote the development of an organized rural health-care delivery system and to increase the role of individual states in the implementation and management of such a system.

CONCLUSION

The impact of the implementation of the EACH/PCH program will not be known for several years, but it is generating much interest among the states, in order to prepare for the application process. Several foundations have entered at this stage, in order to expedite the planning process. All states that are interested in participating in the program must soon commit themselves to the lengthy and politically sensitive application process.

The effect of the EACH/PCH program on the continuing development of state-based alternative hospital models is also uncertain. The state-based efforts in this direction have clearly generated considerable debate and experience in model development, and have contributed to the federal government's attempt to provide a national model. The fact that only 7 states will be designated to participate in the EACH/PCH program, at least initially, means that state-based models will remain essential to the large number of states that will not be designated.

In addition, the regulations and the exact implementation process for the EACH/PCH program are still being debated. The resolution of these issues may serve to hinder the effectiveness of the program, which would, again, reinforce the importance of continuing activity and interest in state-based models. The research for the California model shows that individual states have considerable power to implement programs that provide financial benefits to rural hospitals, without the participation of the federal government. The many benefits of the EACH/PCH program should be investigated energetically by states interested in participating, but these states should not abandon more locally generated alternative hospital models that might be as, or more, effective than the EACH/PCH program.

5. The Primary-Care Hospital: More and Better Health Care Without Closure

Jeffrey C. Bauer

Since the disappearance of full-cost Medicare reimbursement in the mid–1980s, many small and rural hospitals have discovered that relatively low inpatient volume does not generate enough revenue to meet the minimum costs of operating a traditional secondary-care facility. Hundreds of traditional rural hospitals feel threatened with closure at any given time. Although many interrelated factors are involved, the principal reason small and rural facilities go out of the acute-care business each year is financial insolvency (U.S. General Accounting Office 1991). Many more struggle to raise funds for continued operations by borrowing money, imposing additional taxes, soliciting donations from the local community, or seeking grants from government agencies and private foundations.

This chapter discusses, from the perspective of major public policy goals, the relative merits of hospital closure versus conversion to another operating form. These goals are access to care, cost/efficiency of providing care, and quality/effectiveness of care. The chapter proposes that the key to restructuring is not hospital closure; rather, it is the conversion of marginal secondary-care rural hospitals to primary-care facilities. Both economic and clinical arguments for conversion are presented. A model of a primary-care hospital is described and offered as an efficient alternative to the full service facility in smaller market areas, allowing rural residents to retain access to basic care, while preserving cost efficiency.

ACCESS

Preserving access to care is a major public policy goal. Thus, it has been a key consideration in efforts to prevent or delay the financially caused closure of rural hospitals. Because a community without a hospital is almost certain to be a community without doctors, a hospital has been the traditional prerequisite for receiving any health care in a small town. Therefore, rural residents are willing to do almost anything (except perhaps use it) to subsidize their hospital, out of fear that its closure will ultimately lead to disappearance of all local health care.

Hospital closure generates a great deal of public concern and political interest because many believe that residents of a community that has lost its hospital will have to travel unacceptably long distances to receive care (Hart, Pirani, & Rosenblatt 1991). Federal health-planning guidelines have generally assumed minimal access to a hospital as 25 miles or 30 minutes' travel time from a patient's home to the nearest hospital. These travel and time distances are used as the basis for special geographic designations, which establish eligibility for direct financial assistance or enhanced reimbursement, such as the higher rates paid to sole community providers (Kaiman 1990). However, these parameters are arbitrary; they are not based on objective study of the relationships among time, distance, outcomes, and access to care.

Research on rural health-care consumption patterns suggests that most private-pay patients are willing to travel considerable distances to the hospital of their choice.[1] In one specific case, research on travel time for obstetrical care in rural Alabama found that patients were willing to travel, even when a hospital existed locally, and that per capita income was associated with increased travel (Bronstein & Morrisey 1990). Rural health planning is complicated when the access problem differs for public patients who are unlikely to leave town for care and private patients who are unlikely to stay. This situation suggests a need for creative efforts to support better transportation and alternative models of care in communities where a traditional hospital is not financially viable.

However, efforts to subsidize financially threatened rural hospitals have considerably less justification in terms of the other two major objectives of public policy: cost/efficiency and quality/effectiveness. Scarce resources are being wasted because many existing rural hospitals operate at inefficient scale (U.S. Congress, Office of Technology Assessment, 1990). Indeed, from both economic and clinical perspectives, policies to restructure rural hospitals in an effective and efficient manner would result in an improved overall level of health services at a lower cost, an outcome desired by all concerned with the nation's rural health.

COST/EFFICIENCY

One of the few areas of consensus among health economists is that hospitals, like other production facilities, exhibit economies of scale. Production costs are a function of plant size and capacity utilization. A U-shaped long-run, average-total-cost curve (LRATC) is generally believed to exist within the hospital industry. This situation represents a range where per-unit costs of output decline as production of output increases. All other things being equal, least-cost output is produced in an acute-care hospital that is considerably larger than today's typical rural hospital (Carr & Feldstein 1982). By this measure, rural hospitals are more likely to be economically inefficient, in comparison to larger hospitals that operate in a lower range on the LRATC curve. By virtue of being relatively small, rural hospitals have higher per-unit costs in producing their services than larger hospitals that are experiencing economies of scale.

However, economy of scale is not the only issue related to efficiency. Utilization of capacity is also significant, and experience has generally suggested that any hospital, independent of its position on the LRATC curve, tends to produce at its own least-cost output when it is operated at approximately 80 percent of capacity. Small and rural hospitals, as a group, are now operating well below capacity, with occupancy in the 40 percent range common during the 1980s (Mick & Morlock 1990). Size and low occupancy were noted as factors related to hospital closure risk by the U.S. General Accounting Office report to Congress (1991). Therefore, rural hospitals are also likely to be inefficient by virtue of being underutilized.

In recognition of the inefficiencies associated with small scale and underutilization, many rural facilities are beginning to reduce or eliminate some of the most costly services associated with designation as a traditional, full-service hospital. However, a reduced level of operations does not relieve the hospital of the fixed costs associated with licensure as a secondary-care hospital. Surgery is the clinical area where rural hospitals are most likely to reduce services. Yet, if they continue to do any surgery at all, the hospitals must still meet minimal state licensure standards in staffing, equipment, and facility safety. Obstetrics, critical care, and emergency services are other clinical areas where reduced operations can lead to very high costs per-unit of output (service) because fixed overhead expenses are spread over a low level of output.

A further cause of economic inefficiency in many small and rural hospitals is technological obsolescence. Rural hospitals tend to be older than their urban counterparts, and they are less likely to have been extensively remodeled to keep pace with changes in modern hospital design and technology requirements for space. The typical small and rural hospital's heating, ventilation, and air conditioning (HVAC) systems are much more expensive to operate than the systems found in a newer facility. Also, rural hospitals normally have linear nursing units where patient rooms are located along straight corridors. This puts the most remote rooms at a considerable distance from the nursing station. More recent hospital design favors a circular arrangement for cost-effective use of nursing staff. When the nursing station is in the middle of a circle of rooms, all rooms are close and equidistant. Further, this arrangement allows nurses to observe all rooms from the center of a circle, an efficiency lost when the nursing station is on a straight-line patient-care unit.

The high costs of small, underutilized facilities were the basis for the rural health lobby's plea for elimination of the Medicare rural-urban payment differential. This differential was part of the original Diagnosis Related Groups (DRG) prospective payment structure. The federal policy behind DRG-based reimbursement was based on the assumption that rural hospitals deserved lower payments per DRG because they had lower input costs. This misguided policy was conceived by policy analysts who apparently do not understand the relationship between the cost of inputs and the cost of outputs. Low unit costs of inputs do not necessarily translate into low costs per-unit of output; less expensive labor and higher overall costs of production are not inconsistent in cases of low volume or related inefficiencies. Overhead expenses that do not vary with hospital size, such as licensing fees and costs of basic equipment, are particularly significant. Thus, a nurse may receive a higher hourly wage in an urban hospital, but the urban nurse's costs are spread across a greater volume of patients. Consequently, the urban hospital can provide a bed day of care at less per-unit expense, even though it pays higher wages and benefits to its nurses.

Rural hospitals with small scale, low utilization, technological obsolescence, and high fixed costs can have relatively high production costs for specific hospital services. The same services could be provided more efficiently in a more fully utilized hospital. Because transporting patients to well-utilized hospitals costs less than subsidizing hospitals that are too small to operate efficiently, total spending on health care can be reduced by hospital consolidation on a regional basis. The less efficient hospitals that cannot justify continued existence as secondary-care facilities are candidates for conversion to primary-care hospitals.

EFFECTIVENESS/QUALITY

Effectiveness is a measure of the extent to which health care accomplishes its desired purpose. Effective care makes a difference; the patient is better off with the care than he or she would have been without it. Ineffective care has either a neutral or negative impact, meaning that the patient is either unaffected or is made worse off by virtue of having received the care. Because it contributes nothing to well-being, ineffective care, be it neutral or negative, is not worth any amount of money.

Effective care, by contrast, has value. However, effectiveness is relative; some types of care are more effective than others, just as some settings for care are more effective than others. This point raises the issue of whether effectiveness is a function of hospital size—that is, whether small and rural hospitals are significantly different, in terms of effectiveness, than their larger counterparts. Subsidies for rural hospitals will be hard to justify if they are not effective, if comparable quality of care is not produced for each dollar spent.

Because the effectiveness of care in rural hospitals has never been quantified—either absolutely or relatively—with respect to urban hospitals, this issue must be approached indirectly. Health services researchers tend to argue about measurement, whereas clinicians generally define effectiveness and quality in terms of safety, appropriateness, and outcomes. In layman's terms, quality care is the right thing, done the right way, with the desired outcome. It is a correct diagnosis, followed by a matched therapeutic intervention that does not put the patient at unnecessary risk and improves the patient's health status.

A growing body of research is beginning to show positive correlations between hospital size, volume of services, and quality of care (Luft, Bunker, & Entoven 1979, Fink, Yano, & Brook 1989). For example, all other things being equal, a hospital's rate of success with coronary bypass surgery is strongly associated with the number of times its teams perform the surgery. Hospitals that are perceived most effective at performing any procedure also tend to be the busiest at it. More research on the effectiveness and quality of care in rural hospitals is needed, however, before firm conclusions can be drawn.

Nevertheless, the quality of care will be increasingly questioned for low volume services provided in small and rural hospitals. Low volume for any given service will not always mean that the quality of rural hospital care is unacceptable, but it will often indicate that the quality of care in the low-volume rural hospital is not as good as the quality of the same care provided in another hospital that provides the same service more frequently. Surveys suggest quite convincingly that rural patients with mobility and resources will continue to travel to larger, high-volume facilities to get their care because they perceive that "bigger is better" (Bauer Group 1991, Bronstein & Morrisey 1990). Thus, the situation will continue to deteriorate for low-volume rural hospitals that have disproportionately high volumes of less-mobile Medicare and Medicaid patients because private patients go to bigger facilities in search of quality.

Initial findings of quality-volume studies suggest that small and rural hospitals with low volumes may be relatively ineffective, in addition to being absolutely inefficient in providing acute-care services. Due to reimbursement policies, the outmigration of paying patients, and growing technology that favors outpatient surgery in nonhospital settings, these hospitals have little reason to expect improvement in their financial performance. These hospitals have every reason, on the other hand, to restrict the number of services they provide in order to improve both efficiency and effectiveness. These facilities are the prime candidates for conversion to primary-care hospitals.

THE PRIMARY-CARE HOSPITAL

The primary-care hospital may be defined by contrasting it with the traditional secondary-care hospital. In conventional terms, the difference between primary and secondary care is often the setting. A procedure performed in a doctor's office, and therefore considered to be primary care, would be secondary care if performed in a hospital with an overnight stay. Thus, secondary care is essentially that provided in a hospital setting that offers life-saving backup if the need arises.

Regardless of the imprecise definitional distinction between primary and secondary care, the fundamental difference between the traditional model and new model of primary care discussed here is the availability of critical-care services. The primary-care hospital is a hospital without critical-care capabilities. It does not maintain an intensive-care unit, an emergency room, an operating room for critical surgery, or other on-site services dedicated to life-saving intervention.[2]

The primary-care hospital is equipped and staffed to meet the acute medical needs of patients who require institutional levels of observation and support, but whose lives are not currently threatened. It is also equipped and staffed to monitor these patients in order to detect potentially serious changes in vital signs. Further, the hospital has the capability to transfer patients immediately to a hospital with the appropriate critical-care facilities when changes in their condition suggest the possibility of an impending medical crisis. Between 25 and 50 percent of all patients in a typical secondary hospital do not need critical care, making the primary-care hospital an appropriate facility for many patients.

In the model suggested here, the primary-care hospital will generally insure the availability of 10 services. Following is a brief description of 5 of these services that should be provided directly by the hospital.

1. The first of the 5 in-house services is a *hospital-based primary-care practice*, employing 3 or more primary-care providers, which can be a combination of physicians, physician assistants, and/or nurse practitioners. The hospital-based primary-care practice should offer extended office hours and should insure the on-call availability of urgent-care services at all other times.

2. The second key characteristic is *observation beds* to provide overnight care for patients who are not expected to need critical-care services, independent of length of stay. As long as a person who needs acute institutional care does not need critical care, but does need services that cannot be provided adequately at home, s/he is an appropriate occupant of a bed in a primary-care hospital.

3. The third essential component is a *hospital-based ambulance* with state-of-the-art critical-care capabilities. This ambulance must be ready, on a moment's notice, to transfer a patient who unexpectedly needs the critical care services of a traditional hospital.

4. The fourth essential attribute is a *modern diagnostic service* so the doctors and nurses in the hospital-based clinic have immediate access to state-of-the-art laboratory facilities, medicine, and radiology at the levels required by modern primary-care practitioners. Due to ongoing advances in communications, the necessary equipment need not be located in the rural facility, but access by the rural practitioners must be assured. Modern technology is continually opening new avenues for meeting this need (Cordes & Straub 1992).

5. The fifth and final component is *formal clinical affiliation* with secondary/tertiary provider(s). This affiliation is a mutually beneficial relationship guaranteeing that all primary-care services will be provided in the primary-care hospital.

Five additional services, summarized below, must be locally available components of the primary-care hospital system. These can be provided either directly by the primary-care hospital or under contract by outside agencies.

1. The first is *home health care*. The primary-care hospital must be able to insure full-service support for patients who are discharged to their homes. The service must be able to meet the needs of rural residents who can be treated at home without prior admission to the observation beds.

2. *Durable medical equipment* is an essential adjunct to the home health-care services. Recent technological advances have led to the development of portable equipment that can transport basic hospital services (respiration therapy devices, intravenous therapy equipment, cardiac monitors, etc.) right into the home. By insuring local availability of this equipment, the primary-care hospital can substantially diminish unnecessary outmigration of patients.

3. *Long-term care* is probably the best-known alternative use of acute hospital beds no longer needed for secondary care. The long-term care beds will be a part of the primary-care hospital in most cases; however, they can be provided by a nearby nursing home if the conversion does not have room for long-term care.

4. The primary-care hospital must insure *pharmaceutical services* on a 24-hour basis. If a retail pharmacy in the community is not available to meet the expanded needs for prescription drugs at affordable prices, a pharmacy must be included in the primary-care hospital.

5. The final service, *outpatient surgery*, is optional, depending on the community's needs and desires for maintaining local surgery. An outpatient surgery clinic can be added at a later stage of the primary-care hospital's development if relatively high costs make it infeasible at the time of conversion.

This general model defines basic concepts of a primary-care hospital. The final configuration of any specific hospital conversion from secondary care to primary care must consider local circumstances. Improvisation based on the general model is important for hospitals that undertake conversion projects in the interests of survival and growth.

CRITERIA FOR CONVERSION

The United States has roughly 2,000 rural hospitals operating, on average, at 40 to 50 percent of capacity utilization (Mick & Morlock 1990). These figures indicate substantial excess capacity and point to consolidation as a viable means for increasing both efficiency (cost) and effectiveness (quality). Roughly speaking, 600 to 1,000 rural health facilities are good candidates for conversion to primary-care hospitals.

Criteria for conversion from secondary care to primary care have not been determined empirically; however, a few general guidelines will help identify hospitals that might be strengthened by conversion. Any hospital falling below these thresholds should carefully evaluate and consider the primary-care alternative:

- a hospital (independent of bed size) with an average daily census of 20 patients;
- a hospital with 10 or fewer private pay patients (patients covered by insurance or other means to pay the costs of their care);
- a hospital with a primary service area population of fewer than 7,500 to 10,000 residents;
- a hospital with a full-time, resident medical staff of fewer than 5 competent physicians.

Distance from the next nearest secondary-care facility is not a factor. Modern communications and transportation are almost always more cost-effective than subsidizing a clinically and/or financially marginal facility simply to insure that residents do not have to drive more than 25 miles to get to a hospital.

ADDITIONAL CONSIDERATIONS

The primary-care hospital will encounter significant obstacles as it moves from idea to reality. Although it is conceptually viable and responds to the health-care needs and economic resources of rural America in practical ways, the primary-care hospital still does not fit into an approved niche in the overall scheme of health-care delivery in the United States. Its newness will also intimidate many established providers, especially in an era when they are fighting to retain their share of an increasingly competitive health economy.

The most immediate obstacle is reimbursement from the federal government. Primary-care hospitals do not meet the conditions of participation under Medicare or Medicaid. Therefore, services provided to public patients under these programs will not be reimbursed until federal policy is changed. However, Congress and key officials in the Department of Health and Human Services have been openly supportive of the concept, and favorable change is possible.[3] Payment qualifications also must be established with private health insurance companies. This may not prove to be a significant obstacle, however, due to the relatively lower costs of care in a primary-care hospital.

State licensure is also likely to be an impediment because existing rules and regulations for traditional (secondary) hospitals do not fit the specific clinical circumstances of the new facility. Exceptions and loopholes in existing licensure laws will permit the creation of primary-care hospitals in some states, but new rules and regulations will be necessary in the many states where a nontraditional hospital is specifically prohibited.

A large, well-organized rural lobby will be essential to the success of these efforts because most state legislatures and health boards are conservative and reluctant to implement change. Additionally, federal leadership to gain acceptance of the primary-care hospital concept will not necessarily facilitate state-level efforts; many state officials are looking with caution at any idea—even a good one—that comes from Washington.

The primary-care hospital, as proposed here, does not require the creation of any new categories of health personnel. However, prospects for the primary-care hospital will be enhanced by liberalization of the scope of practice for nonphysician providers in those states that do not allow meaningful delegation or independent practice for nurse practitioners, therapists, and a range of providers. Also, permission to use cross-trained technicians (e.g., laboratory-radiology, nursing-respiratory therapy) will be important to the economic success of the primary-care hospital in states with rigid certification criteria.

Quality of care is critical to the success of a primary-care hospital. Consumer surveys suggest quite convincingly that rural residents with resources will continue to go elsewhere for their care unless they are convinced that the services available in the local primary-care hospital are at least as good as the comparable services purchased from a larger (usually urban) provider. People who plan primary-care hospitals must not make any compromises in quality, and they must ensure that the local reputation of the secondary/tertiary affiliate(s) is sound. In particular, if a top-quality service cannot be provided locally because of cost or quality considerations, it ought to be provided elsewhere by an affiliate.

Finally, the process of conversion must involve the entire community, especially residents who are taking their health-care dollars elsewhere. Planning for conversion from secondary care to primary care should rely heavily on input from the very people whose use will make the difference between success and failure. Boards of trustees of existing facilities play a key role in facilitating the process and communicating the needs and plans to residents. The planning process affords an unprecedented opportunity for the hospital to garner local support for the future of local health care.

CONCLUSION

The primary-care hospital offers a new opportunity for many communities to improve the quality and to reduce the costs of hospital-based rural health care. It is the most promising alternative to widespread hospital closure over the next few years. Furthermore, conversion can be a major component of local economic development. A good primary-care system can retain at least 80 percent of all health-care spending in the local community, an increase of at least 30 percentage points over current figures. The primary-care hospital alternative gives many rural communities an opportunity to change their perspective from the fear of losing an old hospital to the excitement of shaping a new and different one that will improve both the fiscal and physical health of the community.

NOTES

1. Since 1984, the Bauer Group has surveyed over 20,000 residents in approximately 110 rural communities throughout the United States to identify the extent and causes of outmigration of private-pay patients who leave town for health-care services available locally. Unnecessary outmigration in the 70 percent to 90 percent range is not uncommon. With few exceptions, these surveys have found that more than half of the patients with resources (insurance and cash to pay their hospital bills) and mobility go elsewhere to purchase their health care. Conversations with other researchers and many rural hospital representatives have corroborated these figures.

2. The model presented here was developed by the Bauer Group. It is not identical to the Rural Primary Care Hospital model authorized in the federal budget passed by Congress in November 1989. The Bauer Group actively supports this new federal program, but it believes that hundreds of rural hospitals should be considering the primary-care hospital now. Even fully appropriated, the new federal program will only fund conversion projects in a few dozen hospitals in a small number of states.

3. The Omnibus Budget Reconciliation Act of 1989 authorizes the Health Care Financing Administration (HCFA) to develop a system for reimbursing primary-care hospitals for care provided to Medicare and Medicaid patients. However, the level of appropriations will allow only a few dozen primary-care hospitals to be covered by the program. The future of federal reimbursement for primary-care hospitals was uncertain at the time this was being written.

PART III

The Supply of Rural Health Care—Labor Inputs

6. Medical Education and Preparation of Physicians for Rural Practice

Kevin M. Fickenscher

During the 1980s, change permeated the health-care delivery system. The environment in rural health care has been particularly stressed by these changes, which have created enormous pressures for new approaches, new methods, and new systems for delivering health care in rural areas. The pressures have been exacerbated by an inability of academic medical centers to respond adequately to the needs of rural America. Physician shortages and difficulty in recruiting primary-care doctors have been ongoing features of rural communities, in spite of an increased supply of doctors overall.

This chapter discusses the role of primary-care physicians in rural medicine, and illustrates how fulfillment of this role has not been realized. The focus of this chapter is on medical education and its responsibility to rural practice. Academic medicine is challenged to be innovative and responsive to the current and future needs of medical students and rural primary care. These needs are shaped by significant shifts in rural demographics, economics, and medical technology. The training and preparation of physicians, for the current and future environment, can no longer be standard and traditional. At issue is the accountability of medical education if rural needs are not met.

PRIMARY-CARE PROVIDERS—THE CASE OF RURAL MEDICINE

Despite greater national reliance on institutions and technology in the delivery of health care, America's rural population depends on primary-care providers for a majority of its health care. Primary care generally includes family practice, internal medicine, and pediatrics. The primary-care physician is the provider of first contact for patients, and the provider of continuity of care for the patient and the family. The physician makes an initial assessment and attempts to solve as many of the patient's problems as possible by coordinating the health-care team, which often includes ancillary health personnel and consultants (Petersdorf 1975).

The reasons for the predominance of primary-care providers in rural ares are varied, but population is one important factor. Although specific criteria vary slightly, it is generally agreed that a larger population base is needed to support specialty practices than is necessary for primary-care providers. The range of population base required to support the practices of specialty providers is typically not part of rural geography (Moscovice & Rosenblatt 1985b).

Kindig, in a comprehensive analysis on the geographic distribution of physicians, notes that "more common or routine care [should be] available in all geographic areas or within a certain distance or travel time" (Kindig 1989, p. 12). Further, a general consensus has emerged indicating that compared to other specialists, primary care physicians (particularly general and family practitioners) are distributed more evenly relative to population. The end result is that rural communities depend more on primary-care physicians, and thus they are more affected by trends in the supply and distribution of primary-care physicians.

GROWING SUPPLY AND SUSTAINED RURAL SHORTAGE

During the past 40 years, the supply of physicians in the United States has increased substantially, nearly doubling between 1960 and 1985 (that is, a total physician increase of 210,000 or 64 percent of all active physicians). The supply is predicted to increase from 227 physicians per 100,000 population to 280 physicians per 100,000 by the year 2010 (Kindig 1989). Nevertheless, the growth in overall supply has not been accompanied by a concurrent growth in the supply of primary-care physicians, nor in the distribution of physicians to some of the most needy rural areas. According to Amundson (1991), the estimated physician growth of 22 percent by the year 2000 will only increase the supply of family physicians by 9 percent. Without changes in physician distribution and specialty training, efforts to provide physicians for rural America will continue to fail.

Recent studies support the notion that most rural areas have experienced either a stable or declining number of physicians during the last several decades. Kindig (1989) cites evidence that the rate of physician growth in rural areas was about one fourth the rate of growth for urban areas, and that the growth was insufficient to meet rural needs. He notes that up to 25 percent of the rural physicians in sparsely populated areas will retire or relocate within the next 5 years, a fact corroborated by other recent studies. He concludes:

There remain geographic areas of the country which are relatively undersupplied with primary care physicians. This is certainly the case for certain subspecialties as well, but has been less well-documented. Most areas have shown increases over the past decade as the result of the overall increase in physician supply, but rural and inner city areas have shown lower rates of increase for primary care physicians. There is significant variation in MD/100,000 population for counties less than 50,000 population, with the southern states having the lowest regional levels. (pp. 50–51)

Another important issue is the demographic distribution of family physicians in the nation. Family practice exhibits a classic bimodal age distribution of physicians. Many older physicians and younger physicians have entered family practice; however, there are many fewer in the middle years, of ages 40 to 55, who have chosen this specialty. Consequently, during the next 10 to 15 years, most family physicians in the older age brackets will enter an era of inactivity through death, disability, or retirement. There is an insufficient supply of physicians in family practice to replace those who will retire. There has also been a decline in recent years in the number of graduating medical students going into this specialty. Finally, many of the physicians that reside in rural areas are the older family physicians; thus, these areas will no doubt be disproportionately affected by the decline in family practice supply.

The marked trend of increasing liability premiums for all physicians has a unique and double impact on family practice physicians and on the communities they serve. With a generally lower income, liability costs represent a greater burden to family practice physicians (Korczyk 1989). In addition, the dramatic rise in premium and liability risks for obstetrical practice has resulted in significant decreases in the percentage of family practice physicians who include obstetric services in their practice (Council on Long Range Planning and Development 1988).

RECRUITMENT EFFORTS OF RURAL COMMUNITIES

There is a need to recognize that society has changed and with it the medical community. The profile of the physician population differs vastly in terms of values, career expectations, and practice settings than even a decade ago. Dual-career families are becoming the norm for medical families, as they are for the rest of society. Many physicians have professional spouses who require equally rewarding employment opportunities. Rural America must face the issue of how to recruit the professional spouse as part of the package for attracting the physician.

Most rural health professionals agree that it is more difficult to recruit physicians to rural areas today than 5 years ago. Reasons for the increased difficulty include changes in delivery patterns, increased reliance upon technology, the general unavailability of ancillary professionals for many rural areas, lack of financial incentives to practice in rural settings, and an educational system that emphasizes subspecialization rather than primary care as the model for future practice.

In addition to these issues, other more specific community concerns affecting the availability of physicians in rural areas must also be addressed. A rural community must decide whether it can support a physician and must estimate the potential for physician-generated revenue. Doekson & Miller (1987) have shown that for every physician in a rural community, 18 related jobs exist. Similarly, a typical hospital in a rural community of about 7,700 could account for about one quarter of the community's jobs through the direct and indirect employment effects.

Factors which influence the choice of a physician's practice site must be actively considered. Although physicians generally prefer permanent practice locations, recruitment and retention are affected to varying degrees by such factors as geographic origin, location of residency training, personal and professional needs of the spouse, special considerations such as National Health Service Corps (NHSC) obligations, specialty training, and long-term goals.

Other practical considerations in the recruitment of physicians include working hours, on-call schedule, and opportunities for continuing medical education. Young physicians who are now completing their training and looking at practice opportunities have different expectations from those of the past. They do not want to be on call every third night and every third weekend, nor do they want to work 80 hours per week. As a result, they accept opportunities at lower salaries in fixed situations, or opt for group practice and employee status; however, these forms are more common in urban areas. Thus, the physician supply shortage in rural areas is further compounded by a substantial rise in the formation of prepaid health systems, which recognize that one of the ways to restrain costs is to utilize primary-care providers as "gatekeepers." The growth of the gatekeeper model in urban areas has resulted in an increased number of primary-care physicians choosing those locations.

In response to these considerations, an important organizational change in health care in recent years is the demise of the solo physician. Solo practice leaves the physician little control over hours and time away. In addition, contemporary health care is a complicated enterprise practiced by a team. The delivery of high quality services requires the availability of many health professionals who can provide a range of services in many different settings. As a result, the solo doc of yesteryear is ill-equipped to practice in the rural America of today. These are major considerations that must be addressed by the rural community if recruitment is to be successful.

Over the last several years, rural health has received increasing attention from the nation's policymakers. The academic medical community can anticipate growing pressure to assist in alleviating the problems of rural health. Indeed, Amundson (1991) suggests medical schools are responsible and should be held accountable for the outcomes of physician distribution. The next section expands on physician location by analyzing the influence of academic medicine.

THE ROLE OF MEDICAL EDUCATION

The academic medical center is in a unique position to assist in meeting the greater needs of society. Such a notion is based on three premises. First, academic medical centers, as the purveyors of medical and health education, are responsible for meeting certain societal needs. The responsibility extends beyond the confines of the traditional biomedical model. The nation is experiencing multiple challenges within the health-care delivery system that will continue to alter the face of health care even more markedly during the next decade. It is anticipated that health care will remain the dominant domestic issue of the 1990s because the existing system has failed to address a host of health-care problems. Much of society believes these problems fall within the purview of the academic medical center.

Second, rural residents, who represent 25 percent of the nation's population, deserve access to the same level and quality of health care as their urban counterparts. Although simple in concept, the notion of equity is an important element in selecting solutions for meeting the challenges of rural health-care delivery.

Third, any changes adopted within medical education will be ineffective without concomitant changes in the overall system of health-care delivery in the United States. With rural health, as with other equally complex problems, such as health care for the uninsured, the health-care delivery system is failing as much as the educational system. Although there are many individual success stories in rural health, success in pieces is not a success of the whole. Small, isolated solutions will not meet the health-care needs of the nation's rural populace.

We can do better. We must do better. Society has invested substantially in the notion that we will do better. Schroeder, Zones, & Showstack (1989) point to several areas of strong performance by academic medicine, including advances in biomedical research, technology development and diffusion, progress against certain target illnesses, disease prevention, health services research, and innovations in health-care provision. Areas of weak performance cited were national health status, national health-care expenditures, quality of medical care, the distribution and mix of medial manpower, long-term care, and disability.

In particular, it is essential to note that the most important change in health care is that it is no longer an isolated exercise practiced by the solo physician of yesteryear. The delivery of quality health care requires the cooperative efforts of many health professionals. The failure of academic medicine to meet physician manpower needs for rural America is not the only issue; it has failed just as dismally in training the ancillary health professions for rural practice and in promoting interdisciplinary practice. Academic medicine is not alone; rather, it is simply the leader of the pack.

There is an expectation that academic medicine will help in solving the rural health problem. In a recent response to the article by Schroeder, Zones, & Showstack (1989), which reviewed areas of strong and weak performance by academic medicine, Dr. Robert Petersdorf, president of the American Association of Medical Colleges, states:

One locus where academic medical centers fail to exercise control effectively and where their actions have not accrued to society's benefit is in influencing physician manpower. In particular, the gap between the number of physicians attracted to the primary care disciplines of family practice, general internal medicine, and general pediatrics, and those in the specialties and subspecialties, seems to be widening at a time when the public perception is that we need more generalists and fewer specialists. This issue requires urgent attention and a plan for ultimate resolution. (1989, p. 826)

Before proceeding with suggestions for how academic medicine can respond and the types of programs which could potentially resolve the problem, it is instructive to elaborate on the reasons for failure.

FAILURE TO MEET THE RURAL HEALTH CHALLENGE

Reasons for the failure of medical education to meet the challenge can be summed up in three words: selection, training, and support.

Selection. It is widely, if not universally, believed that medical schools have a crucial role in issues related to the preparation and selection of students—the nation's future physicians. The inherent criteria of the selection process are too often biased against students from disadvantaged backgrounds, including students from rural backgrounds. The reasons for this can be traced to the focus of high school training (Crandell, Dwyer, & Duncan 1990). Rural high schools without a quality science training program do not provide the foundation necessary to encourage students to enter medicine or the other health careers. This lack of adequate training is further compounded by a lack of good counseling related to careers in the health professions.

The issue takes on added importance when combined with the clearly documented fact that rural students have a much higher likelihood of returning to rural communities (Bruce 1990). If we only train students from large cities, we will only have physicians in cities, just as we will have insufficient numbers of physicians to deliver health care to minority patients if we fail in our goal to train more minority physicians.

The usual response of the academic medical centers is to reject responsibility for the educational system, claiming that they have little control over the system. Although they may not have full control, they are vested with a special responsibility to train physicians for our nation. The responsibility is not finite and does not begin artificially at admission to medical school. Medical schools must support initiatives that identify and encourage the disadvantaged and rural students. In the same manner that schools have responsibility for maintaining the education of physicians through continuing education, they have a responsibility for supporting the composition of the physician pool through proactive educational support.

Training. The second major reason for failure is training. The training issue is the crux of the problem and is part of another phenomenon, the retrenchment of the academic medical center as the core for medical education in America. There is currently a movement toward a biased view of the medical center as the preeminent source of medical education, after several decades that allowed diversity and flexibility within the education system.

Such a trend is disturbing and represents a shift of the pendulum toward a myopia of self-preservation of the academic medical center for the sake of the institution, rather than for the sake of medical education. The self-contained academic medical center, usually urban, is attempting to become the "citadel" of education and training and, more importantly, referrals. The increased reliance upon practice dollars to sustain the academic medical center seems to be the driving force behind the retrenchment of "the university" as the referral point of tertiary care. Medical education, at all levels, appears to be pulling in the direction of modified rules for membership in the club, rules that reflect an understanding of the medical center and its needs.

The promulgation of these standards—most often by representatives of the academic medical center and in the form of the accreditation process—is jeopardizing the viability of equally important medical education centers with different missions, different purposes, and different constituencies. These medical education centers have been providing quality medical education by all available parameters for over two decades. The difference is that they look different, they act differently, and they respond to needs differently from those of the traditional academic medical center.

Although the tertiary and now quaternary academic medical center possesses a unique and crucial role in the health-care delivery and educational system, allowance for diversity and flexibility must not be dismantled in an effort to sustain such centers. Not all medical education centers should be full-fledged academic medical centers. In fact, not all should be quaternary centers. In the same manner, not everyone should be involved in rural health or perhaps even primary care. Many medical schools are incapable of responding to primary-care needs, and some others are unwilling to do so. This dilemma was recognized with this observation by Lewis & Sheps (1983):

The academic medical center must give high priority in its teaching, research, and patient-care programs to the major health problems of the population of its area and to practice in the community. (p. 227)

Those centers with a community focus, a primary-care need, and service-delivery agenda must have a policy of both flexibility and diversity in their training of physicians for rural areas of the nation. Rural health focuses on the community—it is primary care, and it is service for people in need.

A second element of the training issue is the undue emphasis on a segmented, rather than an integrated, approach to medical education. That segmentation of the curriculum among the various disciplines results in an undue priority being placed on the training of "ologists" (subspecialists), rather than on primary-care providers.

Finally, the training problem for physicians is compounded by a concomitant failure of health sciences schools to train adequate numbers of support personnel for rural areas. Although physicians are often considered central to a community's provision of health care, they are outnumbered by an array of other essential providers, especially nurses and multiskilled, allied health practitioners. The success of rural health-care delivery would be improved by a more coordinated effort among all the training programs to prepare students for interdisciplinary practice.

Support. One of the singularly most important reasons for failure resides more with the health-care system perhaps than with the academic medical center. Our health-care system has simply failed to provide sufficient support for rural physicians. The most glaring example is in the payment system. Several studies have demonstrated that federal reimbursement programs systematically discriminate against rural residents and providers, and act as impediments to a more equitable distribution of medical services (Fickenscher 1985). It is a cruel irony that the need to provide health services to the rural and underserved areas is recognized through strong support programs such as Community Health Centers, the Indian Health Service, and other efforts, whereas physicians who practice in these settings are rewarded with payments of up to 50 percent less than their urban counterparts for exactly the same service. The disincentives are clear, regardless of any efforts initiated by the academic medical centers.

Aside from the financial issues, the lack of peer support is also a prevalent problem for physicians practicing in rural areas of the nation. Outreach is effective only to the extent that it meets the referral needs of the academic medical center. More support should be given to primary-care providers in rural America. An example exists in the form of an innovative telecommunications project at Texas Tech Medical School. They have instituted a new program for rural physicians providing obstetrical care, whereby fetal monitoring strips can be sent via facsimile to the central campus for interpretative support, thereby reducing the need to transfer women in labor. As this example clearly illustrates, the technology has evolved, yet a 1960s approach is still practiced in too many situations.

THE NEEDED RESPONSE

The triad of education, research, and service is rhetorical. In terms of interest and commitment, it is, for many medical centers, only a diad— education and research. Service, in the form of private practice by the faculty, is provided only to the extent that it meets the need to support the faculty.

Patient-care service has become the sine qua non for sustaining the academic medical center, since private practice is driving our educational system. Students and the process of medical education in too many cases have simply become the theoretical reason for the medical center to exist. Although service is clearly needed for many rural areas, the service aspect of the medical center is only couched in terms of "patients." However, beyond that aspect, rural communities need a service of assistance, a service of guidance, a service of solutions for meeting their many health-care delivery needs. Such service, although often needed, is too often ignored; such is the support academic medical centers provide to rural communities.

Dr. Tom Johnson (1989) noted at the Midwest Great Plains Council of Deans that the triad of education, research, and service is unstable. Like the three-legged milk stool that topples easily so the milker can avoid the cow's kick, so the academic medical center is unstable for a new era of accountability to society's needs. He suggested that an additional leg of social responsibility to the public, who support our institutions, be added.

A new response is needed to reach out actively to our base communities, and to adopt a broad perspective that recognizes the complexity of rural health within the economic, social, and cultural context of the community. The current educational structure is too linear and does not allow for the exploration and development of new strategies.

There are several potential solutions that could be initiated by academic medical centers to meet the needs of rural and underserved people. A short list follows.

1. Medical centers should insure that an adequate pool of "potential" rural practitioners is selected by the nation's medical schools. A special emphasis on a proactive admission process for rural students will help meet future rural physician personnel needs. Head & Harris (1989) concluded that students raised in rural areas and inclined to rural practice are underrepresented. Special support programs must be presented at the undergraduate level to assist rural and disadvantaged students prior to their application to medical school. Students who share the following characteristics should be actively recruited: students who have a small town or rural background, are over 25 years of age, preferably are married, have attended public college, have evidenced a strong motivation for direct, patient contact, and have exhibited a preference for humanistic over scientific interests. Rezler & Kalishman (1989) identified these as factors associated with lasting commitment to family practice.

2. Medical centers must modify current student attitudes toward primary care. Although the attitude of students is complex, role models play a key role in addressing the issue. Kindig (1989) cites evidence for a declining positive attitude toward primary care based on responses to the annual Association of American Medical Colleges (AAMC) senior student questionnaire. The student preferences for primary care decreased from 36 percent in 1982 to 25 percent in 1988, a 32 percent decline over the 6-year period. The diminishing interest was more prominent for general internal medicine (-43 percent) than for family practice (-28 percent). Special initiatives to decrease the negative impact of subspecialty training must be implemented for successful training of primary-care physicians.

3. Medical centers must respond to new graduate and undergraduate requirements that decrease the degree of acceptable flexibility within the curricula. Innovation and creativity in responding to the rural health problem will come from local efforts, not from a centrally designed standard.

4. Medical centers must recognize that four years of socialization cannot be reversed with a single, isolated clinical rotation late in the fourth year of medical school. Longitudinal experiences at designated rural sites must be integrated into the curriculum if an effective educational experience in rural health is to be provided. It is inefficient and inappropriate to train future rural physicians in tertiary referral centers where little emphasis is placed on the type and level of services to be provided by primary-care physicians. A new model, which incorporates rural sites as the primary training center, is a crucial direction.

5. Medical centers need to facilitate cross-disciplinary training of health professionals. It seems clear that the practice of medicine is a team process, yet our approach to training and education, as it relates to maintaining such a team, is dysfunctional.

6. Medical centers should continue to explore the use of computer modeling in education. The appropriate use of computers will allow universities to cross the geographic boundaries in order to increase their ability to provide quality educational experiences in more rural areas. The portable computer can become the rural educators' best potential tool.

7. Medical centers need to explore and expand telecommunication linkages. The Texas Tech MEDNET project and other similar efforts should be expanded to

allow for greater experimentation in the training of health science students in rural areas. Tying together the resources of the academic medical center with those of rural communities into a unified educational network can create a quality educational system for remote areas, as well as a support base for practicing physicians. Such efforts can be initiated only by the academic medical center.

8. Medical centers need to understand that social responsibility implies more than education and research. It also implies that medical centers accept an important and crucial role in providing support and technical assistance to rural communities in need of viable, local, quality health-care services.

9. Despite the best efforts of medical centers, some rural and underserved areas of the nation will continue to have marked shortages of providers. Medical centers must understand that meeting these needs is not purely an educational issue. It requires programs like the National Health Service Corps, which can provide a pool of committed physicians for practice in rural and underserved communities.

The importance of medical education in focusing the nation's health makes policymakers increasingly scrutinize the results of the nation's investment. In an era of constrained resources, it is especially critical to embrace the concerns of society by responding to the needs of certain constituencies such as rural areas. Amundson (1991) notes that it is not unreasonable for the public to expect solutions, not simply responses, from medical schools to which they have extended trust and generous funding.

INNOVATIVE STRATEGIES

Efforts to enhance rural practice, such as through reimbursement modification and assistance with malpractice premiums, will only achieve modest success without strategies aimed at medical education. Individual states are becoming more progressive with rural health strategies. They are putting pressures on legislatures to give more direction to academic medicine. Furthermore, many states have initiated programs to encourage students to enter primary-care specialties and to select underserved areas for practice. For example, the Minnesota Rural Physician Associate Program for Medical Students (RPAP) combines rural experience during medical school with rural role models and stipends to encourage students to practice in rural areas (Verby 1988). The program has existed for 18 years, with general success in encouraging medical students to enter primary care, thereby improving the distribution of physicians in rural Minnesota counties.

The University of Nebraska Medical Center (UNMC) has increased its commitment to preparing primary-care providers for rural practice through a proposed UNMC Rural Health Education Network (University of Nebraska Medical Center 1991). The network is organized as a hub-and-spoke model, whereby health science education is centered in the "hub" community of the medical center and clinical training takes place in the region's smaller "spoke" communities. The purpose of the network is to alter how and where primary-care students are educated; it requires a partnership among the rural communities, the institutions providing care, and the higher education system of the state's medical center.

Texas has a state initiative that uses an interdisciplinary approach to rural provider shortages (*Rural Health News* 1991). Cooperation among schools of medicine, nursing, and allied health and teaching hospitals is the focus in creating an expanded rural preceptorship program. In addition to the standard features of these programs, such as rural rotations, there is a continuing education relief service, through which the state's Center for Rural Health recruits temporary replacements for those who want to attend educational events. These tactics, as well as utilization of existing communication technology, help overcome the complaint of rural-based providers about the lack of continuing education opportunities.

Gibbens & Olson (1990) outline state legislative strategies that focus on education for the purpose of alleviating rural physician shortages. Legislative establishment of new medical residency programs is one strategy used by several states. These residences provide physicians with experience in rural medicine, and offer communities opportunities to recruit the residents for permanent practice. A second strategy, the development of new Area Health Education Centers (AHECs) to prepare primary-care physicians for underserved rural areas, has been contemplated by several states. One advantage of these programs is ongoing use of rural preceptors, which strengthens ties between the urban teaching institutions and rural practice sites.

Four states, Alabama, Minnesota, Pennsylvania, and New Mexico, are focusing on premedical school strategies, with attempts to interest high school students and adult rural residents in medical careers. These efforts are based on the philosophy that students originating from rural areas are more likely to return for practice. Alabama has advanced this method through its successful Biomedical Sciences Preparation Program (Bio-Prep) to prepare high school students to enter science-based occupations.

Although not a new thrust, nor one aimed specifically at education, it should be noted that the National Health Service Corps has received federal reauthorization, which should renew the rotation of new physicians into underserved rural areas (Kaiman 1991). Funding for the corps for FY1991 was over $91 million, an increase of $41 million from FY1990.

CONCLUSIONS

There is a need to encourage a pluralistic approach in medical education, rather than a unified paradigm. Each approach must stand on its own merits. It is important to recognize the contribution of the community-integrated medical education system as one key in meeting the health personnel needs of the nation, especially in rural, underserved areas. Just as primary-care centers would no doubt fail in training ultraspecialists, so too the academic medical center, without new directions, will fail to train primary-care providers. If we fail to allow for diversity and a pluralistic approach in our educational system, we are at risk of training a generation of technologists rather than physicians. The new technologies evolving in education will radically alter the standards of medical education over the next decade and allow us to consider new and innovative approaches for training the nation's future physicians.

Finally, as part of any considerations in meeting the nation's physician supply needs, the primary reason for medical education must be kept in focus—that is, to train physicians to care for people. Without incorporating innovative strategies, we are at risk of losing that foundation.

7. Preparing and Recruiting Nurses for Innovating Rural Practice Roles

Eileen M. Weis

The nursing profession will undergo significant challenges during the 1990s. Nornhold (1990) predicts the nursing environment will be affected by additional hospital closings, refinement of the traditional nursing role, and increased power for nurses in the near future. Nurses have been central to quality health care in rural areas; it is important that changes in the profession not leave a void in delivery of care.

This chapter focuses on the changing rural health-care scene as it pertains to recruitment and retention of registered nurses. Described are several issues and suggestions for facilitating the transition, for utilizing, and for expanding the contribution of nurses and nurse practitioners in the rural health setting. If approached correctly, organizational change in rural facilities can create innovative practice opportunities for nurses.

CHARACTERISTICS OF RURAL NURSES

Typical nurses, working in a rural hospital, differ from their urban peers both in terms of the role they take in patient care and in terms of demographic characteristics. Nurses who choose to work in rural hospitals normally function as generalists. Because most rural facilities are relatively small, nurses must have the background and adaptability to work in many different areas, from the labor and delivery room to the emergency room to the medical-surgical unit. This rural nursing environment is complex and diverse, requiring a wide variety of skills and the flexibility to adjust to new demands at a moment's notice (Moscovice 1988).

Furthermore, research performed by St. Clair, Pickard, & Harlow (1986) shows that the rural nurse is usually older, has less education, receives a lower income, and scores lower on self-actualization measures than urban counterparts. Rural nurses also tend to be more complacent and resistant to change. Moreover, the authors state that rural nurses have different relationships with patients and families. The meaning of "different" is unclear in the article, but it most likely refers to the more personal and familiar interactions that rural nurses have with patients.

RECRUITMENT AND RETENTION ISSUES

Rural hospitals have trouble retaining nurses, as do other hospitals and nonhospital employers. Nationwide, an excess demand for nurses has existed since the mid–1980s, and many qualified nurses have chosen to leave the profession. According to Helmer & McKnight (1989), the most common reasons for this exodus, in order of importance are these:

1. long hours and understaffing;
2. the treatment nurses receive from administrators and physicians; and
3. low pay and inadequate benefits.

As a result, the vacancy rates for registered nurses in hospitals have more than doubled since 1983. More than 75 percent of all hospitals report some shortages, and 19 percent report a severe shortage. Projected demand for registered nurses is twice the anticipated supply for the year 2000 (Hart 1989).

Rural hospitals, especially hard hit by staffing shortages, are at a disadvantage in competing for nurses on the basis of compensation. These facilities traditionally offer lower wages, fewer benefits, and limited opportunities for advancement, relative to their urban counterparts. Thus, many nurses, living in rural areas, travel to urban areas for employment because the working conditions and the pay scale are more favorable. The rural hospital is then left with worse staffing conditions. This, in turn, creates even more stress for the remaining staff and increases the likelihood of more nurses leaving rural hospitals.

TRANSITION

Many rural hospitals experience significant financial stress because of low census, patient migration to other communities, and low reimbursement levels. Although some hospitals have closed, others are changing their organizational structures, as a means of retaining local access to health-care services. A common pattern is for hospitals to merge or form alliances with other community hospitals in order to create viable organizations (Christianson et al. 1990). Others convert their operations from secondary to primary care in an effort to meet the majority of local health-care needs, while cutting costs at the same time. The structure that emerges creates a new work environment. In addition, the transition phase requires adaptability on the part of nurses and other personnel. The negative aspects of this phase need to be minimized in order to prevent further erosion of staff.

Easing the Transition

Prior to the conversion process, the nursing staff usually experience considerable stress related to a low and fluctuating census. Short-staffed conditions are common. Rumors of layoffs and hospital closure run rampant. The morale of professional nurses often suffers when they frequently have to stay home, without pay, on low census days. Nurses experience many different responses to these stressors, such as fear of job loss, suspicion of management's motives, and depression or irritability.

Hospital administration has several methods available to counter the negative feelings commonly experienced by staff members. First, frequent and open communication providing accurate and timely information about transition plans helps dispel rumors. For example, administrators can meet once a week with staff members, providing updates of progress and answers to questions. Informing staff about the hospital's financial status can also help garner support for change. For example, when the staff hear that the hospital barely made payroll last month, its members usually are more receptive to new options. Secrecy on the part of administration is sure to backfire and should be avoided.

A common complaint expressed by nurses about their profession is their lack of control in the work setting. Offering nurses an opportunity to provide input into the restructuring process, through a participative management approach, enables them to feel more in control of their destiny. Involving nurses in the strategic planning process, as well as in the implementation and operational phases, will help promote the image of the converted hospital as a place that meets nurses' professional needs, thereby reducing turnover. The converted facility will be better able to compete for nurses since it provides a work setting where they have more input into their future than in traditional settings.

Nursing input can be formally collected by utilizing the director of nursing (DON) as a liaison between the planners and the nursing staff. The DON can collect ideas and feedback from the staff, and relay the information to the planners. The DON can also be very useful in providing input for the reassignment of personnel in the event that the service structure is changed. For example, nurses who have worked in the medical-surgical inpatient unit may prefer to work in the new outpatient clinic in the converted facility.

A nursing advisory committee that reports to the hospital board can also be formed to ensure that a formal communication channel exists between the two groups. A committee will ensure that staff ideas are conveyed directly to the board. This is particularly useful in facilitating nurses' empowerment.

Participative management encourages nursing involvement and counters the traditional one-way communication channels. With participative management, nurses are recognized as key players on the health-care team. This fosters an environment whereby physicians consult nurses frequently about patients' conditions, using their input to direct patient management (Stein, Watts, & Howell 1990).

Rural facilities, undergoing organizational change, are ideally suited for creating innovative practice opportunities for nurses. As the institution changes, new roles and responsibilities are created that fit the organization's new purpose. The entire delivery system is reevaluated and altered to create a more efficient and consumer-friendly system. Thus, many job opportunities appear that were nonexistent in the previous system. Nurses are well-positioned to create new jobs and responsibilities that expand their capabilities. They can utilize collaborative practice protocols with participating physicians, enabling them to widen their scope of practice.

Through collaborative practice, nurses are granted decision-making authority in areas that historically have been primarily the physicians' domain. Protocols set the criteria by which nurses make clinical decisions. The protocols identify nursing actions that can be taken, depending on the patient's symptoms and medical history. These protocols, which are usually specific to the institution, are determined on the basis of the capabilities of the local nursing staff and the physicians' agreement to participate. The protocols are always written, as opposed to being verbally understood, in order to minimize the risk of liability to all involved clinicians.

Although a hospital undergoing conversion may eliminate certain existing services such as traditional inpatient care, a converted hospital also creates new services, such as clinics, an infirmary, emergency medical services (EMS), home health, and long-term care, among others that replace acute inpatient care. The provision of a wider range of services in a new type of rural facility helps counteract the perception of the converted hospital as a first aid station. New jobs and services provide intellectual stimulation for the staff by presenting them with an opportunity to be trained in new capacities.

A successful transition to alternate uses usually depends on retraining existing personnel for new positions. This presents nurses with the opportunity and the motivation to expand their skills in areas of interest and availability. For example, nurses trained in inpatient care can learn skills for clinic work (for example, managing a larger flow of patients, screening a wider variety of illnesses), and infirmary work (for example, managing less intensive illnesses).

The costs of retraining personnel should be covered by the hospital, with assistance from a secondary or tertiary affiliate if possible. These hospitals can provide support in educating nurses about services that are new to the converted facility. Staff usually expect to be reimbursed for the time spent learning new skills and the materials used to support the effort.

Inevitably, during transition, some nurses will decide to leave the institution to pursue work elsewhere; many will use the opportunity to transfer to a larger, urban hospital. Nurses may leave because of fears associated with the risk in converting to a new delivery system. However, the possible loss of personnel should not be viewed solely as a negative consequence. Many of those who leave could be a hindrance to the conversion if they stayed; negative attitudes can hinder and undermine progress.

The evolving transition structure will require innovative personnel who view the situation as an opportunity for professional growth. Staff members can use the transition as an opportunity to be leaders in rural nursing and health care. New styles of nursing practice can be developed in this progressive environment, and recruitment campaigns can emphasize this leadership role. Many nurses will be interested in working in transition facilities because they are innovative state-of-the-art models of health-care delivery, and are favorable settings for participative management.

NURSE EDUCATIONAL PREPARATION

Traditional educational preparation for professional nurses may act as a barrier in the new rural health-care environment because of its focus on specialization. The education process must be flexible enough to prepare nurses to work in a converted or consolidated hospital, as well as in a variety of other settings. Nurses preparing specifically for rural practice should learn to function in many different roles—that is, to act as generalists. They should be trained to have dual responsibilities, such as working in urgent care and EMS, or in long-term care and an infirmary. They should also be prepared to function under many different health-care organizational structures: clinics, hospitals, infirmaries, home health delivery, EMS, and long-term care.

Traditional educational programs for nurses include a 2-year associate degree program, a 3-year hospital diploma program, and a 4-year university degree program. Common to all three programs is a curriculum based on the traditional model of nursing services—an inpatient, hospital-based setting. As a result, many nurses are unprepared to work in ambulatory settings and must be retrained to function in primary care. In the primary-care setting, nurses must be skilled in treating illnesses that do not require critical-care capabilities. They must also be adept at monitoring patients with minor illnesses. Nurses working in an ambulatory setting must be skilled at recognizing when patients should be transferred to a secondary-care facility for more intensive treatment.

A related problem for rural areas is that few nursing programs offer courses or practicums that orient nurses to the special demands of rural practice, nor do they provide opportunities for experience with innovative models of such practice. A recent survey of nursing programs across the country revealed that only a small percentage offered a rural track or a component designed to orient nursing students to rural practice (Frels & Straub 1991). According to Reimer & Mills (1988), the focus on specialized, hospital-based practice in urban settings means that nursing graduates develop job standards more suited to urban employment during their courses of study.

In recognition of the uniqueness of rural practice, some medical schools are beginning to break away from the hospital-based model by offering family practice programs that operate only in ambulatory care settings. Rural health care would benefit if some nursing schools would do the same. A number of options exist for nursing schools, such as the development of clinical rotations in converted primary-care hospitals. However, in the current nursing market of excess demand, there is little incentive for nursing programs to undertake changes to accommodate rural need, unless these changes can be viewed as a method of increasing enrollment, by attracting students from different groups, such as older women and men.

When addressing the rural nursing shortage, one option a hospital may choose is a "grow from within" recruitment tactic, whereby people already living in a particular community are trained for positions in their local facility. Many rural hospitals realize that employees with greatest longevity are typically those from their own local areas. It is much easier to recruit a rural resident to work in the local hospital than to recruit an urban person to relocate to a rural area. This tactic makes it incumbent upon rural hospitals to insure that the local educational system can accommodate residents who want to pursue health careers.

ADDITIONAL RECRUITMENT AND RETENTION SUGGESTIONS

Recruitment into and retention of health-care professionals in rural areas continue to present a major challenge to residents and health administrators. Success frequently depends on finding employment for the spouses of nurses and other practitioners. One potential approach is for the hospital or clinic to work with the community's economic development agency to help locate employment opportunities for spouses. Alternatively, the hospital can develop its own career service, designed to provide free job search assistance to spouses. Educational assistance can also be provided to spouses who desire to enroll in courses at a local college. A hospital may benefit from an arrangement with local educational institutions to create new programs that appeal to career-oriented residents.

To aid in the retention of nurses, the hospital should create a working environment that emphasizes learning. The staff should be exposed to the latest in nursing procedures and issues—for example, nursing diagnosis, and new acuity and charting systems. Furthermore, because regular interaction with medical residents is intellectually stimulating to nurses, the converted rural hospital could also pursue inclusion in an affiliate's residency program, which would entail rotating the residents through the rural site. The residents could help maintain the educational atmosphere that so many nursing students become accustomed to during their training.

In addition, the development of specialty clinics, through which urban specialists visit a clinic on a predetermined basis, can help provide clinical stimulation to nurses as they learn and practice new skills and procedures. Patients also enjoy the convenience of purchasing specialty care at their local health facility.

According to Princeton & McGrath (1989), decentralized education programs, such as Area Health Education Centers (AHECs), have proved to be very effective in improving the quality of rural nursing education by making continuing education and degree programs accessible to nurses. The AHEC concept was developed in 1970 as a federally funded program to provide health education to professionals in the fields of nursing, dentistry, pharmacy, public health, and medicine. These programs, now also funded by state and local monies, remain viable in many states (Princeton & McGrath 1989). Prior to the formation of AHECs, nurses had to travel long distances for education, and many decided to forgo the experience altogether because of the inconvenience and cost.

The presence of an AHEC in a region allows nurses to access continuing education in a manner that is both convenient and less costly to themselves and their employers. The AHECs provide a variety of programs to rural nurses and health sciences students, from baccalaureate programs to continuing education for license renewal. AHECs have also been used to attract and encourage nursing students to practice in rural institutions, by providing them with selected clinical experiences in rural areas (Princeton & McGrath 1989).

The range of courses that contribute to rural nurse retention should encompass more than just clinical material. In response to studies showing that many rural nurses score low on self-actualization measures, continuing education programs should offer courses that facilitate the development of positive self-concepts and self-esteem. Roberts (1983) suggests that courses should also be included that focus on effective communication skills, assisting nurses in overcoming self-defeating behavior. Related topics for continuing education include assertiveness, decision making, leadership skills, self-esteem, and new nursing models (St. Clair, Pickard, & Harlow 1986).

Career ladders are another valuable tool that stimulate and reward nurses for staying in the profession and in a specific institution. The placement of personnel in new positions, following hospital conversion, should be based on interest, seniority, and qualifications. Examples of new positions which may be implemented, if not already in place, are quality assurance director, utilization review director, inservice director, clinical nurse specialist, researcher, and member of a nursing advisory board. Further, nurses with seniority and competence should be rewarded with more schedule flexibility. Nurses pursuing additional clinical skills may also be rewarded with higher pay, a main feature of the differentiated nursing model.

Financial assistance for educational pursuits is often an effective incentive for employees to advance professionally. In addition, the hospital might consider offering educational assistance for health-care related courses to local residents who would like to work in the health field as part of a recruitment effort. In exchange for educational assistance, the student could commit herself or himself to work in the local hospital for a designated period of time. Loan repayments could be forgiven, depending on the length of service given.

A major difficulty facing rural facilities is the need to compete with the salaries and benefits offered by urban counterparts. Many rural hospitals already offer urban salaries for physical and respiratory therapists; these same rural hospitals may discover that they also need to offer urban wages for nurses to remain competitive in the nurse market. If financial constraints prohibit this alternative, then rural hospitals should concentrate on making existing nonfinancial concerns, such as scheduling, more attractive to nurses. Further, some rural hospitals have paid their nurses salaries as opposed to hourly wages, to help combat the "blue collar" feeling that sometimes accompanies hourly work.

Rural institutions will improve retention by offering attractive solutions to the most frequently expressed complaints by nurses in both rural and urban settings. Salary compression is a relevant complaint expressed by many nurses, regardless of where they work. Salary compression occurs when pay increases are granted in the first 5 to 7 years, and then level off for the rest of a nurse's career. A rural hospital could counter this trend by granting raises for longevity that are tied to performance.

Another concern sometimes expressed by nurses is that the compensation for short-notice overtime work is inadequate. To counter this problem, a rural hospital may consider offering nurses time-and-a-half pay when they are called to work with less than 24 hours notice.

However, rural institutions will benefit from recognizing that salary is not always the most important issue to nurses. Administrators should learn more about nurses' interests in other work-related issues, such as the quality of the work environment, schedules, day care, employment of spouses, and continuing education opportunities. Responding to these nonwage-related needs may yield a low-cost benefit to retention.

To create a more humane environment for the nursing staff, every effort must be made to retain allied health professionals. When these professionals—for example, respiratory and physical therapists—are absent, nurses must assume many of their duties. Many nurses resent this extra work because they feel that they are carrying too heavy a load; they also resent being used as substitutes in areas for which they have not been trained. Rural hospitals should realize that the work environment and the workload are critical factors for both recruitment and retention.

The nursing profession requires that its members constantly give of themselves, as is expected in many caretaking professions. However, it is often overlooked that nurses themselves need to be emotionally satisfied. Nursing efforts, small and large, should be noticed and acknowledged by superiors, physicians, and peers. Hospital administrators should consciously and consistently provide positive feedback to nurses for work well done. A Nurse of the Month program is one method that rewards nurses for the small, caring actions that often go unnoticed.

In spite of the national nursing shortage, some hospitals have no difficulty recruiting nurses. A study by Helmer & McKnight (1989) discovered that these hospitals have the following factors in common:

1. a nurse-patient ratio that assures quality patient care;
2. flexible staffing to support patient-care needs;
3. flexible scheduling and elimination of rotating shifts;
4. a strong, supportive nursing administration;
5. primary nursing;
6. clinical advancement opportunities (so that RNs can stay at the bedside, but still advance professionally);
7. participative management;
8. open communication in all directions;
9. inservice and continuing education opportunities on all shifts;
10. good nurse-physician professional relationships;
11. longevity benefits for staff RNs; and
12. tuition reimbursement.

Rural hospitals are in a position to provide an environment that would incorporate many of these characteristics, especially during and after transition to alternate structures. With nursing input in the planning and implementation stages, two-way communication is established, and participative management becomes a reality. The groundwork is then laid to develop the other components. Nurses can work with management to develop working conditions that promote quality patient care and create a satisfactory work environment.

NURSE PRACTITIONERS IN THE TRANSITION MODEL

The skills of midlevel practitioners, especially nurse practitioners (NPs), are increasingly being requested in many transition models. Part of their rise in importance is due to their ability to function very similarly to family-practice physicians. Midlevel practitioners, which include physician assistants, nurse practitioners, certified nurse midwives, and certified registered nurse anesthetists, are currently being presented with more opportunities to practice because of vacancies created by a shortage of family-practice physicians in rural areas. The shortage of these physicians will likely increase, because the number of physicians choosing family-practice residencies is declining, compared to those choosing specialty fields (Mulhausen & McGee 1989).

This section will focus only on the role of nurse practitioners in the rural setting. Much of the material on recruitment and retention of nurse practitioners is the same as that for registered nurses because of their similar backgrounds. In the coming years, NPs may be easier to recruit to primary-care facilities than physicians because NPs are primarily trained to function in outpatient settings, whereas physicians train in hospitals and often prefer to work in secondary-care settings.

Research has demonstrated that patients often prefer nurse practitioners over traditional health-care providers for many health concerns. Some of the reasons for this preference, mentioned by Stilwell (1987) and Touger & Butts (1989), are that nurse practitioners have better listening skills, spend more time with patients, delve more into psychosocial issues, and are better patient educators. In one hospital conversion site, the clinic staff consists of only nurse practitioners and no physicians, at the community's request. The nurse practitioner functions independently, consulting with a physician at least once every two weeks, as mandated by state law (Bauer & Weis 1989).

NPs are capable of performing a wide range of patient activities:

1. obtaining medical histories and performing medical examinations;
2. diagnosing and treating common health problems such as infections and minor injuries;
3. diagnosing, treating, and monitoring chronic diseases such as diabetes and hypertension;

4. ordering and interpreting diagnostic (for example, laboratory and radiology) tests;

5. prescribing medications;

6. providing prenatal and family-planning services;

7. providing preventive health care through annual physicals, patient education, and counseling; and,

8. consulting and collaborating with physicians as needed.

NPs can be trained to specialize in treating certain patient populations, but, as with RNs, rural NPs usually function as generalists and are familiar with the illnesses and concerns of many different patient groups. A U.S. Congress, Office of Technology Assessment (1986b), document reports that the pressure of NPs has expanded access to care for schoolchildren, the elderly, and low-income women and adolescents in underserved areas.

NPs are licensed, registered nurses who have completed advanced courses of study in particular areas, and have met the certification requirements of the state nursing and state medical boards. NPs depend on state statute to define their level of independence and right to practice. This includes the right to diagnose and the details concerning physician supervision. Some states do not recognize NPs, while others allow them to practice autonomously, with the stipulation that they consult a physician on a predetermined basis. In fact, in some states, NPs can perform as independent contractors, setting up their own practices and using physicians as consultants. The NPs' scope of practice is frequently determined by their capabilities and by the practice agreements between the NP and physician.

There are several limitations to meeting the increasing demand for nurse practitioners in rural areas. One is deficiency in supply, coupled with higher earnings in urban settings (Ahmed & Muus 1991). Another is regulatory restriction in regard to scope of practice and reimbursement. Deficiency in the supply of midlevel practitioners has been cited as one of the reasons rural health clinics have not achieved their full potential and are continuing to struggle to increase access to primary care in medically underserved areas (U.S. Congress, House, 1989). The supply of these providers must be adequate to keep up with current and future demand, as more innovative practice forms evolve in rural areas. One way to help ensure a steady supply of NPs is by promoting the merits of this type of practice, and encouraging student nurses to continue education through nurse practitioner programs.

In addition, the practice environment for nurse practitioners must become more supportive. Nursing lobbies and concerned citizens can petition their state legislators for educational subsidies and additional programs to prepare these practitioners. A well-defined scope of practice and mandated third-party reimbursement for midlevel practitioners are imperative for effective utilization of their services. Patients are more likely to seek out these practitioners if they know that their insurance carriers will cover the costs.

In regard to transition periods, NPs perform many of the same primary-care services before, during, and after transition to primary-care centers. Their clinical roles do not change significantly. However, they can become involved in their facilities' strategic planning efforts by providing a clinical perspective on operational matters.

NPs are valuable primary-care providers in rural areas. They offer a type of health care that differs from the traditional medical model. When NPs are added to a predominantly all-physician staff, patients have a choice in the type of provider they prefer to use. Value is also added to the span of rural care through the NPs' willingness to serve low-income patients; the U.S. Congress, Office of Technology Assessment report (1986b), found over half the rural clients seen by NPs had annual incomes less than $10,000.

CONCLUSION

Rural nurses can be recruited and retained, as long as efforts are made to meet their needs for satisfactory employment. When a hospital consolidates with another facility or converts to a primary-care clinic, support by the nursing staff is central to making a successful transition. Some ways to garner nurses' support are (a) to maintain constant and open communication between nurses and administration, (b) to enlist their input in the development of strategic plans, (c) to encourage them to expand their skills in areas of interest, (d) to foster community support for change, (e) to work within the educational system to prepare future workers for new health-care delivery systems, (f) to encourage and facilitate educational endeavors, and (g) to nurture the educational and practice environment for midlevel practitioners.

Recruitment and retention of nurses will be further aided by the following actions: helping spouses find work, creating a work environment that emphasizes learning, utilizing career ladders, providing competitive salaries, retaining allied health professionals, and providing positive reinforcement. Nurse practitioners are increasingly important providers in transitional rural health-care facilities. Their knowledge, skill, and style of primary-care practice are essential components to innovative rural health-care facilities.

The nursing profession is undergoing its own transition in determining its direction for the future. The extent to which its contribution to rural health care remains significant depends on its ability to shape the rural health-care environment so that it mutually benefits nurses, other providers, and the rural population.

PART IV

Technology to Optimize
Provision of Rural Services

8. Changing the Paradigm of Rural Health-Care Delivery

Donald L. Cordes and LaVonne A. Straub

The system for delivery of health care in rural America is in transformation. In the 1980s, scores of rural hospitals closed, denying residents in these areas of services they had come to expect. Rural health care and its associated problems are a microcosm of what is happening to many aspects of life in rural America. Essentially, much of rural America is losing its economic and demographic base, and data suggest this trend will continue (Wiener 1990). Dwindling resources have made it increasingly difficult for rural communities to offer comprehensive health-care services. Consequently, those who can afford to do so are seeking care at more sophisticated medical facilities, or at facilities perceived as being more sophisticated. Other residents may postpone care, leading to more severe medical complications in the future.

This chapter opens with a review of the health-care system in rural areas. Current solutions to stemming the erosion of this system are reviewed; these tend toward modification of the existing structure. However, problems with the system cannot be rectified with currently proposed solutions. This chapter suggests that the rural health-care delivery situation be examined from a completely new perspective. This new perspective, seen as a paradigm shift, accepts the shrinking economic base and the demographic trends, and incorporates a range of available technologies which can and must be applied to problems affecting rural health care. Examples are provided to show where pieces of this alternative system are functioning effectively. The chapter suggests that, in accepting a new view of rural health, timing is critical.

LIMITATIONS OF THE EXISTING SYSTEM

Defining rural health care as a crisis is relatively recent. In the not-too-distant past, the differences in health-care availability in rural versus urban facilities were minimal. Today, however, the level and types of care available differ significantly, and the differences are growing. Why has this dramatic change occurred?

The key underlying differences between rural and urban health care are based primarily on medical technology and specialization. Sophisticated modern day health care is inextricably linked to and highly dependent on technology-based medicine. This fact has contributed to the current state of crisis in rural health care (Parker et al. 1989). Because rural America is losing its economic base, its health-care facilities are unable to procure increasingly expensive medical technology. Without the technology, potential patients from the community go to other, better equipped facilities, further reducing revenue flows to the local facility (Lape & Harris 1989). Eventually, a perception about lower quality of care overall reduces the demand for even routine care available locally.

In addition, it becomes increasingly difficult to recruit and retain qualified health-care professionals who, understandably, want to deliver state-of-the-art health care. Physicians and other health-care personnel receive training in settings with ample technology; consequently, their capability to practice depends on having these complementary inputs. They may also feel at risk for malpractice in less technologically advanced settings. Related to this increased emphasis on ever more sophisticated technology is the subspecialization of medical care. It is simply not possible for a subspecialist to practice high quality medicine in a setting with an insufficient patient load to support that specialty.

All of these factors combine to stress further an already uncertain rural health-care system. Resolution is complicated by a natural desire for each community to have a share of the system and by the dual role of rural health. Maintaining health-care providers in the local community relieves worry about access to care, and it generates employment and revenues. The ability of local providers to attract and retain dollars for the local economy is not trivial.

The present model of health-care delivery in the private sector is basically a competitive, market model, with some important features missing. This model has served us well in many respects and not so well in others. It has continuously expanded the capability of medical and surgical services, but it has also produced a system that is becoming prohibitively expensive.

A free market model can work only if it is driven by unfettered supply and demand. This assumes a range of products that match individual preferences and ability to pay. Unfortunately, health care, especially rural health care, is affected by a variety of other factors. These factors, such as government regulations and court-determined definitions of health care, impede the appropriate functioning of the model. Because urban residents overall are wealthier than their rural counterparts, rural areas fare less well in the current pseudocompetitive model.

The following analogy illustrates the point. Imagine for example, inviting a food distribution conglomerate to provide food to an agriculturally poor developing country, but allowing only luxury food items, such as caviar, smoked salmon, and pâte de foie gras. It is likely that very little food would be sold, and this would undoubtedly lead to malnutrition and related hardships. In a free market economy, the food company would probably assess the socioeconomic level of the population and market a range of appropriately priced foods. It would certainly not use an international standard of luxury for food and suggest that those unable to afford this get nothing. However, in American health care, decisions by the courts and regulatory bodies have helped to create a standard of care which is unattainable in much of rural America.

One example of this situation exists in availability of obstetric-care services in Illinois. Overall, the state has a favorable obstetric physician-to-population ratio, yet the distribution is distorted. In 1989, 46 rural counties (of 102 counties in the state) did not have a practicing obstetrician. Although many counties have family practitioners, fewer than half provide obstetric care (Cronson 1991). The absence of an adequate number of obstetricians in rural areas has not generated sufficient alternatives, due, in part, to regulatory restrictions. Certified nurse-midwives must collaborate with a licensed physician, and only a few are in rural practice. Thus, residents, because of the difficulty of obtaining prenatal and obstetric care, either receive less care or travel significant distances in seeking it.

This example is only one indication that the health-care system has created false expectations about availability of health care. High technology, specialized medicine has been promoted as the standard; simultaneously, true costs have been suppressed through a system of third-party payments and cost shifting. The result is an expectation that equates quality with technology and discounts the real cost of medical technology.

The competitive model creates additional problems. If health-care consumers are lured from less sophisticated to more sophisticated health-care facilities, eventually all who could afford it would be going to the most sophisticated center. This is the classic Mayo Clinic Syndrome. The result is that health-care consumers in rural communities often do not use their local facilities, even for their basic health-care needs. If enough people follow this example, it eventually causes the rural health-care facility to close. Competitive advertising, on the rise in health care, is aimed at consumer confidence. Even if advertising is completely positive, it implies lack of competence in those competitors who do not possess the particular diagnostic or treatment facilities advertised.

Furthermore, even if a free market health-care system could operate in rural America, a plausible case can be made for not using it. This is because competition does not always produce the best results for either consumers or providers of goods or services. Health care should not be viewed in the same manner as other consumer goods or services. When people do not get the health care they need when they need it, their health problems often worsen. Individuals suffer the medical consequences, and society often incurs additional costs in the form of more costly health care later.

CURRENT APPROACHES

Current solutions proposed for the rural health-care crisis tend to fall into two general conceptual areas. One approach suggests that provision of rural health care be made economically viable by limiting the level of care and the range of services provided to rural consumers (Moscovice 1989a). This has the advantage of maintaining a certain level of health care for rural dwellers and providing jobs in the local community. Advocates of this approach generally suggest that only primary care and basic emergency services be provided in rural localities. A major disadvantage is that rural dwellers must travel long distances, without the aid of public transportation, to access specialized medical care. This represents a major barrier to the elderly and other less mobile residents. Also, those with resources would probably bypass local facilities altogether and go to more sophisticated medical facilities for all of their care, thus decreasing the economic viability of the local health-care facility.

The other major conceptual approach is to add external resources to make local or regional health-care facilities economically viable and more able to render a wide range of service (U.S. Congress, Office of Technology Assessment, 1990). This requires increasing Medicare and Medicaid payments, or some other form of subsidized resource distribution to rural facilities. A major problem with this approach is the difficulty of finding available funds in these days of detrimental budgeting. Neither the state nor the federal government is willing to devote the money needed to sustain this approach.

These approaches to the rural health-care crisis are based on out-of-date expectations. They both fail to address certain fundamental issues unique to the rural health-care situation. In order to insure access to quality health care for rural America, it will be necessary to rethink the system as a whole. This rethinking will require a paradigm shift.

THE ALTERNATIVE SOLUTION: PARADIGM SHIFT

A paradigm is a set of rules or beliefs that defines the boundaries of a system. A paradigm shift represents a change in the boundaries, resulting from rule or belief changes (Kuhn 1970). An example of a paradigm shift is the change in American buying patterns of Japanese goods. Forty years ago Japanese products were perceived as cheap replicas or junk, ignored by most buyers in spite of their low cost. Now, they are perceived as worth their higher cost, because they are good quality and use the latest technology. Such shifts are currently occurring in health care as well. For example, confining the mother to the hospital for one week following a normal delivery was formerly acceptable practice, now new mothers often go home the same day. The beliefs changed, the rules changed, and the paradigm shifted. It is now possible to conceive of managing a normal delivery in a different way. This would not be possible if the paradigm had not shifted.

The rules and beliefs that govern rural health care today are rooted in past attempts to provide health-care access under different conditions. Part of the difficulty in updating these beliefs lies in the fact that current approaches were valid in the quite recent past. However, a paradigm shift to a new conceptual model is required because current approaches simply are not working. Many of the new models being tried today appear to be based on the old paradigm and therefore continue to be fraught with implementation problems.

The time is appropriate for a paradigm shift to occur because advances in a range of technologies have made care options and resources available which, until very recently, were not feasible. Taken as a whole, this new technology is a tool that allows a transformation in the entire process of delivering health care in rural areas. Delivery methods not possible a few years ago are now not only possible but also affordable. This shift must be initiated soon, before the necessary rural health-care infrastructure erodes further. A solid base in rural primary care must be retained to implement the change fully; further erosion will make its recapture nearly impossible. Thus, the time is not only appropriate but critical.

This new technology is the key component that makes possible the integration of rural and urban health-care systems, thus allowing for a networked approach to the delivery of health care in rural America. However, this does not mean that the paradigm shift simply constitutes the deployment of a vast array of sophisticated new technologies. Rather, the effective use of technology changes the current paradigm by applying a completely different set of parameters to the rural health-care problems.

THE SUGGESTED APPROACH

The paradigm shift being suggested is that a collaborative, rather than a competitive, model be used to deliver health care to rural Americans. The collaborative model considers radically different approaches since the various providers of health-care services do not compete for the same dwindling fiscal resources. This model would encourage and foster inter-dependence as opposed to independence.

This also makes it possible to view rural health-care delivery in system terms. A system in which health-care facilities render the level of care that they are best suited to deliver while passing off the more or less advanced care to the appropriate facility. It means further that new goals for the rural health-care delivery system can be honestly debated and then established. This model calls for efficiency, with as much medical care as possible rendered in a location nearest the patient's family, friends, or other support people. Effective utilization of each level of provider contributes to the model's efficiency.

This type of model is possible now because of advances in communication and medical technologies which are both available and affordable. Current technology makes possible:

1. highly integrated networks to be assembled and managed;
2. high quality clinical decision making to occur so patients can quickly get the level of care appropriate to their needs;
3. health-care practitioners in a rural setting to be fully integrated into the decision making concerning any and all of their patients as they proceed through the network; and
4. all practitioners on the network to have continuing education, consultation, and professional development opportunities available on a regular basis to ward off professional isolation in the more remote facilities.

Collaborative models work only if those involved understand the workings and implications, have an opportunity to participate in development of the plan, and share in the model's benefits.

TECHNOLOGY-LINKED COLLABORATIVE NETWORK

How might a collaborative model for rural health care work? The underlying concept is that a network of rural, regional, and tertiary health-care facilities be assembled to meet the health-care needs of rural Americans. Health care is rendered to patients at the facility appropriate to their needs whenever possible. A patient from a rural area would be seen at the local facility. If the patient's needs can be met at that facility, they would be. If not, the patient would be sent to either a regional center or the tertiary center, whichever is best suited to manage his or her care. Decisions to treat or move patients are based on mutually agreeable protocols and procedures. The network would be fully integrated and linked by current technology. The use of technology would enable rural practitioners to access much of the power available to urban practitioners. Although this form may appear to resemble currently proposed demonstration models involving networking the delivery of services, as well as the AHEC (Area Health Education Center) concept, the application of technology is the key component that differentiates this approach. Technology is not simply added on at random but integrated into the entire framework of the model.

What are the barriers to the adoption of this model? Although this model may appear to be a rather simple, straightforward approach, its implications are far-reaching. If those who have a stake in rural health do not understand either the parameters that must be changed or why it is beneficial to adopt a new mind-set, it will not be possible to implement this course. Golladay & Liese (1980) suggest that since rural health-care workers have less experience with the development of new technology, much care and sensitivity must be taken toward the specific needs of the rural health organization and the individual health professionals themselves. They suggest that both formal and informal group work is necessary to assure a genuine buy-in to the use of new technology and new systems. Finally, the fear that many have about technology in general and the ever-present resistance to change must be overcome.

For the paradigm shift from a competitive to collaborative model for rural health care to be successful, patient care must not be viewed in a zero-sum context. Rather, collaboration must, on the whole, be more beneficial than the existing situation. It must also provide a minimal level of mutual benefits. In other words, it cannot be one-sided with all of the benefits going to some components of the network at the expense of some of the others.

A scenario can be described in which all components of the current rural health-care situation receive benefits in a collaborative network. Consumers of health care benefit by having high quality health-care services available in their local area. They travel to a regional or tertiary center only when local capabilities are insufficient to meet their needs. The community benefits by retaining more jobs and resources locally. Regional and urban medical facilities benefit in that they are made more efficient by expanded use of technology. Specialists in these facilities have the opportunity to provide diagnostic and therapeutic services to patients at rural centers that they would otherwise never have the option of seeing, all without any travel costs or time expended (Staab et al. 1985).

The network promotes an instantaneous sharing of records, including recently completed medical/laboratory tests, thereby saving time and eliminating costly duplication when a referral is necessary. It further allows for more consultations to be provided in a given time period, resulting in additional consulting fees. Secondly, it also allows the rural center to screen out those patients who do not need the expertise of a specialist or subspecialist. If a referral is necessary, it ensures that the regional or tertiary center sees the patient in time to achieve the best possible health outcome for the patient.

Health-care providers at all levels benefit by being able to perform at the optimal level. At the rural center, providers have greatly increased diagnostic and treatment capability because of the network's technology and expertise. This allows them to do more and with greater confidence. They also have greatly increased regular interaction with other health-care professionals as well as frequent opportunities for continuing education. In the regional center the providers of care see many more challenging cases that heretofore went to the urban centers. Providers in tertiary centers see only the most difficult and scientifically interesting cases, with ample time to manage them as well as leaving more time for dedicated research and development. The most efficient use of resources at each level is a potential outcome of this model.

The whole of rural health care also benefits from the use of a collaborative model. The collaborative network is in a position to meet many more health-care needs in a timely fashion. It should prevent a rural health-care consumer from postponing medical care—because of transportation problems or the inability to be away from home—until the disease has progressed beyond successful treatment.

Is current technology really able to support a full-blown, integrated network today, or is this just another exotic Tomorrowland that never seems to arrive? The vast majority of the technology needed to operate a fully integrated health-care system is already in use in other networks or in certain existing remote health-care applications. It is important to note, however, that certain communications infrastructure, such as fiber optic lines, do not yet exist in rural America. The following section presents current examples of how pieces of this approach have been implemented.

EXAMPLES OF IMPLEMENTATION

The state of Oregon has established a Biomedical Information Communication Center (BICC) headquartered at its Health Sciences University in Portland. Through the BICC network, any Oregon health-care professional can access the information resources of Oregon Health Information Online in a simple, straightforward manner. This system makes possible entry to virtually all health data bases existing today. As the BICC expands services in the future, health professionals will use BICC work stations to access such information as patient records and lab test data. As this system becomes fully integrated, it can be a collaborative health-care network (Eye on Orhion 1991).

AT&T, in conjunction with Bowman Gray School of Medicine and North Carolina Baptist Hospital, has developed a sophisticated system that will do image compression and voice recognition. This enables the radiology department to share information with relevant individuals either inside or outside the medical center (Quittel 1988). This is only one example of a practical information-sharing model.

In rural Texas, the Kellogg-Affiliated Remote Environments Network (KARENET) was initiated in 1985 to provide critical support to physicians and other health-care professionals via an on-line computer network accessed by telephone and modem. The network provides such programs as consultation regarding treatment protocols, recording and monitoring patient-care information, health-care research, and continuing education. Hardware used by the network includes two-way interactive video, personal computers with special modems to transmit X-ray images, audio teleconferencing and telefacsimile capability. Although this was not designed as a fully integrated network, it does contain much of the technology needed to support a fully integrated network (U.S. Congress, Office of Technology Assessment, 1991).

There are good examples of less extensive rural-urban networks that are working well. Many states with large rural areas, such as Nebraska, Ohio, Wisconsin, and South Dakota, to name a few, operate comprehensive teleconferencing networks in conjunction with their medical schools. These link large numbers of rural hospitals and clinics for training and information-sharing purposes. These networks facilitate regular interaction between practitioners at rural hospitals and medical school faculty, often resulting in the referral of difficult medical cases.

There are situations where rural health-care facilities link up via technology to urban centers for the benefit of rural patients. One such example is the Medical Information System via Telephone (MIST) operated by the University of Alabama at Birmingham Medical Center. This system allows rural health-care practitioners to access, via a toll free call, the latest research, clinical findings, and protocols. It enables individual practitioners from rural areas to discuss specific cases and develop working relationships with faculty members. It allows the rural practitioner, with the assistance of the faculty, to provide quality patient care on a consistent basis. If the patient needs to be admitted to the medical center, the rural practitioner remains an integral part of the health-care team.

Current health-care applications literally send data and information halfway around the world. The technology not only exists but is mature in the sense that it is beyond the testing phase and has reached a high degree of reliability. Additional applications relevant to remote diagnosis and treatment are being developed and marketed every day. The combination of high definition television and expanded bandwidths based on fiber optic circuitry makes extensive future development even more likely (Szafrom & Kropf 1988).

COST OF TECHNOLOGY

It is already much less expensive (in dollar, time, and personal costs) to transmit data and information than to move people. Added to this are energy savings through reduced travel and minimized fuel consumption (Parker et al. 1989). The good news is that costs for operating these networks are decreasing while the costs of almost everything else, including travel, are rising—and this pattern will likely continue. Additionally, new transmission capability through fiber optic circuitry is coming to rural America. When in place, it will greatly expand technological capability and further reduce costs. The technology is available, and the overall price is right.

However, the rural health-care delivery system does not operate in a vacuum, so any analysis of costs and benefits must be comprehensive. For instance, consideration of net return in the context of reconfiguring rural health care to take full advantage of technology must include the indirect and social benefits from doing so. The gains to rural communities, such as through expansion of fiber optic circuitry and electronic transmission capability, go far beyond improving health-care delivery.

The potential for economic development and quality of life represent sizable externalities-spillover benefits to others besides the direct users. For example, studies show that the indirect gains for rural business and social services from telecommunications are greater than their costs, with ratios ranging from 5–1 up to 100–1 (Parker et al. 1989). Private decisions about investment (in technology or other productive aspects) do not take these social benefits into account when comparing costs and benefits, but rural public policies should do so. These authors conclude that given the importance of telecommunications networks to economic development and quality of life, they should be considered part of a community's basic infrastructure—indicating the need for public decisions regarding these investments.

This philosophy can be expanded to include the range of technology implementation discussed in this chapter; the existence of large social gains justifies government intervention and policies to help rural communities offset the related costs. Policies to assist these communities will not only improve the delivery of health care to local residents, but will empower the communities in their overall economic and social service development. In the absence of government policies to assist rural areas in implementing technology, the gaps between the haves and have nots will expand. This gap does not simply refer to urban and rural, but the gap among rural communities; those that can implement technology and improve their infrastructure will have a significant advantage over those communities that cannot.

CONCLUSION

The changes suggested in this chapter will not be easy. There are significant mitigating factors on both sides of this issue. The factors against making this paradigm shift are the following:

1. Social/professional inertia; neither society nor professional groups have a history of readily embracing fundamental change.
2. A completely new modus operandi must be established and working relationships developed within the rural health-care delivery mechanism.
3. Capitalization costs will be necessary, and they must come from an already stressed system.

The factors in favor of making this shift:

1. The present system is not able to meet current health-care needs in rural America.
2. Minor modifications of the present system have no hope of improving the situation and probably cannot stop further erosion of services.
3. The technology of the information age creates possibilities for efficiency and effectiveness which were impossible only a short time ago.
4. Lay public support for a major change in the area of health care is presently on a rising tide.

What will it take to rethink rural health care and make the paradigm shift? Initially, and this may be the most difficult, there must be an honest acknowledgment on the part of all involved that the present health-care system is not working for many Americans, and that it especially disadvantages rural America. For consumers, the lack of satisfaction is verified. A recent study completed by researchers at the Harvard School of Public Health indicated that American health-care consumers were the least satisfied with their health-care system of 10 industrial nations studied (Blendon et al. 1990). This finding is even more significant when the per capita spending on health care is considered, for the United States outspends the rest of the world. Public opinion research indicates, in 1990, 44 percent of Americans felt fundamental changes are needed to make the health-care system work better, and 25 percent said it needs to be completely rebuilt. Furthermore, public support favors reform that does not involve government operation of health insurance (Blendon et al. 1990). For others, this acknowledgment may be more difficult, because those who must reach this conclusion are the people who may either have a hard-earned investment in the present system or have been responsible in the past for trying to make existing systems work.

Secondly, it will require solid leadership from all sectors at all levels. From the governor and legislators on down, states with significant rural populations will have to truly understand the problem and be willing to support collaborative activities. This includes the professional societies, public and private health-care facilities, state health departments, relevant colleges, universities, and professional schools, consumer groups, and especially health-care professionals at the affected hospitals and clinics. They must demonstrate a willingness to negotiate in a climate of genuine give-and-take. Another role for the leadership, and perhaps it is most significant, is to convince rural health-care consumers that interdependent health networks can provide quality care at all levels.

Can we afford to make this paradigm shift from a competitive to a collaborative rural health-care model? Perhaps the better question is, can we afford not to make it? The present system is not getting the job done, and there are ever decreasing fiscal resources with which to work. At the same time, technology offers us dramatic new opportunities. Although technology allows the large-scale integrated networking necessary to change the present system, human beings must decide whether to embark on this fundamental change. Is there really much of a choice?

9. Medical Informatics—Technology for Rural Health Care

Richard L. Thorp and Donald L. Cordes

Health-care providers working in a rural environment face many obstacles. An important consideration is the isolation faced by these workers, which may erode valuable practice skills and professional competency. Alleviation of many negative aspects of isolation is now possible through continually expanding communication and information technologies. These technologies, known collectively as medical informatics, have the potential to change the entire concept of rural practice.

This chapter focuses on the capacity to access information as a critical factor in retaining quality rural health care. It is proposed that timely access to quality information can improve cost efficiency, quality of services, and equity in the distribution of health-care services. The introductory section presents brief examples of applications of existing medical informatics. The chapter then discusses the range of technologies currently available for consideration in rural practice sites. The list is not exhaustive because innovation is still going on in this field, and new applications are coming on-line with great speed. Application of these technologies can directly benefit both providers and recipients of care. In addition, management and administrative personnel, as well as members of governing boards can benefit from more efficient use of time, money, and resources. The chapter closes with a brief discussion of policy considerations, exploring the larger social and economic gains to rural areas.

TECHNOLOGY AT WORK

The availability of advanced technology expands the capability of rural providers to diagnose and treat patients with assistance from specialists elsewhere. Following are brief examples of technologies currently in use.

1. An emergency medical technician uses a radio data link to transmit a patient's vital signs and EKG from an accident site to an emergency medical physician, who directs the initial delivery of care from a console in the emergency room miles away.

2. A nurse, unfamiliar with the many special-care requirements of a spinal cord injury (SCI) patient, uses an interactive expert system to receive point-of-care information concerning the prevention and treatment of pressure sores.

3. In the middle of the night, a radiologist receives high resolution images on a terminal at home. They are from a remote, small-town hospital. The radiologist is able to read the images and transmit a written report without leaving home.

4. A cardiologist in a major metropolitan area checks and adjusts a rural outpatient's pacemaker through a telephone data link.

5. A stroke patient in rural California receives biweekly speech therapy at a small clinic near her home. The therapist is located more than 200 miles away in San Francisco. Without this technological extension, the patient would not have access to the intensive therapy required to regain speech.

6. A rural physician uses a personal computer to access the latest information in the Physicians Desk Query—Prevention (PDQ–P), an interactive cancer prevention and treatment data base maintained by the National Cancer Institute in Rockville, Maryland.

7. An emergency medicine specialist refers to a display screen in the emergency room for expert guidance while treating a head injury. The specialist's verbal orders for X rays and lab work are automatically digitized and converted to text, which is displayed on emergency terminals in radiology and in the laboratory. Treatment protocols are compared with expert solutions prepared by a panel of multidisciplinary specialists.

MEDICAL INFORMATICS

Medical informatics is a generic term that encompasses various technological and informational systems used for training of personnel—and administration—as well as for the delivery of health care. It includes sophisticated technologies, such as computers, satellites, and data links, in addition to devices as simple as the telephone and telefacsimile (FAX) machine. Medical informatics is the application of modern technology to the practice and administration of medicine. This application can generally be classified into four areas: (1) training, (2) point-of-care expert systems, (3) storage and retrieval of data, and (4) remote operations. The technologies that make up medical informatics form a matrix with these applications, and there is a great deal of crossover.

The ability of rural providers to benefit from each of these technologies varies with the situation. Certain of the advanced systems require significant investments in equipment and training beyond the scope of some rural settings. Others require establishment of statewide or regional user groups and adoption of equipment standards. The creation of an integrated network, as described in the previous chapter, provides for optimal application of medical informatics. The following brief descriptions of the technologies comprising medical informatics are arranged in order, beginning with the least expensive and the least complex.

Telephone. The telephone represents an old technology with significant unused potential in rural health-care settings. It is not generally recognized as a tool for setting up systems to provide difficult-to-access information. Its current uses are limited to systems such as 9–1–1 access or poison-control centers developed by the telephone company or the community. An excellent example of an effective and innovative use of the telephone to provide access to key medical information is the Medical Information Service via Telephone (MIST), a program that has operated in Alabama since 1973 (Fisher 1984).

The MIST system utilizes a special telephone network to provide toll-free consultation with physicians and other health-care professionals. This system operates 24 hours a day, 7 days a week, and can be activated by a single telephone call. Callers have immediate access to the faculty and staff of the University of Alabama/Birmingham, a major medical complex in the Southeast.

Although the MIST approach may not be suitable for every state, those with significant rural populations might consider some version of it. If a statewide approach is not feasible, a regional system may be considered, whereby a rural community hospital arranges to receive crucial medical information in a timely fashion via telephone from a medical school or referral hospital in the nearest city.

Another creative use of the telephone is being applied in rural Utah. A consortium of rural hospitals, established with a grant from the Robert Wood Johnson foundation through Interwest Quality of Care Inc. (IQC), will use a telephone-based "quality management hotline" (Cordes 1991). This hotline will utilize recently retired physician and nurse volunteers trained by IQC staff to provide immediate response to clinical and administrative questions from personnel in consortium hospitals. The volunteers will work in a center equipped with the latest in medical decision support technology. An 800 telephone number will be available around the clock for rural practitioners to get immediate answers to pressing problems.

An obvious advantage of the telephone is that it uses existing technology. There is no requirement to expend resources for hardware or operating personnel and little training is necessary for those who use the system. Residents of rural and remote areas recognize the benefits of this technology, and rural telephones are basic to emergency assistance.

Telefacsimile. A telefacsimile (FAX) machine enables users to send or receive printed information to or from any other FAX machine over standard telephone lines. This equipment, already in use in most hospitals and physician offices, will continue to expand the capability to send and receive printed material quickly and at low cost.

Libraries, including medical libraries, use FAX machines on a regular basis. As with the telephone, the potential for rural health-care providers to receive information via FAX is limited only by creativity. A simple application is for the library at a local community hospital to work out an arrangement with a medical school library to perform targeted information searches, and then to FAX relevant articles back to the hospital. In the Utah hospital consortium mentioned above, each telephone inquirer receives the most relevant, critical information or articles immediately by FAX.

Audio Teleconferencing. Audio teleconferencing is group voice communication among three or more individuals or groups via telephone. Most audio teleconferencing uses standard telephone lines. Special teleconferencing equipment typically consists of conference telephones and a bridge, which connects all individuals and groups. This connection allows each remote site to hear and speak with other remote sites participating in a teleconference. The special conference telephone is a professional device with certain features that distinguish it from a standard speakerphone. High quality amplifiers, speakers, and press-to-talk microphones make group participation both pleasant and easy.

Besides voice-only, interactive audio teleconferences, there are graphic media add-ons, which produce a type of teleconference known as interactive audiographic teleconferences. Typical technologies used in audiographic teleconferencing include simple 35mm slides, facsimile, networked personal computers (PCs), and slow scan television.

The use of audio or audiographic teleconferencing by rural hospitals can include a variety of applications from training to networking, and information sharing. A number of health science centers, as well as professional and commercial organizations, regularly offer a variety of teletraining courses (Ostendorf 1991). Courses are available for most health-care professions, and many are approved for continuing education credits.

Audio teleconferencing can play an important role in alleviating a major personnel problem in recruitment and retention of providers in rural areas—their need for ongoing education and training. Because of the wide variety of training available via audio teleconferencing, even the most remote rural hospital can meet many of their health-care providers' training needs in a cost-effective and timely manner.

Another exciting potential use for audio teleconferencing is shared information and joint problem solving among hospitals of similar size and type. For example, in a recent Department of Veterans Affairs teleconference, information sharing among dietitians resulted in significant cost savings to several hospitals. Participants learned of suppliers who provide specific goods and food at significantly reduced prices. With hospital budgets becoming increasingly tight, this type of activity can improve operating efficiency. However, for a hospital to participate in an extensive sharing network, proactive work must be done, either by the hospital or some other entity, such as the state hospital association. These efforts include establishing the protocol for use, allocating costs, and defining the scope of the network.

The advantages to the implementation of audio teleconferencing include the fact that it is a mature technology. It has been used for more than 25 years in continuing medical education and for specific applications in business and industry. It is an easy and relatively inexpensive tool to implement (Chute & Elfrank 1990).

Satellite Video Conferencing. Satellite video teleconferencing (also known as video conferencing) advances beyond the audio mode by providing the opportunity to communicate via full motion television in either a one-way or interactive mode. Currently most video teleconferencing is one-way video with two-way audio, meaning a conference originates at one site and is seen at multiple sites. Remote site viewers participate either by a telephone bridge or by simply calling in questions or comments via an 800 telephone number. This technology uses a satellite to transmit the signal from the studio to the viewing sites.

Video teleconference networks use either a C band or a Ku frequency band to transmit their signal. Although both are regularly used, Ku band is becoming the more popular format and is generally considered to be the wave of the future (Chute & Elfrank 1990). In both cases, the studio uses an uplink to transmit a signal to a specific satellite, which in turn amplifies the signal and beams it back to earth, where it is received by downlinks at participating stations. Special scrambling equipment is sometimes used to ensure that only those who are legitimate participants can tune into the video teleconference.

For a hospital to take part in video teleconferencing, special equipment, knowledge, and skills to operate the equipment are needed. However, these are not unduly complicated, and with minor training should be easily handled by the management personnel responsible for biomedical communications, medical media, or audiovisual activities. A typical "television receive only" (TVRO) setup includes an antenna (satellite dish), a satellite positioner, a satellite receiver, a feed control, a TV modulator, a TV descrambler, a TV set, and normally a video recorder. There are cabling requirements to connect all the equipment, and there may be need for other switching equipment, if it will be connected to an existing hospital closed circuit television (CCTV) system.

Many organizations provide continuing education via satellite video teleconferencing for health-care professionals (Ostendorf 1991). The programs vary from one-time, one-hour programs on a specific topic, to an annual subscription service for a variety of training services. Nursing programs by way of video teleconferencing have already been established offering college credit toward a nursing degree (Ostendorf 1991). This programming gives rural areas an effective means of upgrading lesser skilled nursing personnel, while at the same time responding to demands of rural nurses for more training opportunities (Straub & Frels 1990). Contractual arrangements for video teleconference programming vary greatly, as does quality. Vendors often offer an opportunity to preview past programming to evaluate the extent to which it will meet needs.

To support the development of both credit and noncredit teleconferencing, the National University Teleconference Network (NUTN) has been created (Dunning 1989). This organization offers colleges and universities, interested in teleconferencing, all the training and support necessary to develop and offer high quality training.

Video teleconferencing research and development efforts are likely to yield major breakthroughs in the near future (Parker 1990). Initial results show that use of this technology has allowed companies to reduce costs and improve quality, simultaneously and significantly. Digital television and signal compression techniques will soon reduce the cost of equipment and allow program originators to offer programming at a greatly reduced cost. Fiber optic telephone lines are now commonplace throughout the country; these will permit two-way video and audio teleconferencing without need for expensive satellite equipment.

One of the most appealing aspects of teleconferencing, either audio, video, or a combination of both, is that the receiving location, relative to the faculty or the organization sponsoring the program, is practically irrelevant. Virtually any location in the United States that can support a hospital can receive and interact on a teleconference. In the past, finding the courses suited to a certain hospital or a particular need was a difficult and time-consuming task. This task has recently been made much easier with the publication of a directory of both credit and noncredit teleconferences (Ostendorf 1991).

The Computer. The computer is what makes advanced medical informatics systems possible. Fortunately, most medical informatics systems are based on microcomputers, common in the home and office, and do not require expensive mainframes.

Computer-assisted instruction (CAI) and computer-based training (CBT) refer to educational programs (courseware) that will run on standard computer systems without special auxiliary devices or interfaces. The courseware is distributed on diskettes, and the majority of available CAI runs on an office computer. Advances in CAI courses allow for the use of real color photographic images. For example, the Department of Veterans Affairs recently commissioned a visually enhanced CAI course on the Oral Manifestations of HIV/Aids (Internal VA Memo). The one-hour course, which includes VGA full-color images of HIV-related oral pathology, is professionally narrated. The images were prepared by converting color slides to digital files. An electronic exam for evaluating continuing education credits is included.

Most professional organizations, many medical schools, and countless commercial vendors have CAI programs that can help rural health-care providers remain current (Locatis 1990). CAI provides an inexpensive way for staff members to receive ongoing training. Furthermore, this method of delivery allows the training to be integrated into their work schedule.

Modem Access. With the addition of an inexpensive modem, the PC becomes a gateway to vast stores of information and resources to assist in practicing medicine. The modem permits computers to communicate with each other over standard telephone lines, opening up a variety of opportunities for information exchange. For example, users can complete literature searches on-line and print out a synopsis of relevant articles. Modems are currently being used to access and share treatment information via the national Tumor Registry data base. Similarly, vast amounts of treatment data can be obtained from the Physicians Desk Query data base. The use of modems also allows professionals to participate in a Special Interest Group (SIG) bulletin board, which permits them to communicate with professionals with similar interests and to share the latest information in the field.

Subscription to a general purpose data service is another initial step. Compuserve is one example of such a service. It includes electronic mail, access to news services and reference libraries, and participation in over 20 medical practice related SIGs. For example, the Rehabilitation Medicine Database available on Compuserve allows users to search for rehabilitation devices or to search and review abstracts of articles from the *International Journal of Research and Rehabilitation Medicine*, or to correspond electronically with leaders in the field.

A PC equipped with a modem can help to eliminate the sense of professional isolation that plagues rural health-care providers. Access to a world of information is inexpensive in terms of both time and dollars. Furthermore, the mere fact that rural practitioners are taking advantage of this technology can help alleviate potential patient concerns about the quality of care in remote settings.

Automated Reference Systems. Medical-health-related publishing, worldwide, has expanded to the point where the National Library of Medicine (NLM) subscribes to 21,557 publications annually (U.S. National Library of Medicine 1990). Given the rigorous set of criteria a publication must meet to be included in the NLM, it is fair to assume that this number represents only a fraction of the medical journals currently published. This crushing load of information poses especially difficult problems for rural health-care practitioners. However, processes are being developed to make medical and health related information more accessible and useful to health-care practitioners.

Information synthesis is a process that has been developed to assist in matching demands to the supply of information. Information synthesis is the process of reviewing relevant literature, within a specified area, and synthesizing the results into a less voluminous and more accessible format. This is normally done by experts in a particular field or specialty. Good print versions of this process have existed for several years through *Scientific American Medicine*, and the *Lange Medical Series*, two of the best-known publications in the medical area.

With the arrival of new data storage capability in the rapidly expanding microcomputer arena, information synthesis is now available on computer compact disks. Through technology, known as CD-ROM, a huge data base of information can be formatted for a special computer disk. Almost all rural hospitals and clinics have microcomputers capable of supporting a CD-ROM player. The use of CD-ROM technology enables physicians and other health-care providers to search for and locate quickly the latest information available within the various medical specialties and health-care disciplines. The information stored on the compact disk can be accessed and retrieved in a variety of ways. For example, from the data base, users can scan the tables of contents of all books and journals on a topic, review any book or article on a topic, or search books and articles for a key word or phrase.

In minutes it is possible to cover a literature data base that, in the past, would have taken hours or days. An added benefit is that updated disks are sent regularly to subscribers to ensure that the latest information is available to the practitioner. Current sources of information synthesis, or reference libraries available on CD-ROM, include Stat-Ref, Med-line, and the Physicians Desk Query (PDQ).

Expert Systems. Expert systems (also referred to as performance support systems) are detailed knowledge bases available at the point-of-service delivery. For example, an expert system in emergency medical care assists physicians in the emergency room, or provides guidance to an emergency medical technician at a field emergency scene. A true expert system captures the thought process of an expert or a team of experts in a field. The system provides for easy user input. Devices such as touch-screens, voice recognition, or infrared wireless remote controls are used to accept input while the user is otherwise occupied.

A well-designed expert system represents an extremely valuable resource to rural practitioners. It is like having an expert at the side of a practitioner to assist with diagnosis or patient management. The end-user practitioner remains in full control, and decisions based on personal knowledge are augmented with on-the-scene observations. The information contained in the expert system provides a powerful on-the-spot resource to support performance.

Technically, expert systems are training mechanisms. However, instead of training that occurs at a specific place for a predetermined length of time, an expert system is available to deliver the right information when it is needed. In other words, it provides key information at the "teachable moment." The advantages to providers in more remote locations are obvious. Typically, new learning comes from attending a course or seminar, then returning to practice. Initially the information gained is fresh, but it erodes with lack of use, and weeks or months later, when a situation is encountered that requires the knowledge, it may be dated or difficult to recall.

Many expert systems are multimedia—that is, a computer-controlled presentation system that combines one or more audiovisual presentation techniques with computer data, text, and information. Tremendous amounts of data, both visual and audio, can be stored in an expert system. A logical computer system controls access and permits end-users to access the exact information required directly.

Videodisc. Videodisc is a popular expert system format. A recently developed expert system contains compressed versions of 30-minute videotapes on various topics related to the care of spinal cord injury. Information is stored in graphic and text form on a hard disk, text is combined with or overlaid on visual information and is narrated by audio retrieved from the laser disk. The presentation is displayed on a special multiscan monitor capable of displaying both analog video segments from the laser disk, and digital graphics and text from the computer disk. Encoded audio from the laser disk adds tremendous capacity to the system, permitting hours of verbal explanations. This system is being developed and refined under an NIH grant and is called Nursing Pressure Sore Prevention Expert System. It is currently being field-tested at Beaton Hospital in Baltimore.

Other multimedia systems used in expert system development include CD-ROM (Compact Disk Read Only Memory), CDI (Compact Disk Interactive), and the latest, and perhaps most exciting of all, DVI (Digital Video Interactive). The CD-ROM is a 5-inch optical disk that holds 600 megabytes of information, roughly the equivalent of 500 floppy disks. Current work on a CD-ROM project for the Pan-American Health Organization demonstrates the capacity. Upon completion, a single CD-ROM will contain over 1,500 high resolution color images of pathology related to HIV/AIDS along with detailed case studies and reference text.

CDI is designed primarily for the home entertainment market. Although it has the ability to be used for training and expert systems, both programming complexities and high initial development costs are slowing its acceptance and widespread use.

DVI will likely become the standard for training and expert systems for the future. DVI offers all of the advantages of laser disk without the high initial development costs. DVI enables courseware developers to include full screen motion video, high resolution still pictures, graphics, computer data, and FM quality audio in expert systems.

DATA STORAGE AND RETRIEVAL SYSTEMS

In the next ten years, there will be a revolution in methods used for the generation, storage, retrieval, and transmission of patient records. X rays, Magnetic Resonance Imaging (MRI), and other advanced diagnostic images will be stored in a high resolution digital format. High density non-volatile solid state memory will permit virtually unlimited storage of images and patient records, and will allow for access at the speed of light. At a keystroke, practitioners will be able to switch between images. They will be able to conduct visual matching queries of enormous shared national data bases to find matching images automatically to aid in diagnosis and treatment.

An ever-growing pool of case management information, including treatment protocols and predicted outcomes, will be available to physicians in rural as well as urban areas. Fiber-optic networks, both internal at medical centers, and nationwide through telephone service, will make instant transmission of images possible. Small town practitioners will be in touch with specialists at major medical centers by use of 2-way video transmissions. Long distance consultations will be as commonplace as case discussions with colleagues at local medical centers. Today, it takes approximately 6 minutes to transmit a high resolution X-ray image via telephone modem; when the expert advice required is several hours in travel time, this is the much preferred alternative.

REMOTE OPERATIONS

Like the emergency medical specialist who controls treatment of a patient at a remote accident site by means of a two-way data link, technology offers numerous ways to provide expert care where it would not have been possible in the past. Data collected by allied health-care personnel or in some cases by the patients themselves can be transmitted via inexpensive data links. Effective utilization of paraprofessionals and delivery of primary care in rural locations are more feasible with existing technology. For example, village health aides are critical to care in remote areas of Alaska where satellite circuits and earth stations at remote villages allow aides to be in constant contact with regional hospitals (Parker et al. 1989). The aides diagnose and treat patients, assisted by doctors at the distant hospital. This capability could relieve pressure in many other remote rural areas of the country.

Remote operations also provide an affordable and convenient method for carrying out regular checkups. For example, pacemakers can be checked and adjusted remotely. Patients can be monitored in their homes. Blood sugar levels, heart rate, blood pressure, and other critical information can be routinely checked without requiring the patient to travel to a medical facility.

SEEDING THE FUTURE

There are numerous efforts, currently underway, to use technology to improve the delivery of health care and information. As a means of harnessing this creative explosion of hardware and software, a part of NLM (National Library of Medicine) known as the Lister Hill National Center for Biomedical Communications has created an Educational Technology Branch with a Learning Center for Interactive Technology (Locatis 1990). This center collects and displays exemplary products that use interactive technology for health professions education. It also provides a learning laboratory where health sciences faculty can experience, firsthand, the current technology. Much of the technology being tested and developed at the Lister Hill National Center is ultimately applicable in the rural hospital or clinic.

POLICY CONSIDERATIONS

The prospects for implementation of these new technologies in the rural health setting are both exciting and discouraging. They are exciting because of the contributions that can be made to retention of quality care in rural areas, but discouraging because there are some obstacles to full realization of the potential. In general, the limitations are cost, regulatory constraints, and acceptance. These are interrelated, and the search for solutions is somewhat compounded by the fact that many of the technologies require decisions beyond those that can be made by a single unit—a provider or even a community.

An appropriate framework for assessing the costs of implementing communications and information technologies to benefit rural health care is to consider the impact of telecommunications on the survival of rural America. In addition to the direct benefits to rural residents, the indirect gains to rural business and social services from telecommunications technology have already been documented (Parker et al. 1989). The measurable benefits have been substantial, exceeding costs and contributing directly to economic output. Yet, rural communities are now lagging, and telecommunications policies are not responding to their needs.

According to Parker et al. (1989), the 1980s transition to a competitive telecommunications market has created serious hardships for rural areas.

Under the previously regulated monopoly, cross-subsidization offset some of the costs. This is no longer the case, and competition within telecommunications is a new ball game. In the absence of policies to assist, there is potential danger that, at some future time, rural America will realize it is not prepared to compete in the national economy.

In spite of this, it is important to remember that rural telecommunications policies can be formulated such that rural communities (a) can achieve better economic performance by providing the basic infrastructure, (b) are able to make the transition to the competitive telecommunications marketplace, and (c) will be empowered with equal opportunity to participate in the national economy. What is suggested is not that the government fully fund the rural telecommunications infrastructure, but rather that it take a strong leadership role and reduce structural barriers. Government help is needed to create policies for devising a broad system, including incentive fund pools and technical help, so that the private sector will be motivated to become involved. There are several ways in which policies can be changed. For example:

1. Improvements can be made to the planning and coordination among all federal agencies involved in rural development.

2. Additional funding for telecommunications services can be authorized.

3. State social service agencies should include telecommunications issues in their planning.

4. State governments should establish a centralized telecommunications policy office (if they have not done so) which will assist all state agencies in telecommunications planning, and coordination of policy among the various agencies, including the public utility commissions (Parker et al. 1989).

In short, the burden of implementing an infrastructure for insuring that rural areas are able to take advantage of technology should not rest solely on these communities. The overall economic and social benefits are substantial and should be factored into any equation when benefits and costs of preparing rural areas for technology are under consideration.

There are other limitations and issues that must be worked out in implementing a range of technologies to sustain quality health care for rural residents. Details, such as third party payments and malpractice responsibilities when providers work at a distance, require special attention. Finally, investment in these enhancements does not guarantee success; it is necessary for providers, administrators, and consumers of health care in rural areas to accept and utilize them.

CONCLUSIONS

In many ways, rural America is not truly participating in the information age. With only minor changes in information technology, a practitioner located in a rural setting could easily avoid living a professionally isolated existence. For a practitioner with a preference for a nonurban life-style setting, the cost does not have to be a sacrifice of collegial relations. For patients, lower quality and standards of care do not need to be accepted as a trade-off for local care. The world is engaged in a major electronic revolution. The capabilities that are currently available provide options never before imagined. New technologies make it possible to rethink how health-care professionals perform their jobs, interact with peers, and keep pace with ongoing advances in their disciplines.

Rural health facilities may view embracing these new technologies as a great challenge; however, their very survival may depend on their accepting this challenge. There is justification for government(s) to reduce structural barriers and take a leadership role, thereby assuring that social and economic benefits accrue to the rural area at large.

10. Rural EMS System Development: Innovative Technological Approaches

Paul B. Anderson

The emergency medical service (EMS) system serving a rural area has a frontline role within the overall health delivery system. Many small, rural communities have an EMS response organization, but do not have a local hospital or even a medical clinic. The importance of EMS capability to the rural community is increasing, due to the large number of rural hospital closures experienced in rural areas in recent years.

The movement to develop EMS systems in the United States began in 1966. The United States Congress that year enacted the Highway Safety Act, which identified EMS as a priority area and stimulated the development of EMS programs in each state (Johnson 1966). Also in 1966, the National Academy of Sciences, National Research Council, completed a study and published a report which became known as the EMS White Paper. This was a landmark event that stimulated action from leaders at the national, state, and local levels, including the medical community.

The need to develop multiple component integrated EMS systems throughout the nation was the thrust of the Emergency Medical Services Systems (EMSS) Act of 1973 (P.L. 93–154). This act provided substantial federal funding to states, and led to a concerted nationwide effort to develop over 300 regionalized EMS systems nationwide. Also in 1973, the Robert Wood Johnson Foundation (RWJF) grant program awarded over $15 million to 46 applicants throughout the nation to develop regional EMS communications systems (Robert Wood Johnson Foundation 1977). Both programs heavily impacted rural areas.

In 1980, the federal government terminated the categorical EMS program as part of a shift to a block grant approach, thereby transferring the leadership responsibility for EMS systems development to the state level

(Omnibus Budget Reconciliation Act of 1981, P.L. 97–35). A 1986 report by the United States General Accounting Office (GAO) gave generally high marks to states for their EMS systems development efforts. However, the GAO expressed concerns about a lack of uniform progress among the states and a relative lack of resources allocated for EMS development in rural areas.

As the 1990s unfold, the state leadership position in EMS system development continues. The strongest continuing federal EMS role is that of the National Highway Traffic Safety Administration (NHTSA) (National Highway Traffic Safety Administration 1990). The Trauma Care Systems Planning and Development Act (P.L. 101–590), enacted in 1990, continues to focus on state and regional roles (Legislation Focuses on Nation's Regional Trauma Care System 1991).

This chapter presents an overview of EMS systems and notes unique features and limitations of rural systems. The major thrust of the chapter is the potential to apply existing technologies to offset these limitations. Examples of applications and potential uses are given. These are classified as technology to improve delivery of services or technology for education and training. The benefits of technology to the provision of EMS in rural areas are discussed.

CHARACTERISTICS OF EMS SYSTEMS

Rural EMS systems share several characteristics, such as a high dependence on volunteer staff members. Another is the large geographic area typically served by a rural EMS unit, resulting in relatively long response and transport times. Also, the definitive care facilities in rural areas most often provide only basic levels of emergency and critical care. Thus, the need to transfer patients, by air or ground transport, to higher levels of emergency and critical care is quite common.

Another and unfortunate feature of rural EMS systems is that their funding is relatively less than in most urban areas. In some cases, small rural communities provide almost total financial support to maintain the EMS service for an entire geographic area of several hundred or more square miles. In other words, the low population density of rural areas makes it more expensive, on a per capita basis, to provide emergency medical coverage. Furthermore, rural communities do not have the EMS-run volume and profit potential to sustain private for-profit EMS operations (U.S. Department of Health and Human Services 1990a).

Another characteristic shared by rural areas is that the injury problem resulting in a request for EMS is more severe than in urban areas. There are wide geographic variations in motor vehicle crash mortality, with the evidence showing an inverse relationship between population density and mortality. More than half (56.9 percent) of *fatal* traffic crashes occur in rural areas, whereas only about one third of the population resides in these areas. Motor vehicle crashes do not occur more frequently in rural areas, but persons involved in rural crashes are three times more likely to sustain serious or untreatable injuries than those in urban areas (National Highway Traffic Safety Administration 1990).

Rural prehospital coverage is primarily provided at the basic life support (BLS) level by personnel certified as basic emergency medical technicians (EMTs). Although basic EMT certification standards are consistent throughout the nation in both rural and urban areas, the rural EMT is rarely a full-time paid professional. In contrast, most urban areas have advanced life support (ALS) EMS coverage provided by EMT paramedic personnel.

Most rural areas in the country are served by volunteer services operating at the basic life-support level; however, there are other models. A particularly noteworthy example is the Acadian Ambulance Network, which serves 22 parishes (counties) in Louisiana (Acadian Ambulance Honored 1990). The Acadian Service has an annual subscription campaign that generates much of the revenue necessary to sustain the service, which includes many ground and air ambulance units staffed by paid, advanced life-support personnel. Although there are other examples of innovative rural EMS operational approaches, the Acadian Service is the largest in terms of the geographic area and number of rural communities served.

There are many obvious contrasts between urban and rural EMS systems. The executive summary of a 1990 study of rural emergency medical services stated that EMS in rural areas has not advanced to the same level as in urban areas (U.S. Department of Health and Human Services 1990a). The report concluded that EMS becomes increasingly critical as traditional rural health-care delivery services erode. It represents the safety net, and is often the only primary care available, yet EMS services are difficult to provide.

Almost all urban residents are now served by first responder units (often fire department first responders from the nearest substation) that arrive within a couple of minutes of the call to 9–1–1. These units are normally followed by the arrival of an ambulance unit, usually staffed by paramedics. Initiating first responder units in small communities could reduce the time between the call for help and the arrival of the first EMS unit by 15–20 minutes or more. For patients in critical condition, this reduction in time may mean the difference between life and death. The initiation of first responder units, staffed in most cases by volunteer basic life-support personnel, represents a low-tech model to improve rural EMS systems. A pool of individuals who are willing to take EMS training and can be available to respond to emergency calls is the most important ingredient.

A report on EMS in North Carolina (Cline 1990) profiles ways in which rural systems differ from urban systems. These include geographic factors, differences in the population, types of emergencies, and the basics of field triage. Many aspects of rural geography, including remoteness and lack of access to transportation and phones, make the delivery of emergency medical services more difficult.

RURAL LIMITATIONS

A number of factors limits the effectiveness of rural EMS systems. Seven top problems for rural EMS were identified by a national survey conducted cooperatively by the National Rural Health Association Rural EMS Task Force, the National Association of State EMS Directors, and the Center for Rural Health at Georgia Southern College. They include (1) financing, (2) recruitment and retention, (3) training, (4) communications, (5) trauma care systems, (6) optimal standards, and (7) medical control (U.S. Department of Health and Human Services 1990a).

The financing issue for rural EMS systems has historically been a problem. Two decades ago, Owen (1971) pointed out the relative lack of financial and system support for EMS.

With respect to emergency medical care, however, we are still in the dark ages . . . . In fact, to me the sense of values of the community seems to have been misdirected. For example, in answer to a fire call, equipment worth tens of thousands of dollars arrives on scene in minutes to save a house, which can be replaced. In the event of a theft, well-trained police and investigators are there immediately to help repossess stolen jewelry, which can be replaced. But, if one has a heart attack, we cannot be certain a trained and well equipped ambulance crew will arrive on the scene to save the life which cannot be replaced. (P. 7).

In testimony before the United States Congress, the small town of Stanley, Idaho, was offered as one example of a rural community having difficulty in financing EMS services (*Congressional Record* 1975). This town has a population of only about 150 persons, and the nearest hospital is 60 miles away over a mountain pass. The immediate area, the Sawtooth National Recreation Area, experiences a visitor influx of over 1,000,000 visitor days a year. Yet, the financial burden of supporting the Stanley ambulance service is almost entirely on the shoulders of the 150 permanent residents of this rural community. Certainly, this is a dramatic example, but it is not unique. Throughout the United States numerous small communities provide the financial support and volunteer staffing necessary to operate this essential public safety service, used primarily by outsiders. As the cost of new ambulance vehicles has escalated into the $40,000–80,000 range, it is increasingly more difficult for very small communities to replace them as they wear out and become unreliable. Some states have enacted special fees to fund state and local EMS programs, as shown in Table 10.1.

Although financial support of rural emergency medical services systems is a very important issue, there are many others that also need attention, and most are not independent of financing. The rural environment handicaps resolution of many problems; however, technological developments offer genuine help.

APPLICATION OF TECHNOLOGY

One of the most promising approaches to solving some of the key problems of rural EMS systems is expanded application of existing and new technology. Although not all rural EMS problems can be solved through the use of technology, there are examples to illustrate the significant potential of innovations in using technology to address most problems.

This section discusses several technology applications by focusing on their use primarily to improve the delivery of rural emergency medical services or primarily as tools to enhance education and training.

Application of Technology to Improve Delivery of Services. The ability to continue the provision of high quality care in remote locations is affected by increasing demands on limited resources. Being on call day after day results in burnout for rural EMS personnel and interferes with work, family, and outside activities. The use of radio communications technology to improve response times, and to give rural volunteers freedom of movement within their community while on call, is one solution. This technology allows for the immediate deployment of units, and removes the need for the dispatcher to contact each on-call EMT individually (Anderson 1981).

This use of improved radio communications has other positive impacts as well. It allows instant communications capability for rural EMS units when they are on all types of runs, even in very remote areas or rugged terrain. The unit can remain in contact with the dispatcher, to request additional assistance at the scene (for example, a rescue-extrication unit or a helicopter), to notify the destination hospital of the patient's condition, and to be available for another call when returning to quarters. In some areas, without the microwave links to mountain-top radios, most of the rural EMS units would not have communication capability when operating in their service call.

Several states (Idaho, New Mexico, Maryland, North Dakota, and Utah are examples) have taken action to provide statewide EMS communications networks that include coverage of vast rural areas, yet much of rural America still does not have this capability. Ambulance and rescue vehicles often are out of radio contact when they go on a call. However, in some states, such as Alaska, the cost of installing a statewide mountain-top radio system would be prohibitive.

A teleconference bridge terminal, with two-way audio teleconferencing capability, has valuable uses for a statewide EMS system for delivery of

Table 10.1
State-Imposed Fees for EMS Support

State		Traffic Violation Fee Imposed
Arizona	$ 30	on every fine, penalty, and bail forfeiture imposed and collected by the courts for driving under the influence
	5	on every fine, penalty, and bail forfeiture imposed and collected by the courts for other penalty assessments
Florida	5	driver damaging vehicle or property
	5	reckless driving
	25	DUI
Indiana		drunk driving offenders pay for uncollectible EMS expenses from motor vehicle accidents in which they were involved
Minnesota	10	for failure to wear seat belt
Mississippi	5	from each person fined or forfeiting bail for any hazardous moving traffic violation
Utah	3.50	for each reportable traffic violation when a fine is imposed or bail is forfeited
State		**Vehicle Registration/Driver's License Fees**
Colorado	$ 1	per vehicle registration
Florida	0.10	per vehicle registration (to fund administration of trauma care program)
Idaho	1.25	per vehicle registration ($1 to state and $0.25 to county of origin)
	2	per driver's license
New Mexico	1	per vehicle registration
Virginia	2	per vehicle registration

Source: Kleinholz and Doeksen 1991.

services, as well as educational purposes. A terminal located in the state-wide EMS communications center is available for 24-hour emergency use. For example, in complex hazardous-materials emergencies, the bridge terminal is used to convene all of the various environmental health, law enforcement, fire-rescue, EMS, and other agencies involved in responding to such situations. It is available for other complicated emergency situations as well, such as aircraft search and rescue missions and mountain rescues. In addition, the teleconference bridge terminal may be used on a scheduled basis to convene EMS committees such as the statewide physician committee, statewide trauma committee, EMS field offices, and other groups. The teleconference method allows such groups, with participants widely scattered over a large, rural state, to convene without the necessity for costly and time-consuming travel to reach meetings.

Another application of the computerized teleconference bridge terminal is to conduct retrospective critiques of major EMS incident situations. When major incidents with multiple patients occur in rural areas, typically a number of EMS units from different towns respond, and the patients are transported to rural hospitals, to the regional trauma center, or other major referral centers. In addition to ground EMS units, one or more EMS aircraft, rotary or fixed-wing, service is usually involved in handling the incident, along with other agencies. Without this technology, it would be very difficult to convene a retrospective critique session after the incident is over because of geographic dispersion. However, by using this technology, the emergency responders involved in the actual response can be easily convened for a teleconference critique session.

Computer technology has also been used to study and design rural EMS systems. In the mid–1980s, the National Highway Traffic Safety Administration (NHTSA) funded a multiyear, interdisciplinary effort to design, implement, test, and apply a computer simulation model of a rural emergency medical services system (Wolfe 1988). The resulting computer model, Ruralsim, provides a realistic representation of the demand for emergency services in an area and the EMS system's response to that demand under alternative configurations of system resources. Ruralsim is designed as an aid for system planners in evaluating different modes of delivery of emergency medical services.

Another example of the use of computer technology having a very significant impact on rural EMS systems is the use of microprocessors as the "brains" of automated cardiac defibrillators. These smart defibrillators are able to analyze the cardiac electrical status of a patient and inform the EMT if the rhythm is "shockable" or "nonshockable." The computer microprocessor compares the electrical rhythm obtained from the patient with an algorithm that is based on the analysis of many thousands of cardiac strips obtained from actual patients.

The use of automated defibrillator technology illustrates the impact of this type of innovative advance on delivery of services in rural areas. Manual defibrillation programs require considerably more training because the EMT personnel have to be taught rhythm interpretation. Also, it is necessary to have frequent cardiac arrest simulation sessions in order to assure that knowledge and skills are maintained. In the context of overall requirements of maintaining EMS certification, automated defibrillators reduce the burden on volunteers (Ham 1991).

These high-tech devices are a reality today, and more rural EMS units are obtaining them. National medical organizations support the use of cardiac defibrillators by EMS units (Defibrillation by EMTs 1991). On the one hand the cost of about $5,000 for a defibrillator appears high for a rural EMS unit that is struggling to pay the insurance bill on its EMS vehicle. Yet, when viewed in the context of the overall expense of obtaining and operating an ambulance service in a rural community (an unequipped ambulance vehicle now costing $50,000 or more), the incremental cost of adding the automated cardiac defibrillator becomes less significant.

Placing cardiac defibrillator units not only in ambulance vehicles but also in first responder vehicles has been shown to be very effective. The time from collapse of the patient to delivery of defibrillation shocks is the most important factor in survival from cardiac arrest. Equipping first responder units with the automated defibrillator devices saves valuable time.

The development of a nationwide air ambulance network is another example of use of high technology to significantly impact rural EMS patient care. In particular, the initiation of rotor-wing EMS services, most of which are based at urban tertiary-care hospitals, provides surrounding rural areas with advanced life-support critical care for both on-scene and interhospital transfer types of calls. In one study, a 52 percent reduction in predicted mortality occurred in a group of 150 consecutive trauma patients, many from the rural areas surrounding an urban tertiary-care center (Baxt & Moody 1983). The rotorcraft clearly has the capability of bringing a high level of medical expertise to the patient at the site of injury or illness over a broad geographic area.

Application of Technology for Education and Training. Providers in rural areas are continually faced with the problem of skill retention and keeping up with knowledge in their fields. Limited access to programs increases the risk of practice for providers, and adds to the difficulty of recruitment and retention for rural areas. Technology is a key factor in alleviating this disadvantage of rural practice locations; following are several examples of applications.

Advances in communications technology can improve audio teleconferencing capability for rural EMS systems. This technology facilitates the delivery of continuing education courses to rural areas. In the early 1980s, the Idaho EMS System installed a computerized teleconference bridge terminal in order to have high-quality continuing education programs delivered to many rural area locations (Anderson 1984). Prior to use of audio teleconferencing, it would typically be necessary for rural area EMS personnel to travel 100 to 200 miles one-way to reach continuing education conference locations. A particularly attractive feature of the Idaho program is their teleconference bridge terminal, which allows up to 48 local community classroom sites to call the bridge simultaneously to join the teleconference. The teleconference network now includes over 150 classroom locations. The sessions are repeated to accommodate all the sites, and over 1,500 EMT personnel participate in each program. The speaker may be a nationally or internationally known EMS expert, and can be at a location thousands of miles away while making the presentation to local classroom sites.

In the initial years of teleconferences, each site was furnished with a set of slides for use during the lecture portion of the class; however, in recent years, the slide portion of the presentation has been replaced by videotape presentations. This has reduced overall costs, and the videotaped presentations have been very favorably received by teleconference participants. The Idaho EMS teleconference network has shown that a rural EMS system can use this technology effectively to produce high-quality continuing education programs delivered to thousands of widely dispersed, rural EMS personnel (Anderson, Bjornson, & Wayne 1982).

Satellite technology offers certain distinct advantages for educational programming, such as the capability of providing video conferencing. In 1990, the Virginia state EMS program started using the satellite method to deliver one-way video teleconferences to sites throughout the commonwealth, including to EMS units in outlying, rural communities (Garza 1990). A toll-free telephone method is used to allow site participants to ask questions of the faculty member. The Virginia satellite teleconference programs have been enthusiastically received by rural EMS personnel.

Delivering quality EMS continuing education by teleconference does have limitations, however. In particular, although it has been shown (by using pretests and posttests) to result in learning uptake rates comparable to those obtained with the faculty member present in the classroom, the teleconference approach has significant limitations with regard to hands-on skills training.

A number of states have initiated mobile training unit programs to improve the delivery of hands-on skills training to rural area EMS personnel who do not have the benefit of large volumes of critical patient encounters to maintain their skills (Anderson 1990). The programs operate by having the mobile training units visit local community EMS organizations periodically. The mobile EMS training programs emphasize the use of very realistic simulation of actual emergency situations to compensate for the lack of frequent exposure to such patient cases by rural EMS personnel. The mobile training unit (MTU) approach brings urban area instructors, with considerable EMS experience, out to rural areas to share their expertise.

The mobile training units use new technology, including the latest training manikins, extrication simulators, and other means to obtain very realistic simulations of events. Besides the skill learning stations with instructors, several mobile training unit programs include programmed learning unit (PLU) stations. The mobile training unit experience with the computer learning stations has been positive. Rural EMS personnel have shown a high degree of enthusiasm for the computer based training (CBT) stations (Anderson, Neuman, & Trimble 1986).

When students complete EMT training in rural areas, they do not become immediately seasoned, in terms of actual emergency experience. Rural volunteer EMS personnel thus may be relatively inexperienced for a lengthy period, unless they obtain experience in some other manner. In Oregon, the state EMS program has initiated a formal program termed Project Rustout to bring rural area volunteer EMS personnel into Portland to go on actual runs and gain experience over weekends (Rustout Project Report 1989). However, the program is limited in that it is only able to accommodate a few of the several thousand rural area EMS personnel in the state. Further, whereas Oregon has a major metropolitan area, many rural states do not have a large urban area with high EMS run volumes. This makes it imperative that alternative approaches be developed to help rural EMS personnel obtain the equivalent experience in some other manner.

One approach to providing rural EMTs with more intensive practical experience involves the use of new technology to substitute simulated events for actual events. This use of computers for EMS educational purposes actually integrates the microprocessor with video technology to produce results that are most dramatic. In 1990, one rural state EMS program converted a mobile trauma training unit (MTTU) into a mobile interactive training unit (MITU) (Anderson et al. 1990). The MITU is equipped with eight interactive videodisc (IVD) learning stations, each comprised of a computer central processing unit (CPU), an interactive laser videodisc player, and a touch-screen monitor. The learning material is on a 12-inch videodisc that holds 54,000 video frames, with the text and graphics incorporated as part of the computer software. By using this combination of technology, very realistic simulation of emergency events is made possible. It is analogous to the flight simulator device used by airline pilots to practice handling emergency and other situations that would be too expensive, too dangerous, or otherwise too difficult to do while flying an aircraft. The use of interactive videodisc (IVD) technology holds particular promise for addressing the issue of rural EMS personnel becoming experienced in handling emergencies that they do not often encounter.

The use of IVD technology has an additional advantage in that it allows for evaluation of each trainee's response by capturing every key stroke (actually activated by using the touchscreen monitor). Thus, by using this evaluation methodology, the degree of knowledge, skills retention, and degradation can be determined over time, and compared to retraining intervals, levels of exposure to actual emergency incidents, and other similar related factors.

An example of this technology at work is the Idaho program, developed as part of a national pediatric demonstration grant. Idaho EMS personnel worked with the Dartmouth Medical School Interactive Media Laboratory in New Hampshire. Members of this project team have produced the first pediatric videodisc program, "Respiratory Emergencies in Children."

The pediatric respiratory videodisc program is now being taken, on a circuit rider basis, by the mobile interactive training unit (MITU) to every EMS unit in the state. Bringing the mobile training units to each local community EMS unit has allowed virtually all EMS personnel to participate in the educational sessions. By contrast, when training sessions are held a distance away, usually only a few representatives of each rural EMS unit are able to attend. At a cost of about $6,000 for each IVD learning station, it was deemed practical to obtain eight IVD learning stations, put them on a mobile training vehicle, and take them to each community on a periodic basis.

After the student becomes oriented to the IVD learning station, a video is presented that puts the student in the role of an EMT responding to an emergency by traveling through the community in an ambulance. Upon reaching the scene, the EMT crew takes equipment into a house where a small child is found to be experiencing severe respiratory distress. The EMTs are then presented with alternatives, on the touchscreen, as to what they should do first in terms of assessing the patient, questioning the mother, and other tasks. Then, the EMTs are presented with options in terms of what emergency care measures should be taken. At key points in the presentation, the patient is shown on the video with signs of respiratory distress, including the sounds of upper or lower respiratory compromise, and the condition of the patient changes depending upon the effectiveness of the treatment methods that are used by the EMTs. For instance, if the patient is gurgling and needs to be suctioned, after the EMTs take this action the patient no longer will have gurgling sounds on the video. However, the patient may still be cyanotic, and only after the EMTs initiate oxygen therapy will be degree of cyanosis be attenuated and the patient's color become more normal.

The combination of microprocessor technology and the videodisc is a far more flexible and sophisticated approach to EMS learning than linear video. Linear video, like other more traditional lecture-film methods of presenting information, is a passive method of learning. The interactivity of the videodisc method brings students into the medium to the point that the student virtually feels part of the process. It is not uncommon during an EMS videodisc learning situation for the EMT to verbalize "I can't lose him now," or "hang in there, I'm doing everything I can for you." Obviously, the EMT feels as if it is an emergency scene; this process certainly helps to season the EMT, even though it is not an actual emergency scene.

Studies have shown that students reach mastery levels of learning with the IVD methodology to a higher degree than with traditional learning methods, and in less time (Vada 1986, Beardsley & Davis 1989). For rural areas, as the training hour requirements increase, it becomes more and more difficult to recruit volunteers. Implementation of IVD and similar technologies that result in equivalent or better learning levels in less time, should translate into more adequate staffing levels and more stability for rural EMS units around the nation.

However, cost is a barrier to implementing computer/videodisc technology for rural EMS units. Certainly, this technology will never be available at the cost of a lecture using slides, but there are several possibilities that may result in drastic cost reductions, including compact disc-interactive (CD-I) technology. If the cost falls into the range that many rural EMS units can afford, the volume of EMS courseware reproductions would increase significantly, lowering the cost per disc. The compact disc (CD), with which the public is now familiar in terms of high quality music, also will accommodate video.

In addition to CD-I technology, there are many other technological approaches now being considered that may hold dramatic promise for EMS education in rural areas. These include digitized video interactive (DVI) and other similar technologies. The capability to digitize the video, as opposed to having the actual video frames on the videodisc, is advantageous because it becomes possible to manipulate video to make more realistic situations needed for conducting EMS training.

CONCLUSIONS

It is difficult to predict the extent that technological innovations will be utilized in the rural EMS environment during the 1990s. Certainly, it is clear that the microprocessor chip will be the basis of many of the technological innovations that will impact rural EMS in the future. However, there will be many variations in the use of such technology. Some will be truly space-age, such as the use of satellite technology to improve EMS communications in rural/frontier areas before the end of the decade (Castiel 1990).

Voice (analog) messages will be largely replaced by digitized messages that are sent in bursts that each last only microseconds. The digitized messages will be sent from EMS vehicle keyboards up to a satellite, then down to an earth station, and to the EMS communications center where the message will be printed out at a terminal. The center will be able to communicate on a two-way basis with each rural area EMS vehicle through the satellite network and its components.

It appears that only by developing a multiple state cooperative approach will it be practical, from a financial and technological standpoint, to solve rural and frontier area EMS communications problems using satellites and associated developments. Until technological developments are fully implemented, many situations will continue to occur in rural and frontier areas involving EMS and rescue incidents which are beyond the coverage of existing radio communications systems. Rural and frontier EMS crews will continue to be at risk, because they are out of radio contact when on difficult runs. Patients will continue to suffer because lack of adequate radio communications prevents EMS crews from obtaining the necessary assistance in particular emergency situations. It is apparent that new direction will need to guide rural area EMS system development in forging the multistate cooperative approaches necessary to utilize the latest in available technology.

The issue of adequacy of funding for EMS in rural and frontier areas is, of course, tied directly to political decisions. There must be significant general public support for EMS to assure that elected officials will support programs to the extent that new technological advances will be implemented.

In 1990, Maryland's EMS director emphasized challenges for the future. Among remaining tasks are recruitment and retention of volunteer providers, who are the main EMS source for nonurban areas. The need for two-earner families and concerns about infectious diseases are factors decreasing availability of volunteers. Some communities have found it necessary to pay personnel during working hours; others have considered tax benefits for volunteers.

In spite of the challenges to be faced, a clear focus must remain on the goal: trauma care—the eradication of preventable death and disability is a primary goal of EMS. Another is to define more clearly the meaning of medical direction, which has remained one of the murkiest concepts in EMS for the past two decades.

Comprehensive emergency medical care is no longer a goal. It is a public expectation. In Maryland, the goal and the expectation remain a focus of a comprehensive statewide EMS system that links a strong clinical base with voluntary statewide networking. Maryland's challenge should be viewed in the broader context of the entire nation. Rural areas are especially vulnerable due to continued reduction of traditional forms of delivery. Innovative EMS coverage is not a luxury in these areas, but a necessary component of the health care system. (Ramzy 1990, p. 71).

This can certainly serve as a model for rural EMS throughout the country. With increasing demands on this form of delivery, but a lack of similarly increasing resources, efficient and innovative use of technology represents a key component and a major challenge.

PART V
Linkages

11. The RWJ Hospital-Based Demonstration and State Rural Health Policy

Anthony R. Kovner and Joan M. Kiel

During the 1980s, rural hospitals experienced lower occupancy rates, fewer private pay patients and inpatient days, and increasing dependence on government financing. At the same time, the rural areas they served suffered as unemployment, poverty, and indigent rates increased (Ermann 1990). The maintenance of the rural hospitals in such a setting requires changes from the traditional, full-service, acute-care facility to an alternative configuration of services and multilinkage arrangements. Historical models for such changes are limited because previously there was little need or demand.

The Robert Wood Johnson (RWJ) Foundation's Hospital-Based Rural Health Care Program was developed to demonstrate viable, alternative responses to the changing environment of rural hospitals. The program is a national initiative that supports consortium of hospitals in order to strengthen the ability of rural hospitals to provide high quality care and to promote the financial stability of these institutions through cooperation, not competition. Joining a consortia may be a viable alternative for a rural hospital facing high fixed costs, unused duplicate services, and financial instability.

This chapter is divided into several parts. The first explains the selection process for awarding grants under the Hospital-Based Rural Health Care demonstration program. The second describes key aspects of state health policy that affect rural hospitals. The third discusses the implications of the demonstration for state policy, and is followed by a review of what has been learned in the process.

SELECTION OF THE DEMONSTRATION PROGRAM HOSPITALS

The Hospital-Based Rural Health Care Program began in 1987, when over 400 letters of intent were received from hospitals in 48 states. During the next three months, 180 applications representing 33 states were reviewed. From these, 14 grants were awarded to consortia representing 182 rural hospitals in 12 states (the average grant was $335,223 for 4 years). A short time after the awards were made, the number of sites participating was reduced to 13; one consortium withdrew because of physician opposition to a hospital-sponsored HMO, which was to be their sole program. In addition, a loan program was established for up to $500,000 for each grantee. The University of Minnesota's School of Public Health assumed responsibility for a formal ongoing evaluation of the program.

As shown in Table 11.1, the 13 grantees had varying characteristics. The number of counties served varied from one in northern Maine to 26 in western Texas. Project areas served ranged from 94,600 square miles in Nevada to 3,500 in northeastern New York. Northern Maine, with 5 hospital members, had the smallest consortium, and Texas the largest, with 36. Physician distribution differed significantly among the 13 areas served. Southern Maine had 152 physicians per 100,000 population compared to less than half that number in Montana, Nevada, Texas, and Wisconsin. Demographic variables such as population per square mile, elderly population, and poverty population also varied among the areas.

In 1989, the awards for the second phase of the demonstration for western New York, northern Maine, southern Maine, and Mississippi were not renewed for a variety of reasons. In addition, program scope was reduced in northeastern New York and Montana.

The 13 original grantees initiated 43 different demonstration programs during Phase I, 1988–89 (Table 11.2). During Phase II, June 1990–92, nine grantees are conducting 24 different programs. The number of programs has been reduced for several reasons including program completion accomplished in Phase I (4), lack of program feasibility (6), and changes in program focus. This last reason has resulted in creation of 5 new programs and elimination of 4 original programs.

These RWJ demonstration programs have been affected directly and indirectly by state health policy, as shown in Table 11.3. For example, the North Carolina small-employer health benefits program initiative was affected by a lack of eligibility and inability of employees to buy in to Medicaid. The aim of this consortium initiative was to develop insurance packages for small businesses, which previously had offered few or no health insurance benefits to employees. During 1989, the plan was approved by the North Carolina General Assembly, but it was not funded. Although this was recognized as a setback, the program staff succeeded

Table 11.1
Selected Characteristics of Consortia and Environments of Hospital-Based Rural Health-Care Grantees, 1987

	AL	NM	SM	MS	MO	MT	NV	NN	WN	NC	SC	TX	WI
Hospital members in consortium	6	5	17	16	12	7	10	5	12	16	20	36	20
Physicians per 100,000 population	123	125	152	78	96	66	61	131	100	80	105	67	62
Number of counties served	7	1	10	21	21	6	12	3	7	14	14	26	12
Population (1,000s)	234	89	978	565	549	44	108	148	643	445	906	329	299
Project area, square miles (1,000s)	5.5	6.7	12.3	10.9	14.4	19.6	94.6	3.5	5.4	6.3	8.4	25.4	9.3
Population per square mile	42.6	13.2	79.3	51.7	38.1	2.3	1.1	42.1	119	70.4	108	12.9	32.0
Percent age 65 and older	11.6	10.4	12.6	12.3	15.4	11.2	10.2	13.3	12.5	11.8	9.8	12.6	15.2
Percent below poverty	25.6	16.2	11.4	20.8	16.4	15.2	11.7	12.8	10.6	19.1	17.3	19.3	12.2

NM=Northern Maine; SM=Southern Maine; NN=Northeast New York; WN=Western New York.

Sources: Moscovice, Christianson, and Johnson 1988; U.S. Bureau of the Census, 1983 and 1988; and American Medical Association 1986.

Table 11.2
Program Summary, 1988–89

Program Types	Number of Consortia Phase I (13)	Phase II (9)
Primary/Specialty	9	7
Shared Services	8	5
Management	7	4
Recruitment and Retention of Clinicians	6	3
Acute Care Bed Conversion	4	2
Marketing/Public Relations	4	2
Quality Assurance	3	1
Health Insurance	2	0
Total	43	24
Average Programs Per Consortia	3.3	2.3

Source: Robert Wood Johnson Foundation 1988, 1989.

in sensitizing state policymakers to the need for insurance coverage for the growing number of low income, uninsured residents.

State-specific characteristics make it difficult to generalize about the demonstration progress, and to predict how similar programs might be successfully transferred to other states. This is compounded by variations in state policies regarding health care.

KEY ASPECTS OF STATE HEALTH POLICY

In this section the key aspects of state health policy that affect rural hospitals are discussed. These aspects include Medicaid, financial subsidization of clinicians, subsidization for capital and technology, certificate of need and incentives for reconfigurations of services, and technical assistance from state agencies.

Medicaid. Although much attention has focused on the impact of the Medicare reimbursement differential on rural hospitals, the structure and

Table 11.3
State Policy and Rural Hospitals

State Policy	RWJ Programs
Medicaid	Health Insurance
Financial Subsidization of Clinicians	Recruitment and Retention of Clinicians
Subsidization of Capital and Technology	Acute Bed Conversion and RWJ Loan Program
Certificate of Need and Incentives for Reconfiguration of Services	Shared Clinical Serves and Referral Services
Technical Assistance from State agencies	Management, Finance and Information; Quality Assurance; Marketing and Public Relations

Source: Robert Wood Johnson Foundation 1990.

level of Medicaid payments is also important to rural hospital finances. Approximately half of all rural hospitals receive between 9 and 14 percent of their net revenue from Medicaid, and 9 percent of rural hospitals receive over 15 percent from this source (American Hospital Association 1989). The dependency of these hospitals on Medicaid is exemplified in Texas, which ranks last in per capita Medicaid payments in the nation and first in hospital closures. Currently, Texas Medicaid covers only 25 percent of the poor, which is less than in any other state (Kennedy 1989). To respond to this problem, House Bill 1345, the Medicaid Enhancement Bill, was introduced in the Texas legislature. This bill will provide coverage for additional recipients and services. It is estimated that enactment of this legislation will cost the state $166 million dollars annually. Although the legislation was costly, other states are passing similar legislation to enhance access to needed services.

Alabama has recently legislated an expansion of Medicaid benefits for maternal and child health care. The West Alabama Rural Health Consortium, an RWJ grantee, will be involved in the implementation of this policy change. This consortium is located in an economically troubled and medically underserved area, and includes 3 of the 20 poorest counties in the country. The major programs of this consortium are shared clinical services and specialty clinics. These programs are intended to improve access and local utilization of care. Specialty services which will now be provided locally include cardiology, surgery, orthopedics, gynecology, and urology. The West Alabama Rural Health Consortium has also implemented shared services among 3 county hospitals for the provision of mammography, ultrasound, surgery, and physical therapy. Through these shared services, this consortium has responded to the needs of the communities it serves. The hospital leadership recognized that these poor counties could not support the services on their own, thus, by forming a consortium, the 6 rural hospitals have improved access to care in an efficient manner.

Other states that are similarly changing their Medicaid policies to enhance rural health care include Maine and Iowa. Maine's House Bill 1643 extends coverage to children under age 5, with eligibility up to 100 percent of poverty level. The state also provides a subsidized health insurance program that will cover the indigent population with incomes below 150 percent of the poverty level. Similarly, Iowa began increasing Medicaid coverage for children up to age 6 on a phased-in, year-by-year basis on January 1, 1989 (Alabama Department of Public Health 1989). Rural hospitals must respond by coordinating the services that the state is willing to expand and fund, and by giving feedback on how the state policies affect their hospitals.

Rural hospital administrators are approaching state policymakers to change Medicaid reimbursement mechanisms. Arkansas proposed to the Health Care Financing Administration (HCFA) that they reimburse rural hospitals, with 99 or fewer licensed beds or those with an average daily census of 50 or fewer patients, on a cost basis. Utah also recognized the financial difficulties its rural hospitals faced, and now uses separate reimbursement mechanisms for rural and urban hospitals. Rural hospitals are reimbursed on the basis of 95 percent of charges, whereas urban hospitals are paid prospective rates (Phillips & Luehrs 1989).

The consortia of the Hospital-Based Rural Health Care Program are committed to assuring access to care for the poor and medically underserved. Solo rural hospitals do not have the "political clout" to influence state legislatures, nor do they have the flexibility to respond to policy changes. As shown here, consortium members can make their needs known to the state in an "interest group" fashion. Then, when changes occur at the state level, hospitals can coordinate among themselves how best to provide the services and satisfy the needs of the community.

Supply of Clinicians. Individual states control the process of licensing health-care professionals. For physicians, nurses, technicians, and allied health professionals, this jurisdiction extends from testing, to continuing education, to tax levies for use in recruitment. Recruitment and retention of professionals have been difficult for rural areas, especially when competing in markets experiencing shortages, such as for nurses. Nationally, in rural areas, there is a pronounced physician distribution problem. For example, the Nevada consortium serves an area with 61 physicians per 100,000 population and covers 94,600 square miles (Table 11.1). Montana has only 66 physicians per 100,000 population, and when hospitals lose their only physician, they are forced to close, at least temporarily. In response to this crisis, the Montana consortium initiated a program for physician recruitment and retention.

In 1990, a survey was conducted to assess the attitudes and behaviors of physicians in Montana. Reconfiguration of hospital services, continuing professional education, and coverage relief for physicians were identified as important factors influencing physician recruitment.

In another program-sponsored initiative, the Rural Health Care Partnership of Northeastern New York, based in Albany, designed the Health Care Personnel Recruitment, Retention and Continuing Education Program. This program is designed to improve local access to care, as well as quality of rural health services through enhanced recruitment, retention, and continuing education for health personnel. The program is being developed in conjunction with the Albany Medical Center and the Health Systems of Northeastern New York.

The first step of the program was a survey conducted among the three local, rural hospitals to assess their personnel needs. Second, a continuing education needs assessment was made among the hospitals' physicians, nurses, and allied health professionals. The results of these studies assisted in the implementation of 40 interdisciplinary, educational programs offered by various rural hospitals. It was important to the physicians that the continuing education programs be brought to them, thereby substantially lowering their cost of participation in these programs. These educational opportunities have had a positive impact on rural hospital physician recruitment and retention. In 1989, 4 physicians were hired: 2 family practitioners, 1 pathologist, and 1 psychiatrist. Also recruited were professional ancillary staff, including a consulting psychologist and social workers. Not only have the recruitment and retention improved, but so too have professional relationships and collegial support.

The previous examples demonstrate how the consortia survey results could be used by states to amend policy. When a majority of a state's rural hospitals present evidence of problems and recommendations for changes, policymakers cannot ignore them. As more physicians continue to settle in urban areas for economic reasons, several states have initiated policies to provide financial assistance for the recruitment of rural physicians. Wisconsin created the Kunicki Rural Health Care Initiatives, which include a program for assisting physicians who agree to serve in rural areas by repaying medical school loans. New Mexico has implemented the Rural Primary Health Care Act, which provides funds to assist in physician recruitment and medical school loan repayment. Georgia initiated the Physicians for Rural Areas Assistance Act in 1989, allowing medical school loans to be repaid through practice in rural areas.

A direct state effort to assist physician recruitment and retention may be achieved through a special state income tax policy. Iowa has proposed a state income tax credit program for health professionals who serve in rural areas. Oregon has already passed a similar law, which establishes tax credits of $5,000 per year up to 10 years (Alabama Department of Public Health 1989).

Nurses and allied health personnel are also in short supply in rural areas. The Ozarks Health Network, Missouri, consortium responded to this problem by designing a personnel float pool. The objective of the float pool is to address staffing problems related to fluctuating patient occupancy rates in member hospitals. The consortium coordinates the training and temporary placement of personnel on the basis of a hospital's needs. The rationale is that high occupancy hospitals can borrow staff from low occupancy hospitals, at a lower cost and in a more efficient manner than by using the services of a temporary agency. By the end of 1989, the float pool employed 34 registered nurses (RNs) and 15 licensed practical nurses (LPNs). Recruitment efforts have been enhanced with newspaper advertising, bulletin boards, and appearances at career days. Presently, 55 percent of all requests for nurses are met. Competition from 5 other nursing agencies and the broader nursing shortage have prevented a higher request fulfillment rate. The program has assisted rural hospitals in resolving nurse staffing problems, and the consortium is now considering a program to encourage recruitment and retention of physicians, physical therapists, respiratory therapists, and pharmacists.

As shown here, states have recognized the crucial rural manpower shortage and have responded in a number of ways. Consortia assist in this, as they can more easily undertake a needs assessment and voice the results more effectively to state policymakers than can a solo rural hospital.

Access to Capital and Technology. Rural hospitals have great difficulty obtaining needed capital and technology. A paradox exists; hospitals want to expand the range of profitable services to increase revenues, but they are deemed financially unstable for receiving loans. Without the loans, the services are not developed, and the revenue pipeline shuts down. For example, Washington State has had a capital assistance program since 1980, but only 1 of 41 rural hospitals in the state has received assistance; the other applicants did not meet the bond rating criteria. The North Carolina Rural Hospital Coalition, on the other hand, has successfully established the needed financial planning to assure acute bed conversion in one eastern North Carolina community. Their goal is to secure and stabilize a health-care delivery system for the community, by expanding primary-care services and converting acute medical and surgical beds to ambulatory and long-term-care services. With a $500,000 loan from the Robert Wood Johnson

Foundation, this consortium has secured $1,250,000 toward a goal of $4,000,000.

Overall, the Robert Wood Johnson Foundation has awarded over $4.5 million dollars to assist consortia financially. One aspect of the foundation's assistance is a loan program that makes loans of $500,000 available to each grantee consortium. In order to secure a loan, the consortium must submit work plans for its proposed project. The foundation then determines the feasibility of the project and makes the funding decision. Several states, including Nevada, Wisconsin, Alabama, and South Carolina are currently preparing work plans to secure funding. Up to this point, the loan program has not been fully utilized due to such problems with proposed projects as feasibility and cost/benefit analysis. However, further assistance is being given to the consortia to develop viable loan projects.

New York State has designed a rural hospital initiative program that has earmarked over $4,000,000 for rural development. The money is designated for funding conversion and expansion of services, networking projects that coordinate the delivery of services, swing beds, and clinician recruitment and retention. New York is recognizing the financial needs of rural hospitals. Other states, including New Mexico, Iowa, Hawaii, and Nevada have initiated similar programs to assist hospitals in attaining capital funds through low interest loans. The New Mexico Hospital Equipment Loan Council has started a financial assistance program whereby they issue tax-exempt revenue bonds to generate funds. This money is then used for low-interest loans and the refinancing of previous loans.

In 1988, after the Nevada Rural Hospital Project consortium received funding from the RWJ Foundation, an evaluation of each hospital's facilities and needs was conducted. The results revealed there was a need to improve access to radiology services in rural Nevada. At that time, only one hospital had a full-time radiologist. Other hospitals relied on part-time radiologists or courier transport of X rays, but none provided 24-hour service. This severely limited patient access to basic diagnostic service, generating unnecessary transfers to urban hospitals.

Quality of care and physician recruitment and retention were also adversely impacted. In response to this, with additional funds from the Health Care Financing Administration and Rural Health Care Transition Grants, a teleradiology system, complete with 24-hour consultation service was established. This service provides transmission of X rays over standard telephone lines; thus, rural physicians have around-the-clock access to radiology consultation. Currently, 9 of the 10 consortium members participate, and the tenth houses the resident radiologist. During the first two months of this service, 25 percent of the inpatients remained in local hospitals, instead of being transferred to larger hospitals.

Texas has established a management information system for the analysis of hospital utilization, staffing, and problem solving. The West Texas Rural

Health Providers Consortium consists of 30 hospitals in 26 counties in the Texas Panhandle area. The isolation of these hospitals led to a need for a communication and information network. A management information system to meet the specific needs of the rural hospitals was designed jointly by an accounting firm and a software company. The implementation of this technology has resulted in a decrease in the time spent on maintaining third-party-payer logs, in improving utilization of personnel, and in facilitating decision making on the basis of more timely data.

Rural hospital consortia must urge states to provide financial assistance for capital and technology. This, in turn, will enhance services, access to care, quality of care, and recruitment and retention of personnel. The success of programs such as those funded by the RWJ grants can be used as leverage when asking states to provide financial subsidies.

Reconfiguration of Services. With the changes occurring in rural demographics and the health-care sector, some rural hospitals are faced with two options: change or close. Between 1980 and 1988, 246 rural hospitals closed leaving some areas with limited access to health care (American Hospital Association 1989). To prevent further closures, rural hospitals have approached state legislatures to change policies on hospital structure.

Among the approaches to rural hospital restructuring are special licensing categories, loosening Certificate of Need (CON) restrictions, networking, and swing beds. Rural hospitals can be categorized into three types:

1. Type A hospitals which are small and remote, have fewer than 50 beds, and are more than 30 miles from another acute inpatient care facility.

2. Type B hospitals which are small and rural, have fewer than 50 beds, and are less than 30 miles from another acute inpatient care facility.

3. Type C hospitals which are rural, have more than 50 beds, but are not a referral center. (Fisher et al. 1989)

More rural hospitals are realizing that cooperation, not competition will lead to greater success. It is of little benefit to have 10 full-service, financially unstable, acute-care hospitals in a rural area that cannot support the full surgical services and the required support services mandated by the state licensing requirements.

As a result, the Rural Health Care Commission in Washington State recommended that its rural hospitals be examined, and that licensure requirements be made more flexible to improve cost efficiency. Florida has already amended the definition of a rural hospital (an acute-care facility with 85 or fewer beds and an emergency room) to ease licensure requirements. Montana has created a new licensing category for Medical Assistance Facilities, which provide care to persons needing immediate care for no more than 96 hours before discharge or transfer to a hospital. These licensing changes were necessary to counteract previous policies, which had created duplicate services and high costs, leading to hospital closures.

Although CON has been amended or discontinued in many states, rural hospitals still covered face difficulties with the regulation. Complaints about the high filing and consultant fees and the time involved to meet compliance are frequent. On the other hand, CON can assist rural hospitals by decreasing the number of satellite services opened by urban hospitals, which then compete with rural hospitals. While debate continues, some states, notably Florida and Washington, are easing their requirements. Florida exempts hospice or home health services provided by a rural hospital from CON requirements, and the CON application fee. State legislation in Washington, Senate Bill 5180, also exempts rural hospitals from certain CON requirements (Fisher et al. 1989).

The major focus of the RWJ program is to encourage configuration of the rural health-care delivery system through consortia. A networking approach has provided member hospitals with access to more services and specializations through sharing agreements. The Alabama consortium, which currently shares services among 3 county hospitals, is in the process of adding 4 more counties. The South Carolina consortium is developing shared services among 2 groups of hospitals: 1 with 2 hospitals and the other with 4. To date, joint data processing, billing, and laundry services have been implemented, resulting in decreased operating costs.

As state policymakers realize the advantages of shared services, programs will be initiated to assist with coordination. For example, in New York the Cooperative Programs and Networks for Health Care Delivery in Underserved Rural Areas established a grant program to restructure the rural health-care delivery system. The emphasis is on long-range coordination of service delivery. Already 7 projects have been funded and an additional 6 more will be funded (Alabama Department of Public Health 1989) in areas such as staffing and bed conversion.

The Northeast Mississippi Rural Health Consortium, which was funded by RWJ until December 1989, was in the process of implementing a facility conversion program. The goal was to convert underutilized acute-care beds to long-term or adult day-care beds. Due to a moratorium on number of nursing home beds allowed in Mississippi, the consortium first had to negotiate with the state. In mid–1989, after overcoming this obstacle, the consortium successfully converted 137 acute-care beds to long-term-care use. With this changeover, costs have been decreased, efficiency increased, and, ultimately, the needs of the community are more readily served. It is hoped that states will realize the benefits of supporting rural hospital restructuring in lieu of closure.

Technical Assistance. With the many policy changes occurring in rural health care, hospitals need technical assistance to form consortia to carry out innovative new programs. Consortia are at an advantage in doing this when member hospitals can specialize in and coordinate one area of technical assistance. For example, the Nevada Rural Hospital consortium members provide technical assistance in various areas. These include developing model quality assurance and physician peer review programs, implementing a model community relations program, and assisting with licensure and strategic planning activities. These programs have assisted in promoting their institutions and in educating their communities about the services they provide.

The West Texas Rural Health Consortia provides technical assistance in the form of a peer support network. This network is comprised of various member hospital administrators who act as consultants. As a team, they make site visits to participating hospitals and offer assistance to strengthen the financial stability, share information, enhance the quality of care, and strengthen the management, board, and community relations. In some cases, this helps the hospital stay open. During the visits, the peer support network members meet with the rural hospital administrator, fiscal manager, and director of nursing. Observations and recommendations are made before the team leaves the site so that information is timely and available for use. Examples include enhancing revenues by increasing room rates and changing the combination of services offered, decreasing costs by negotiating new purchase agreements and utilizing personnel more efficiently, and enhancing the hospital worksite with aesthetic and technological improvements. By making changes on the basis of peer support network recommendations, 86 percent of the hospitals visited during the first 12 months increased their revenues.

A similar technical assistance program is being implemented by the Rural Wisconsin Hospital Cooperative (RWHC). The Financial Management Program coordinates meetings among the consortium members' financial officers. They discuss common concerns, problem-solving techniques, and new legislation, in roundtable fashion. Through the project, a "benchmarking" process has been implemented to identify and replicate "best practices," among the RWHC member hospitals such as for billing patients. This exchange of ideas has resulted in improved Medicare reimbursements, cash flows, and operating cost margins.

The Wisconsin Consortia has another program—Quality-of-Care. With full participation of the member hospitals, this program has collected and provided data on generic outcome indicators and quality indicators on various hospital services, such as emergency care, respiratory therapy, and physical therapy. The consortium also acts as a centralized credentialing agency, and approximately 95 physicians have been granted hospital privileges through this process. Because of this program, Wisconsin hospital administrators and state hospital association members have heightened their awareness of the need for high quality-of-care standards. In turn, the consortium has formed the Physician Quality Assurance Committee, and the Wisconsin Hospital Association has established a Data Quality Task Force.

These technical assistance programs demonstrate the advantages to rural hospitals of forming consortia. Alone, each hospital may not have all of the knowledge, ideas, or critical judgment on issues important for their survival. Together, each consortium becomes an "interest group force" capable of changing and influencing state policymakers. Providing technical assistance in planning and management to rural hospitals and their communities is a low cost state-level solution. Other such solutions include developing a state plan to identify troubled hospitals and financially support them, and developing more flexible state regulations on the basis of the rural hospitals' needs. States such as Colorado, Illinois, North Carolina, North Dakota, Wyoming, and Wisconsin have developed state Offices of Rural Health to implement these "solutions."

DEMONSTRATION PROGRAMS

Although demonstration programs can support various approaches to the rural hospital problem, little funding of such demonstrations is under way by states. Hospitals, in areas other than the demonstration site, may resist the project unless it is available for all hospitals in the state. Also, under current fiscal conditions, there is lack of state monies to fund such demonstrations. Some alternative models, such as medical assistance facilities, are being developed in California under state legislation, and may result in more projects being funded. Demonstrations are needed to make reconfigurations in rural hospitals more feasible, to link rural hospitals with secondary- and tertiary-care centers, and to encourage development of rural emergency-care systems.

Federal demonstrations for rural hospitals have focused on assisting rural hospitals with meeting community needs through financing and conversion mechanisms. In 1989, the Rural Health Transition Grants Program was initiated. Its purposes are to provide funding to rural hospitals with fewer than 100 beds and to assist in implementing change strategies. Health Care Financing Administration (HCFA) oversees this program, and has had difficulty evaluating the programs funded by the $85 million given to hospitals in 1989. Congress has extended the supply of these grants, in spite of the burden on HCFA in overseeing the 182 existing grants. As previously mentioned, flexibility in rural hospital structure must be considered in relation to the needs of the community and the hospital. Other demonstrations, such as swing beds, assist rural hospitals in changing their status from full-service acute-care providers to structures that reflect the community's use.

RECOMMENDATIONS

Much can be learned from the Robert Wood Johnson demonstration consortia. Programs that are seen as successful must be publicized at the state level. In turn, states should realize that in the long run, these measures will help rural hospitals to survive.

The following recommendations, based on experiences with the 13 rural hospital consortia and rural hospital initiatives across the country, are made:

1. States should provide financial and technical assistance to restructure the rural health-care delivery system in order to meet a community's needs most economically and equitably; and

2. rural hospitals should enter into cooperative relationships and form regionalized health-care systems. (Kovner, Runde, & Kiel 1990)

Both states and hospitals must communicate with each other to reach feasible solutions. This may result in some hospital closures, but in turn, it will strengthen the remaining ones. After rural hospitals make their needs known to the state, planning and implementation of alternatives must be undertaken, including both financial and technical assistance. This assistance has been initiated in several states through legislation to enhance physician recruitment by sponsoring medical students and enacting loan forgiveness programs. Several states have opened Offices of Rural Health to focus on the critical issues.

The importance of regionalization and affiliation among rural hospitals is seen in the "strength in numbers" approach. As demonstrated by the RWJ consortia, community needs can be met and financial stability achieved through cooperation. By promoting cooperation instead of competition, rural hospitals can adjust their financial and clinical focus according to the needs of the hospital and the community. They can work together to change legislative priorities of state hospital associations. They can also expand the leverage of community and hospital leaders. It is strongly recommended that states provide incentives, such as the federal transition grants, to enable their local health-care organizations to form affiliations, regional relationships, or other working agreements with larger medical centers. This would help to preserve access to locally needed primary and emergency care, while forming sufficient volume through shared services. Future research and evaluation need to be completed on regionalization, on the effect of state policy changes in support of rural health care, and on the costs and benefits of alternate hospital structures.

12. Developing a Rural Health-Care Agenda for the Future

Larry T. Patton

For rural health-care advocates, the late 1980s were years filled with great promise. After a decade of apparent indifference, federal and state policymakers began to refocus attention toward rural health-care issues. A plethora of rural legislative initiatives have been enacted at the federal and state levels. For example:

the United States Senate established a rural health-care caucus;

the United States House of Representatives established a rural health-care coalition;

the United States Department of Health and Human Services established an Office of Rural Health Policy; and

half the states established an office or focal point for rural health.

This frenzy of activity in the public sector has been mirrored in the private sector. It is reflected in the growth of the National Rural Health Association, a proliferation in the number of statewide meetings, and in the establishment of several state rural health associations. It can also be seen in the activity of a number of the nation's major philanthropic organizations, such as the Robert Wood Johnson Foundation, the W. K. Kellogg Foundation, the Northwest Area Foundation, the Colorado Trust, and the Wesley Foundation, which have developed rural health-care initiatives.

Clearly, rural health is now one of the top issues on the public policy agenda. In fact, the current level of interest may even exceed that of the Rural Renaissance of the early and mid–1970s, the last period in which rural health-care issues captured the attention of policymakers. However, just as in that earlier era, there is no guarantee that policymakers will continue to accord rural health such a high priority in the decade ahead. No matter how favorable recent experience has been, rural advocates must recognize that there is always the possibility that new or recurring issues may move to the forefront at any time.

Although it is not possible to control the public policy agenda, advocacy groups can play a crucial role in assuring that rural America benefits from current opportunities. The effectiveness of these advocacy groups, however, hinges on how well they understand the public policy process, how well they articulate the problems of rural America, and on the scope of the agenda being promoted.

Successful rural advocacy requires more than the mere generation of new legislative or regulatory agendas. Increasing numbers of rural communities face challenges to the organization, structure, and delivery of health-care services in their communities that will not be remedied by facile changes in federal or state policy. An essential focus then is the rural community itself and its struggle to meet external pressures for change.

This chapter proposes that strategies must place as much emphasis on the process of change at the community level as they do on the public policy process. The following sections offer observations on both the public policy process and on the forces of change now at work in many rural communities.

THE PUBLIC POLICY PROCESS

The confluence of events in recent years has provided the rural health-care community with its best opportunity in more than a decade to influence the course of public policy. However, the very success of rural advocates in the last few years necessitates the adoption of a much more sophisticated approach. Unfortunately, the very nature of the public policy process can easily lead advocates to squander their best opportunities. In addition, the evolution of federal policy and the experience of the Rural Renaissance of the 1970s provided key lessons for today's rural advocates. The sections that follow examine both.

The Nature of the Policy Process

For most advocates, the major challenge is to maneuver their issue(s) onto the public policy agenda. For the rural health-care community, the major challenge is managing the public policy process now that their issue has moved to center stage. This is often the more difficult task. The reality is that the public policy process can often prove to be a two-edged sword.

Once set in motion, the process often develops a momentum of its own, generating demands for new ideas and quick solutions to the crisis at hand.

The challenges only escalate with success. As an issue becomes more politically attractive, the number of legislative players increases. Instead of making enactment of an agenda easier, the reverse is often the case. Not only is there an increase in the number of players who must be consulted on every measure, there is also an increase in the number of players who will seek a leading role in resolving the crisis at hand. This creates even more pressure on advocates to develop legislative proposals so that each participant can have ownership of a specific "solution" to the crisis.

This dynamic is clearly recognizable in recent years; its dangers are just as obvious. First, it becomes too easy to focus on short-term, quick-fix initiatives. The need to feed the public policy process continually with new proposals encourages fragmentation. It quickly becomes easier to dust off every old program whose funding has expired and every interest group's pet project, instead of fashioning initiatives with greater long-run potential.

Second, advocates often become mesmerized by their legislative successes; legislative freneticism easily becomes confused with progress. Although the process encourages the creation of a myriad of new initiatives, such activity, by itself, does not constitute an agenda. The challenge is to move beyond legislative laundry lists of narrowly targeted uncoordinated programs to the promotion of a comprehensive vision.

Finally, in a seeming paradox, legislative success can undermine a movement. For example, rural hospitals have been an important source of strength and leadership in the revival of interest in rural health issues in the 1980s. Now that Congress has enacted one of the movement's highest priorities, the phasing out of the differential in Medicare's urban and rural hospital base payment rate, will they display the same level of interest and support for less prominent issues? Only time will tell.

This, then, is the public policy process, and it serves as an important backdrop for the review of federal policy that follows.

The Evolution of Federal Policy

The current crisis in rural health care is, in many ways, a continuation of a long-term historical trend. During most of this century, rural America experienced population decline and migration of younger workers to urban areas. The rural health-care infrastructure has been steadily eroded by the growth in technology and medical specialization, and the decreasing economic strength of rural areas, all of which have served to concentrate health-care resources in more affluent urban areas (U. S. Congress, Senate, 1988; Rosenblatt & Moscovice 1982). There has been a radical transformation in the response of the public policy process to these developments. In the early part of this century, with the exception of a few grants-in-aid programs, the federal government did little to arrest the deterioration of the rural health-care system. This "hands-off" policy reflected the then dominant view of federalism: activities, such as health, that were not specifically assigned to the federal government by the Constitution, were the exclusive responsibility of the states.

This assumption began to change with the enactment of the Social Security Act in 1935 and, during the next three decades, the federal government tentatively entered the health-care policy arena. The first federal initiative to impact rural communities was the Hill-Burton Act adopted in 1946. Although not exclusively a rural initiative, this landmark legislation underwrote a major transformation of the health-care delivery system in many rural communities, supporting the construction, modernization, or expansion of more than 1,500 rural hospitals and, in later years, ambulatory-care facilities. During the ensuing 3 decades, the federal government played an increasingly strong role in health care, but public policy initiatives remained generally deferential to the role of the states. Indirect grants-in-aid programs channeled through state health departments were the norm (U. S. Congress, Senate, 1988).

The final transformation in public policy occurred in the mid–1960s, when the federal government committed itself to a major and direct role in improving access to health care for the poor and medically underserved populations. Medicare and Medicaid were enacted to improve financial access to health care for the elderly and the poor; categorical programs, providing direct support for the education of health professionals and the establishment of a variety of health centers, represented efforts to improve the health-care infrastructure. At the same time, the federal government took its first tentative steps toward the promotion of planning and regional systems of health care for nonurban areas with the creation of the Regional Medical Program and Comprehensive Health Agencies.

Although Medicare and Medicaid significantly improved financial access to health care for many rural residents, these programs tended to institutionalize the lower fees that were paid to rural physicians and thus contributed little to rural provider recruitment or retention. The categorical programs initiated during the mid and late 1960s tended to have a distinctly urban, rather than rural, orientation. Even the regional medical program was perceived as overly focused on urban-based academic medical centers. Thus, as the 1960s drew to a close, there was a growing feeling among rural legislators that these new federal programs had not treated rural America equitably.

The Rural Renaissance

This lack of attention to the concerns of rural America set the stage for the health policy activism that characterized the early and mid–1970s, a period that is now known as the Rural Renaissance. It was a period of renewal for rural America on nearly every front. Reversing the historical trends of a century, the rural population began to grow; surprisingly, the fastest growth took place in smaller rural communities (Rosenblatt & Moscovice 1982). Concomitantly, nearly all sectors of the rural economy began to prosper.

It was during these years that the federal government's increasing willingness to intervene directly to improve access to health care moved into high gear, as summarized in Table 12.1. The decade began with the enactment of the National Health Service Corps; at the same time, the Congress redirected the regional medical program toward issues of access in medically underserved rural and urban areas. In subsequent years, a series of programs focused on rural America were enacted, such as Area Health Education Centers, and older programs, such as community health centers, were greatly expanded.

By the mid–1970s, however, there was increasing concern about the fragmented and uncoordinated nature of the programs that had been developed. In response, a series of initiatives—the Rural Health Initiative (RHI), the Health Underserved Rural Area (HURA) program, and the National Health Planning and Resources Development Act—were established. However, before these efforts could achieve full potential, the political climate changed radically: competition replaced regulation and planning as the political paradigm of choice, the population and economic growth of the early and mid–1970s came to a halt, and public policy interest in rural America began to wane. These factors, combined with predictions of a physician surplus (U. S. Department of Health and Human Services 1981) and studies demonstrating increasing physician diffusion into rural communities (Schwartz et al. 1980), strengthened the Reagan Administration's arguments to end federal intervention. Consequently, many of the programs enacted during the Rural Renaissance were significantly scaled back during the early 1980s, although surprisingly few were eliminated outright.

Yesterday and Today

The current resurgence of interest in rural health was triggered by the precipitous decline in profit margins of smaller rural hospitals in the mid–1980s, when many sectors of the rural economy experienced (or only gradually recovered from) severe economic distress (U. S. Congress, Senate, 1988). By contrast, the starting point for the Rural Renaissance had been an atypical period of population and economic growth for rural America. Considerable energy in the 1970s was channeled into development of programs that addressed short-term crises. For example, concern with shortages of physicians and midlevel practitioners led to programs such as the

Table 12.1
Federal Rural Initiatives

Availability of Hospital Resources

The Hill-Burton Program	1946-1974
Medicare Sole Community Hospital Program	1972-1983
(As revised by Prospective Payment System)	1983-present

Availability of Health Personnel

Health Professions Student Loans/Loan Forgiveness	1965-present
The National Health Service Corps	1970-present
Area Health Education Centers	1972-present

Availability of Ambulatory Care Facilities

Migrant Health Centers	1962-present
Community Health Centers	1965-present
Rural Health Initiative	1975-present
Health Underserved Rural Areas	1975-1981
Rural Health Clinics Act	1977-present

Health Planning and Regionalization

The Hill-Burton Program ("318" agencies)	1964-1974
Regional Medical Program	1965-1974
Comprehensive Health Planning Program	1966-1974
Experimental Health Services Delivery Systems	1971-1974
The National Health Planning Act	1974-1987

Source: Patton and Puskin 1990.

National Health Service Corps. With minor exceptions, these programs failed to address the prerequisites of successful rural practice. These prerequisites include equitable reimbursement, overcoming provider isolation and assuring back-up coverage, and, in the case of midlevel practitioners, issues of eligibility for reimbursement and scope of practice. As a result, provider retention rates have been low, and, coupled with the failure of the projected physician diffusion in smaller rural communities, desperate shortages of personnel continue in many areas.

Even when policymakers did attempt, in the 1970s, to promote coordination, regionalization of health services, and the development of health systems, these efforts often served only to strengthen the hostility of rural communities to planning and coordination. Given the inherent individualism of many rural providers, this result is not very surprising. Rural communities believed, with considerable justification, that planning imposed by the federal government favored larger, urban-based providers who had the necessary personnel and resources to circumnavigate the bureaucracy and paperwork the process imposed. Their experience with the initial set of draft guidelines for the implementation of the National Health Planning Act of 1974, which would have closed the majority of rural obstetrical units, simply confirmed their view. As a result, much of the movement toward regionalization that took place during these years occurred without regulatory intervention (Rosenblatt & Moscovice 1982).

In the last few years, much energy was also expended toward short-term, narrowly targeted, provider-focused amendments that often reflected political, rather than policy, considerations. (A comprehensive list of legislation is in the Appendix to this chapter.) However, legislative initiatives are beginning to emerge that are designed to ensure the long-run financial viability of rural health-care providers. These include the following:

- the phasing out of the differential in Medicare's base payment rate to urban and rural hospitals;
- the adoption of a Medicare fee schedule for physicians based upon a resource-based relative value scale (RBRVS) that promises significant increases in the fees of primary-care physicians, who constitute the majority of rural providers;
- Medicare bonus payments for physicians practicing in medically underserved areas;
- an increase in the cost-based payment ceiling for Medicare and Medicaid payment of rural health clinics; and,
- the extension of a similar payment system under Medicare and Medicaid for community health centers receiving support from the Public Health Service as well as some of their nonfederally funded counterparts.

A second small but important group of initiatives is beginning to address the issue of restructuring rural health-care services, on both an intracommunity and intercommunity basis. The first move in this direction, the Rural Hospital Transition Grant Program, was intended to assist rural hospitals restructure services and focus to serve communities better. In theory, this program can help rural communities in developing a more appropriate mix of health-care facilities, thereby improving financial viability.

The Medical Assistance Facility (MAF) demonstration program in Montana, funded by the Health Care Financing Administration, is one step toward the development of an alternative hospital model. The Essential Access Community Hospitals (EACH) and Rural Primary Care Hospitals (RPCH) demonstration program goes even further by assisting in the development of an organized system of care across several communities in a region or state.

These developments are important because they have the potential to address long-run questions of financial viability for rural health-care providers. In addition, the seriousness with which these programs are taken in many rural areas suggests that profound changes are taking place at the provider and community levels.

FORCES OF CHANGE AND THE RURAL COMMUNITY

An encouraging aspect of these developments is that they are bringing together a host of individuals—rural health-care providers, payers, consumers, and policymakers—within rural communities, which traditionally have too little contact with one another. This is a welcome departure from past custom.

The individual components of the health-care system, even in rural communities, have been too compartmentalized. The locus of activity for providers frequently is the trade association rather than the community. Furthermore, all too often, local or regional rivalries between communities or long-standing feuds between providers or institutions have contributed to provider isolation. Moreover, the experience of many rural communities and providers with health planning and regionalization initiatives in the 1970s merely reinforced these tendencies.

Against this background, a quiet revolution is at work. At the provider level, rural hospitals are increasingly redefining their concept of autonomy in the face of current economic pressures. For years stoicism was the prevalent attitude, but during the past decade, there has been an inexorable move toward new types of alliances. Today, nearly 40 percent of rural hospitals belong to some form of multihospital system (Rosenberg & Runde 1988). Many also participate in more flexible types of alliances that have sprung up in recent years in an attempt to achieve economies of scale. The dimensions of this trend are reflected in the Robert Wood Johnson Foundation's (RWJ) experience with its Hospital-Based Rural Health Care solicitation in 1987. To help achieve an objective of linkages among institutions, RWJ indicated that it would not accept applications from individual hospitals.

The importance of these developments is not reflected in the mere formation of alliances among rural hospitals; nor does it derive from the immediate activities generated by such short-term adaptive strategies. The central point is that these arrangements afford rural providers something less tangible but of much greater significance: concrete experiences through which rural administrators are developing a new sense of trust and confidence in cooperative arrangements. As Tim Size, executive director of the Rural Wisconsin Hospital Cooperative, has argued, trust among providers is the ultimate prerequisite if fundamental changes in existing organizational arrangements are to be successful (Size 1990). Trust among rural health-care providers, although necessary to the timely undertaking of new ventures, is delicate. Development of complex systems requires collaboration and trust, and is inhibited by demands for proof or underwriting at each stage. Impediments, such as the high rate of turnover among rural hospital administrators, mean that the process of building trust needs constant attention. Nevertheless, the development of new types of alliances, such as rural hospital consortia, in which rural hospitals voluntarily participate, may ultimately prove to be an essential step in the evolution of rural health-care delivery systems.

Important changes are also taking place at the community level. Increasingly, rural communities are challenged to shift from a provider-based focus to a community-level perspective. Then, the question is no longer, "How can we save the local hospital?" Instead, the starting point becomes "What is the most appropriate mix of facilities and services to meet the community's needs, given the realistic prospects for recruitment and retention of health-care personnel?"

Many rural communities will conclude that maintaining their existing hospital is the appropriate course of action and will take steps to shore up its financial viability through diversification or better definition of its role. In some cases, communities will conclude that the role of the hospital should be substantially changed or eliminated. Once the decision is made to abandon the traditional hospital, attention can turn to developing an entirely new focal point for the local health-care delivery system.

THE PROCESS OF CHANGE

At the community level, the process of local assessment and change will be the central issue for many rural communities in the 1990s. As Bob Van Hook, executive director of the National Rural Health Association, has noted, two critical changes are essential if new models are to be implemented successfully: (1) rural communities must change their expectations of services from rural hospitals; and (2) rural physicians must change their expectations of the hospital's role in serving their practice needs (Van Hook 1989). His observation is equally applicable to the need for hospital administrators and boards of trustees to change their own expectations and self-images.

However, little is known about how communities and providers can alter their expectations and performance. One demonstration, the Colorado Trust's Rural Healthcare Initiative, is beginning to shed light on this topic. This demonstration has three goals: (1) to promote regionalization (to eliminate hospital underutilization and unnecessary duplication of services); (2) to promote systems development (to address advanced health-care services that cannot be provided economically or safely at Colorado's rural hospitals); and, (3) to enhance and demonstrate the quality of services in rural hospitals (Nowlan 1990).

As the Colorado Trust discovered, the process for change is not easily initiated, even when there is widespread consensus within a community that the existing health-care organizational arrangements cannot survive. They found the availability of grant funds was an important incentive and motivator and that successful change also appears to hinge on education, information, and the development of personal trust among the prime actors (Nowlan 1990). The process can be hindered by a variety of conditions, including doubt as to motives of the proponents of change (i.e., motives tend to be questioned if the proponents of change will benefit by the change), a lack of clarity of the problem to be addressed, insufficient data on the problem and potential solutions, a lack of consensus on the desired outcome or if a sense of interdependence among the key actors is not present.

Translating these "negatives" into affirmative guidelines for community action is a step in the right direction, but it is clearly necessary to identify other communities that have gone down this path. Communities that have undertaken a communitywide debate to examine their experiences critically can act as models. They can guide other rural communities to better understand both the prerequisites for successful community dialogue and the pitfalls that should be avoided.

THE MOVE TOWARD A BROADER PERSPECTIVE

Rural hospitals, and indeed rural communities, are beginning to learn the vital lesson of the 1980s: "You can't go it alone! We're in this together!" The rapid transformation that engulfed medical practice and the business of medicine in the last decade, played out against a backdrop of federal and state budget constraints, make this point abundantly clear. Resources are simply insufficient to allow for rural communities to consider the needs of their hospital, their primary care providers or their long-term care providers in isolation.

It is also abundantly clear that it is difficult for rural communities to embark upon the process of change. The pathway for change is ill-defined, local leadership is often undeveloped, and the levels of trust necessary for widespread, fundamental restructuring of the rural health-care delivery system have yet to be achieved.

Defining the Role for State and Local Advocates

Given these trends and the current evolution of public policy, how should organizations, such as state rural health associations, proceed with defining their role and developing an agenda for the decade ahead? There is no single, appropriate approach, but there are several guidelines.

1. A Dual Focus is Essential. The role of an organization must be as broad as resources will allow. For example, state associations can be both "honest brokers," providing an important forum for education and information, and "catalysts for change," helping to forge linkages among the diverse participants in rural communities.

2. Never Lose Sight of the Goal. In pursuing public policy objectives, the balance of short-, medium-, and long-term initiatives in the agenda must be constantly reassessed. The gold standard, of course, is a measure that will enhance the long-term financial viability of rural health care, or one that will facilitate fundamental change in rural communities. In addition, medium-term initiatives, such as measures that support the testing of alternative models of care, can play an important role. Although political expediency and true crises will lead to the support of a number of short-term initiatives, this opportunity to influence the public policy process will be squandered if an agenda is not weighted to initiatives of medium- and long-term worth.

3. Education is a Primary Role. Rural health associations and advocates must give high priority to the education of policymakers. The issue is not solely that the majority of health policymakers are from urban or suburban areas, but turnover among federal policymakers, and among hot issues makes education a continuing priority. Similarly, there has been increasing turnover in key civil service positions, eroding institutional memory at many levels of the federal and state governments.

Thus, there is a growing number of policymakers at all levels of government with little or no exposure to the rural health initiatives of the 1970s, who have little understanding of what has worked and what has not. Therefore, one of the prime missions must be continuous education of policymakers through the presentation of the results of scientifically based research studies.

4. Articulate a Vision. It is necessary to provide policymakers with an articulate overview of the problems of delivering health care in rural America and with a vision for the future direction of public policy. This vision must be broad-based. The overview should not be limited to health care per se. Rather, underlying issues, such as rural economic development, which have an important impact on the viability of health services as well as in the rural community must be recognized and incorporated. Regardless of what form a future national health-care system takes, it needs to be clear how the rural health-care system fits into the broader picture. Budgetary constraints will continue for the foreseeable future and policymakers are increasingly concerned with the rational allocation of resources, irrespective of geography.

5. Determine Essential Access. It is important to recognize that for most health policymakers, the federal government's primary role in this area is to assure access to health care, not to subsidize rural institutions. Thus, the issue for them is not saving rural hospitals, or any other single aspect of the rural health-care delivery system, but rather, it is trying to identify when essential access to health care is threatened. However, there is little consensus regarding what constitutes essential access or essential institutions, and even old definitions of medical underservice are being reexamined.

Long-run success in the policy arena requires a shared concept (by policymakers and advocates) of the appropriate federal and state roles. It is necessary to apply this framework in making "rural" arguments for specific federal interventions.

6. *Quality Health Care is Key.* The viability of rural health-care institutions rests, in large measure, on adequate reimbursement and the ability to attract patients. In turn, the attraction of patients rests upon the ability of rural health-care institutions to convince local residents that they provide quality care and deserve their patronage. All too often rural providers have become defensive when Medicare, Peer Review Organizations, or other regulatory bodies have attempted to enforce quality standards. Quite frankly, the enhancement of quality of care should be the keystone of advocacy efforts.

As policymakers review evidence that a high percentage of rural residents are bypassing local institutions for nonemergent care, the perception is growing that there is a quality problem in rural institutions. It is not clear whether this concern reflects a true problem or merely an unjustified perception on the part of rural residents. Moreover, it is not always clear whether the portrait painted by these numbers is accurate. For example, the number of rural residents seeking tertiary care that could not have been provided at the local rural hospital in any event, should be factored out. Additional research in this area is needed.

Research examining the relationship between patient volume and patient outcomes, for the conditions most commonly treated by rural hospitals and rural providers, could yield practical advice for how rural hospitals can best build on their strengths. The Medical Treatment Effectiveness Program (MedTep) of the new Agency for Health Care Policy and Research (AHCPR) will be a central focus for this type of research.

Rural health associations should take the lead in developing a regional and statewide dialogue among all health-care providers on how quality of care can best be assured and enhanced. Such efforts would help improve patient care and the viability of rural institutions, while at the same time enhancing the credibility of the state association, in the policy arena.

7. *Recognize the Fragility of Special Programs.* Organizations and associations should be wary of placing too much emphasis on the creation of rural initiatives that are dependent upon the vagaries of the yearly

appropriations process. This approach can be very useful for testing new models or approaches for improving access to care in limited rural areas. However, if the goal is to enhance the long-term financial viability of the health-care system, the focus must be on assuring equity—not subsidy—in reimbursement and entitlement programs. It is important to note that the private sector increasingly follows the federal government's lead in the area of provider reimbursement, and it is that type of system reform that will yield long-term improvements.

8. Avoid Separate but Equal. A corollary to the previous point, and it is bound to be controversial in some circles, is that the ultimate goal of rural health advocacy should not be the creation of a series of special programs or set-asides for rural providers. Although these approaches can be politically expedient in the short-run, the end point of rural advocacy should be the development of federal initiatives that have sufficient flexibility to accommodate the unique aspects of rural as well as inner-city health-care delivery.

While the concept is easier to articulate than operationalize, but "purposeful flexibility" is an approach to policy that recognizes the need for purposeful federal action—federal quality, access, and cost standards—while affording greater flexibility in the development of organizational structures and process measures that are appropriate under differing circumstances. It is easy to envision purposeful flexibility as the starting point for a new dialogue over federal and state regulatory structures.

CONCLUSIONS

Clearly, the status quo in health care cannot be maintained in many rural communities; forces and constraints are at work that are simply beyond their direct control. At the same time, rural health care is ultimately a local affair and the process of change must have its roots in the rural community itself. This suggests that any strategy that does not place as much emphasis on the process of change at the community level as it does on the public policy process will ultimately prove inadequate.

If rural communities are to gain any control over the forces of change and their direction, all elements of the rural health-care community must be brought into a broader dialogue on the future of rural health care. Although such a dialogue cannot be imposed from above, organizations such as state rural health associations can provide a forum to help rural communities better understand the process of change, by learning from one another. Through such actions, it is also possible to promote the development of trust and mutual respect among providers. These are important prerequisites for innovative joint ventures.

Finally, in developing and framing a vision for the future, rural advocates must avoid parochialism. With the surprising resurgence of interest among policymakers in the broader issue of restructuring our national health-care system, rural advocates will increasingly be challenged to explain how their vision accords with systemwide reform.

This chapter has attempted to identify key lessons from the public policy process to guide in developing a rural health agenda for the 1990s. The list presented is not exhaustive; additional considerations will emerge. However, this chapter provides a starting point for the type of strategic planning that must take place.

Appendix: Recent Rural Health Care Legislation

Omnibus Budget Reconciliation Act of 1986 (P. L. 99-509)

1. All hospitals received a Prospective Payment System (PPS) rate increase of 1.15 percent, effective 10/1/86.
2. Create separate pools from which to pay urban and rural outliers. Urban hospitals, having more outliers, are required to contribute larger amounts to their pool, while rural hospitals, having fewer outliers, contribute less.
3. Provides for case weighted rural and urban averages in determining the average costs in setting PPS amounts. Beginning FY1988, the average will be calculated on a case-weighted, rather than a hospital-weighted, basis, thereby better reflecting the higher costs of higher volume hospitals.
4. Extends through cost-reporting periods beginning in FY1988, the volume protection provision for sole community hospitals (SCHs).
5. Excludes SCHs from reductions in capital payments.
6. Authorizes disproportionate share payments to rural hospitals of 500 beds or more that exceed a set minimum percentage of low income patients (set by the Secretary); payment on the same basis as qualifying urban hospitals with more than 100 beds.
7. Extends periodic interim payments (F I P) for rural hospitals with fewer than 100 beds. Allows accelerated payments to PPS ho–pitals with significant cash flow difficulty.
8. Places criteria for rural referral center designations in statute and allows more hospitals to qualify.
9. Requires Secretary to submit a legislative proposal by October 1988 that would improve PPS treatment of outlier cases and variations in severity of illness/case complexity.

Balanced Budget and Emergency Deficit Control Reaffirmation Act of 1987 (P. L. 100-119)

1. Provides rural hospitals with a 3 percent update in PPS rates effective 10/1/87; by contrast, large urban hospitals receive 2.5 percent, other urban hospitals, 1 percent.
2. Hospitals located in a rural county adjacent to an SMSA can be counted as urban depending upon the commuting patterns of county residents; rates of urban hospitals will be adjusted to accommodate this change; rates paid to hospitals retaining a rural classification will not be lowered.
3. Extends swing bed provision to rural hospitals with 50-100 beds, provided that they discharge patients in need of skilled nursing care to a SNF (Skilled Nursing Facility) within 5 days if a SNF bed is available.
4. Permits hospitals receiving SCH status (and thereby qualifying for volume adjustment payments) to continue to receive 100 percent national PPS rates if they prefer.
5. Lowers to 275 beds (from 500) the threshold for designation of a hospital as a rural referral center, thereby receiving urban hospital rate.
6. Establishes Rural Hospital Transition Grant program, providing up to $50,000 per year for 2 years, to assist hospitals in modifying services or mission.
7. Requires Secretary to report on impact of outlier payment changes.
8. Requires ProPac to report on desirability of phasing out urban-rural differential.
9. Establishes rural health medical education demonstration project.

Appendix (continued)

10.   Physicians practicing in class 1 or 2 shortage areas will receive 5 percent bonus payments.
11.   New physicians in rural shortage areas will have their customary payment rate set at 80 percentile (not 50th percentile) of area prevailing charge.
12.   Increases rural health clinics' maximum payment from $32.10 to $46.00/visit.
13.   Psychologist services may be reimbursed in rural mental health clinics and direct reimbursement permitted at community mental health centers is authorized.
14.   Peer review organizations (PROs) are directed to take into account special problems associated with delivering care in rural areas and at least 20 percent of rural hospital reviews are to be on-site.
15.   Provides statutory authorization for Office of Rural Health Policy.
16.   Requires rural impact analysis of Medicare/Medicaid rules and regulations.
17.   Requires set aside of 10 percent of Health Care Financing Administration's (HCFA's) demonstration funds for rural projects.

Omnibus Budget Reconciliation Act of 1989 (P. L. 101-239)

1.   Update for rural hospitals of market basket + 3 percent (total of 9.17 percent), effective 1/90.
2.   Extends all current rural referral designations for 3 years.
3.   Those with < 100 beds and > 60 percent of patient discharges from Medicare will be higher of: 1) 100 percent hospital-specific rate based on higher of 1982 or 1987 base year costs or 2) PPS rate.
4.   Lowers SCH distance criteria from 50 to 35 miles: hospitals have same payment option as #3 above.
5.   Authorized $10 million Essential Access Community Hospitals/Primary Care Hospitals (EACH/PeaCH) demonstration.
6.   Establishes geographic classification review board to review requests from hospitals seeking "urban" designations.
7.   Requires ProPAC to study cost-based reimbursement option.
8.   Requires PhysPRC to study rapid growth in Medicare outpatient payments.
9.   Requires Health and Human Services (HHS) to study adequacy of ambulance service reimbursement.
10.   Requires Secretary HHS to submit legislation eliminating urban-rural differential by 1995.
11.   Provides 10 percent bonus payments for all physician services in any Health Manpower Shortage Area.
12.   Expands number of rural health medical education demonstration projects from 4 to 10 by 6/90.
13.   Continues pass-through for Certified Registered Nurse Anesthetist (CRNA) costs; raises procedure limit to 500 from 250.
14.   Phases in Resource Based Relative Value Scale (RBRVS) over 5 years starting 1/92; full Medicare update for primary care services by 1/90.
15.   Reduces required physician assistant/nurse practitioner coverage in rural health clinics to 50 percent; extends coverage to nurse midwives and clinical social workers.

Appendix (continued)

Omnibus Budget Reconciliation Act of 1990 (P. L. 101-508)

1. Phase-out of the urban-rural hospital differential by FY1995.
2. Rural hospitals receive an updated payment rate of market basket minus 0.7 percent.
3. SCHs, rural primary care hospitals, and essential access community hospitals are exempted from 15% inpatient and outpatient capital cost reductions.
4. Requires Secretary to use updated 1988 area wage index data in computing hospital payments as of January 1991.
5. Deadline for applications by hospitals seeking geographic reclassification extended 60 days after the guidelines have been published.
6. Requires the Secretary to collect data on input prices to develop a non-labor cost index.
7. Directs ProPAC to include in its annual reports recommendations related to payment of rural hospitals, especially on issues related to access to care.
8. In designating the 15 Rural Primary Care Hospitals, the Secretary shall give priority to hospitals that are not in a grantee state but that are participating in a rural hospital network in a grantee state; also authorizes designation of hospitals that closed within the last 12 months and met conditions of participation at time of closure.
9. Requires Secretary to report by April 1, 1992 on the impact of Medicare regulations on PPS hospitals to determine if they could be made less burdensome on rural hospitals without diminishing quality of care; the review must include staffing standards.
10. For the transition to physician payments based upon RBRVS, increases the lower limit for prevailing charges for primary care services from 50% to 60% of the national average prevailing charge.
11. Extends under RBRVS existing exemption for primary care services and services furnished in a rural health personnel shortage area from charge limits that apply to new physicians.
12. SCHs and primary care hospitals are exempt from reductions imposed on capital costs related to outpatient services.
13. All clinical laboratory tests provided in all settings, except rural health clinics, must be provided on an assigned basis.
14. Nurse practitioners and clinical nurse specialists in rural areas will receive direct Medicare Part B reimbursement for services they are authorized to provide under state law or regulation; effective 10/17/90.
15. Requires a General Accounting Office study of the ability of community and migrant health center physicians to obtain admitting privileges at local hospitals.
16. Payments to community/migrant health centers and programs for the homeless will be reimbursed on an all-inclusive rate under Medicare, effective 10/1/91; certification process for rural health clinics will be expedited and waivers will be available to clinics that have been unable to meet the rules requiring a physician assistant, nurse practitioner, or certified nurse midwife to furnish services at least 50% of the clinic's operating time.

Sources: Omnibus Budget Reconciliation Act of 1986, 1989, and *1990, Balanced Budget Emergency Deficit Control Reaffirmation Act of 1987,* and Patton 1991.

13. Rural Society—the Environment of Rural Health Care

Edward W. Hassinger and Daryl J. Hobbs

Discussions of rural health care usually emphasize the deficit in the number of health-care providers and problems in the organization of the health-care system. Passing reference is sometimes made to the rural environment or to rural/urban differences affecting health and health care. Yet, as every health worker knows, and as this volume demonstrates, the rural environment is a key aspect of health care. Too often, this aspect of the equation is neglected.

This chapter, therefore, examines the diversity and uniqueness of the American rural socioeconomic environment with emphasis on the implications for health and the health care of rural people.

THE RURAL CONTEXT

One fourth of the nation's people, spread over 95 percent of its land surface, is identified as rural. Rural residents, and the groups they form, have become an integral part of the larger society (Vidich & Bensman 1968). However, everyday activities, such as making a living, getting an education, and obtaining health care, are not played out at the societal level. These are community activities, and it is at the community level that rural populations exhibit a degree of unique social integration.

Therefore, we must recognize a two-tier rural social, economic, and service context—the larger national and even global environment, and the local community. The two-tier concept helps us to understand better the great social, economic, and spatial diversity of contemporary rural America. Rural communities, and the health care, education, and other services they provide are not autonomous. These services and the institutions responsible for providing them are generally linked to national systems that exert a great influence over them. Understanding today's rural communities requires taking elements of the larger society clearly into account. It also requires a consideration of the unique characteristics of the various rural communities and of how these communities relate to, and are affected by, the larger national institutional sectors.

A two-tier interpretation of the rural environment fits well with the provision of rural health care. Health-care policies, technology, professional training, and a major part of reimbursement for services are provided extralocally. In obtaining health care, however, the community represents a significant link between the individual (family) and the larger society. Even if actual services are located outside the community, they are often initiated and expedited (as with emergency health services) in the community, and patients return to the community where continuing health care is rendered by local providers and families. Whether this linkage works well, and therefore whether adequate and appropriate health-care services are available and accessible to rural people, is a key issue.

RURAL TO NONMETROPOLITAN

Most of the rural population data come from the United States Census of the Population and intervening population surveys. Population in incorporated and unincorporated places of 2,500, or larger, and in densely populated areas around large cities, has traditionally been defined as urban; the remainder has been counted as rural. However, the more recent categorization of the population as metropolitan or nonmetropolitan—based on the United States Office of Management and Budget's designation of Metropolitan Statistical Areas (MSA)—is widely used. An MSA consists of a central city of 50,000 population or more (with some qualifications) and the county in which it is located; it may also include adjacent counties that have a highly urbanized population and are a part of the economic complex of the central city. Using this classification, major cities have become centers of metropolitan regions, incorporating multiple counties. The metropolitan–nonmetropolitan classification has official status and is used extensively as a basis for federal policy and administration of federal programs. The classification has often worked to the disadvantage of rural providers; for example, federal policy directs a higher Medicare reimbursement rate for metropolitan physicians and hospitals than for their nonmetropolitan counterparts.

Although the metropolitan and nonmetropolitan designations have gained official status, they are not without drawbacks. Statistically, nonmetropolitan includes everything from isolated and extremely small ranching communities in the West to small cities having a population up to 50,000. Thus, the "rural" umbrella is very large.

DIVERSITY OF RURAL SOCIETY

Social and economic changes during the past three decades have contributed to metropolitan areas becoming more similar, while nonmetro areas have become more economically specialized and therefore more dissimilar from each other. Efforts have been made to disaggregate rural society by examining regional socioeconomies. This is useful in some contexts; however, rural diversity extends to a finer level, with significant variations between communities, even within the same county.

Social scientists in the United States Department of Agriculture (USDA) have made a major effort to classify nonmetropolitan counties according to the principal source of their economic base, the presence of federally owned land, and population characteristics (Bender et al. 1985). Counties were used for this typology because they are the smallest unit for which most nonmetropolitan data are reported.

Their classification of nonmetropolitan counties and a brief description of each follows.

1. Farming-dependent counties (702 counties, 29 percent of total nonmetro counties). These counties are principally located in the upper Midwest and Plains states. Most lost population during the 1980s.

2. Manufacturing-dependent counties (678 counties, 28 percent of total nonmetro counties). These counties are concentrated in the Southeast and Northwest. They became manufacturing counties in 1950–80, as industries relocated from cities to rural areas, largely because of cheaper labor.

3. Mining-dependent counties (200 counties, 8 percent of total nonmetro counties). These counties are concentrated in the coal fields of Kentucky and West Virginia and in the energy-producing areas of the West.

4. Specialized government counties (315 counties, 13 percent of total nonmetro counties). These counties are generally the location of a military base, state university, or another major state or federal activity. They are quite uniformly dispersed across the nation and most have a growing population.

5. Persistent poverty counties (242 counties, 10 percent of total nonmetro counties). These counties are concentrated in the South, especially in the Mississippi Delta and in parts of Appalachia. They also include many Native American reservation counties. Most have a high concentration of minority population.

6. Federal lands counties (247 counties, 10 percent of total nonmetro counties). These counties, all located in the West, are generally sparsely populated but grew in population during the 1980s.

7. Destination retirement counties (515 counties, 21 percent of total nonmetro counties). These counties attract retirees, relocating because of environmental amenities or lower cost of living. Retirement counties gained population during the 1980s.

Of the 2,443 nonmetropolitan counties in the 48 contiguous states, all except 370 are included in at least 1 of these 7 county groups.

The county groups are not mutually exclusive, but overlaps among them are not considered serious; 57.3 percent of the counties belong exclusively to one group. Another 22 percent are in two of the seven groups, leaving only 6 percent in three or more groups. The ungrouped counties represent another 15 percent. (Bender et al. 1985, p. 2)

This typology of counties, of course, does not exhaust the possibilities for grouping rural areas into socially and economically meaningful clusters. Even counties falling within only 1 of the 7 USDA categories reflect widely varying conditions of economic production and social organization. In its examination of the impact of technological and structural changes in agriculture on rural communities, the Office of Technology Assessment (OTA) divided the nation into 5 distinct agricultural regions: Northeast, South, Midwest, Great Plains, and CATF (California, Arizona, Texas, Florida) (U.S. Congress, Office of Technology Assessment 1986a). The CATF region includes 98 counties dominated by large-scale industrial type agriculture. The criteria for inclusion of counties were that they ranked either in the top 100 counties nationwide in sales of agricultural products, or that they had $2,000 or more per capita income from agriculture. Ironically, many of these top-producing (CATF) agricultural counties are classified as metropolitan.

The OTA analysis confirms that, even among rural counties classified as agricultural, there is wide variation in social, economic, and demographic characteristics, which affect the need for, and the provision of, health-care services.

On the basis of the information in this section, it is clear that a high level of rural diversity exists. The extent to which diversity affects or should affect the delivery of basic services, such as health care, is a question for further investigation.

UNIQUE FEATURES OF RURAL SOCIETY

Despite regional and local diversity in rural America, there are distinctive features of the rural environment. This segment of the chapter examines three of these features and their impact on health care: size and density of population and its effect on social organization and group relationships; economic deprivation; and center/periphery relationships.

Size of Communities and Density of Population

Population density is the basis for the classification of counties as either metropolitan or nonmetropolitan, urban or rural. From the standpoint of delivery of health-care services, one implication of population density is that it usually costs more per capita to provide these services to dispersed populations. There is an added cost to users as well, since they must typically travel farther to obtain services.

However, in addition to the economics of space, low and high density population communities differ in organization. On the basis of differences in community size and population density, Dewey (1960) identifies five organizational characteristics on which rural and urban communities differ. In rural communities, there is less anonymity, less division of labor, less heterogeneity in population, as well as fewer impersonal and prescribed relationships and fewer symbols of status that are independent of personal acquaintance.

The small size of rural communities and organizations facilitates greater informality in relationships of all kinds. Related to the pattern of informal relations are volunteerism, a relatively low tolerance for conflict, and a distrust of experts. In the latter case, experts tend to represent outsiders exhibiting professional norms; furthermore, they are often cast in the role of implementing unpopular state and federal programs or forcing compliance with their regulations. Despite this, Sokolow (1982) points out that professionals and experts are used increasingly in rural communities. It has become a feature of the two-tier system: a necessity for outside support and the regulations that accompany it, but a desire to retain local control.

The two-tier characteristic of the rural social and service organization is increasingly a source of conflict within the rural locality, despite a widely held impression that rural communities decide and do things by consensus. Advocates of growth and change can be found within most rural communities, alongside those who retain a commitment to traditionalism and preservation of the status quo. A study by Cummings, Briggs, & Mercy (1977) examined rural community conflict concerning textbooks used in the schools. In this case, the school symbolized conflict between the local and the mass societies, with traditionalists perceiving the school as an alien institution staffed and controlled by outside experts. Padfield (1980) suggests that these conflicts may be intractable, citing an inherent contradiction between "growth fundamentalism" and "rural fundamentalism."

The apparent tranquillity of rural communities can be deceptive. The preference for informal ways of doing things often creates an impression of consensus, although dissension may lie beneath the surface and erupt in response to some precipitating event or issue. Communities must be able to deal with change and conflict. Indeed, Flora & Flora (1988) found that one characteristic of thriving Midwest farm communities was their acceptance of conflict. During the Hill-Burton era of growth in health-care services, there was little conflict over health-care issues within rural communities. In the current era, however, of constrained health resources and competition among providers, this issue can become a focus of conflict.

For example, agreement on increasing local taxes to retain a hospital may vary among groups according to age, income, and mobility.

Economic Deprivation and Dependency

Although rural Americans are not generally perceived as wealthy, there is a widely held image of rural areas as a stronghold of the good life. Although this may be true for many rural residents, contemporary facts do not correspond with the images. Data reveal that nonmetro median family income is 36 percent less than metropolitan family income, and that nonmetro income has been increasing only 38 percent as rapidly as metro income (U.S. Bureau of the Census 1989a). The principal contributing factor is that higher-paying occupations are disproportionately located in metro areas, and lower-paying occupations are disproportionately located in rural areas (Falk & Lyson 1988).

The metro–nonmetro income differential has persisted for a long time and has been a major factor in the long-term trend of young, more highly educated rural youth migrating to metropolitan areas to live and work. The historical prominence of that trend was emphasized in *The People Left Behind*, a report of the National Advisory Commission on Rural Poverty in the 1960s. The report characterized the rural poor as those who lacked the resources, skills, education, and mobility to relocate from areas of low employment or low-paying employment to areas of higher income and employment (National Advisory Commission on Rural Poverty 1967).

A much greater incidence of poverty continues to be a distinguishing characteristic of rural America. Data on poverty for 1987 reveal that 18 percent of the nonmetro population, compared with 12 percent of the metro population, lived below the poverty line (U.S. Bureau of the Census 1989b). Furthermore, the rural poor were more likely to be the working poor; 70 percent of the rural families living below the poverty line had at least one employed worker, and 40 percent of the families had two or more employed (Greenstein 1988).

The implications of poverty for health and health-care services are immense. Many health indicators for populations of the persistent poverty counties are far above both rural and national norms (Clarke & Miller 1990). Perhaps most grievous is the health status of rural poor children, who are affected by poor nutrition, inadequate prenatal care of mothers, and a shortage of child-related health-care services. Compounding the problem, especially for the working poor, is inadequacy of health insurance coverage. Rural workers tend more often to work for small businesses and to receive lower wages. Data show that only 17 percent of workers in small businesses, of less than 25 employees and earning less than $5 per hour, had employer-provided health insurance coverage (U.S. Small Business Administration 1987). By comparison, 77 percent of workers employed by such firms but making more than $10 per hour had employer-provided health insurance coverage.

The greater incidence of poverty and low-income clearly affects rural health status, both the need for care and the financing of that care. Furthermore, rural areas are populated by a larger and growing elderly population who have a greater need for health care and reduced mobility. Lack of mobility becomes more critical when health-care services are at a greater distance from home, as they are for many rural residents.

Center/Periphery Relationships

Change in settlement patterns. Within the nonmetropolitan population, there is great variation in size of places and density. Frontier counties are those with 6 or fewer persons per square mile; in 1980, there were 394 such counties covering 45 percent of the United States' land area. Alaska is 96 percent frontier, as are 80 percent of Nevada, 55 percent of Utah, 41 percent of Montana, 27 percent of New Mexico and Oregon, and 24 percent of Nebraska (*Rural Health Care* 1986; Hewitt 1989).

Great Plains states and Alaska have many frontier population counties, although most of their population is concentrated in urban places. It seems paradoxical that in low population states, such as Wyoming and Alaska, a high proportion of the population is counted as urban.

The relationship between center and periphery populations and the interdependence between rural and urban areas have long been a focus of demographers, human ecologists, and economic geographers. Many of the early ideas are relevant today. For example, 40 years ago, Kraenzel (1953) analyzed this population pattern in the Great Plains and was especially concerned with the social and economic costs of space. He called the more densely populated areas, which were concentrated along major transportation routes, the Sutland, and the sparsely settled areas, the Yonland. The problem, as Kraenzel saw it, was that the Yonland does not have the population base necessary to maintain a full range of institutional services. At the same time, services are organized on a limited areal basis as part of the cultural holdover from the Eastern settlement pattern. Kraenzel saw a need to adapt service patterns to the settlement patterns.

[There] is also a need for integrating the Sutland and the Yonland, and proper division of labor for many services. Certain services must be made to reach out from the Sutland to the Yonland in mutually accommodating form. For other services, there must be an adapted counterpart in the Yonland that is properly integrated from the Sutland headquarters. (P. 358)

In the Yonland, Kraenzel found generalists providing first level services, with more specialized services concentrated in the Sutland.

In more densely settled Eastern states, services traditionally were provided in trade centers that have a hinterland service area. Galpin (1915) delineated the trade and service areas of rural communities by observing that rural trade centers were quite evenly distributed geographically. They served hinterland populations engaged mostly in the agriculture industry, organized as family farms. The service areas of the several institutional organizations in the trade centers (schools, churches, retail stores, health facilities) could be quite precisely drawn, with clients/customers depending on local services for the most part. There was a strong tendency for trade centers to be similar to each other in the type and range of services they provided. Since agricultural production and providing services to an agricultural population were the principal economic activities, and since transportation was slow and limited, employment was generally confined to the boundaries of the community service area. Thus, the trade-center communities became the location for meeting most economic and service needs. It was in this setting that the solo practicing family doctor found a place.

Very importantly, communities in this era retained a high degree of control over their services and institutions. In addition, close interpersonal relationships strengthened residents' community identity. Literally, residents felt a sense of ownership. This was a period labeled by Dillman & Beck (1988) as the "era of community control." However, as they emphasize, the era of community control was to be supplanted in the period from the 1920s to the 1970s by the emergence of the mass society.

Mass society gave birth to the two-tier rural communities of today. Trade centers have lost their exclusive trade areas, and they have become quite differentiated in the goods and services they offer. Employment of residents is no longer confined to community boundaries. At the same time, scholars have noted a regularity in location of trade centers of different service levels, with services patterned in a hierarchical manner (Christaller 1933, Berry 1967). Thus, simple convenience services (for example, bread, milk, and gasoline) are offered in many locations, while highly specialized services (for example, open heart surgery) are offered in few. Rural consumers now travel widely for goods and services, especially such services as specialized health care.

These changes reflect a massive shift in both the structure and the social and economic environments of institutional organizations. Settlement patterns have taken the form of "larger communities," usually consisting of a larger town or small city that serves as a regional center for a perimeter of smaller towns (satellites), which combine to form a more or less complete service complex. Many community-level organizations, including health-care services, have not survived the shift to a regional trade-center pattern. They have either closed for lack of business or have been consolidated into a larger organizational entity. Problems of service delivery often revolve around the adjustments being made to these locational and organizational shifts. The adjustment regarding health-care services is sensitive, due to the nature of the product and unpredictability of need.

EXTRALOCAL/LOCAL RELATIONSHIPS

Organizations in modern rural communities are inextricably connected with extralocal organizations (Warren 1978). An unresolved question is whether the rural component is simply merging with the larger society toward the urbanization of rural society, or whether a core periphery relationship is a better description.

Local organizations serving rural populations often have necessary but dependent relationships with large-scale organizations at the state and national levels. Bureaucracies in the larger society impose certain accountability and competency (competency in the bureaucratic model) requirements on local organizations in exchange for financial and technical support. Thus, the structure of local organizations tends to be created in the image of the outside bureaucracy. The bureaucracy that administers the Medicare program, for example, requires certification of participating hospitals. This involves quality control, monitoring, and detailed record keeping, which place burdens on rural institutions not able to utilize scale economies in responding.

In some respects, competency in local organizations relates to size. Large-scale organizations often find it inefficient and difficult to deal with very small local units. Such units may lack the resources for good record keeping and may lack the norms of organization that reflect those of the bureaucracy with which they are dealing. Furthermore, in the view of bureaucracies, it is relatively inefficient to deal with a large number of small units, when fewer, larger units could serve the same population. Therefore, consolidation of local organizations is often advocated by large scale bureaucracies, in the name of efficiency, accountability, and competency.

There is likely to be uneven power in relationships between local and extralocal organizations. Extralocal organizations are usually the initiators of the programs or projects undertaken. They establish rules according to their vision; they command major resources, and they have expertise in administration not matched at the local level. In such arrangements, there is the possibility, and certainly the perception, of exploitation of the local entity.

THE EVOLUTION TO INFORMATION SOCIETY

In Dillman & Beck's (1988) analysis, reorganization of rural services into rationalized and hierarchically structured service complexes was a part of the transformation of rural areas from community control to the mass society. Rural services became increasingly professional and more integrated into the national systems characterizing the mass society. They describe this process of rural transformation as follows:

Hierarchies became the model for businesses and social service agencies. Local representatives reported to regional representatives and so on up the corporate ladder. The federal government increasingly extended its reach in American life, from education to transportation.... Rural communities were no longer isolated from urban centers. Relative economic independence was replaced with tight knit interdependence. (P. 29).

These authors contend, however, that the era of the mass society, and its basic principles of specialization, centralization, and standardization, are declining, as a new era—an information era—is ushered in. The information era is driven by advances in communications technology. "Dramatic improvements in computers and telecommunications are enhancing our ability to identify, sort, retrieve, transmit, create and apply information" (Dillman & Beck 1988, p. 30). In this period, information is an added resource and substitutes for other resources. Information technology has facilitated the emergence of a global economy, which affects the nation's farms and each of the different economic bases of rural communities. For example, many factories, which relocated to rural areas during the 1960s and 1970s, are again relocating to other countries attracted by even cheaper labor there.

The information age portends great changes for rural community service relationships; it provides more options for communities and places more responsibility on them. There are increasingly greater opportunities for communities to shape their own futures and reconsider traditional ways of providing rural services. In the era of the mass society, the dominant strategy was to further centralize and consolidate rural services, to make them more "efficient." Thus, rural people experienced added costs in obtaining health, education, and other services, as they were forced to travel farther. Information technologies make it possible to transport the service—for example, diagnostic images or health-care training—rather than the people. However, although these alternatives can restructure the provision of rural services, they also increase the possibility of greater external dependence for rural people and communities.

Dependence, whether in an information era or a mass society era, is largely an issue of control. If a rural community has little control over its services and simply has services extended to it by the institutions of the larger society, there are several possible adverse effects. One is the possibility that the services may not be appropriate to local needs. Services designed for application to a mass society may not meet the specific needs of unique rural communities. A second consequence is the effect that dependence has on a community's ability to act on its own behalf. If a community becomes dependent on services, frequently a sense of powerlessness follows; that powerlessness often extends in to other realms of community life as well (Luloff 1990). Indeed, these consequences of rural community dependency are the basis for many analysts' emphasis on a great need for rural community development (Wilkinson 1986).

Because one era does not entirely displace another, the service patterns of the community-control period persist to some degree. In health services, this is exhibited in the nostalgia for the personal community family physician and the independent community hospital, which together "belonged" to the community and provided most medical services.

Mass society principles, to a greater extent, remain evident and dominant in the current health-care system. Health services represent a clear example of a hierarchy of services: primary-care services consisting of family doctors are widely distributed; more specialized secondary services, typically found in community hospitals and associated clinics, are in fewer locations; and tertiary health services, involving superspecialists practicing in medical centers are found in relatively few locations. There is an expectation, although not always realized, that these various levels of service are coordinated to provide a logical progression of services to a population. The regionalization of services—the loose coordination of differentiated services within a given area—describes these relationships (Hassinger 1982). However, achieving real coordination of these services to provide effective, appropriate, and affordable care remains a central issue in the delivery of rural health services.

The information era is only emerging; its effects on the health-care system could be profound. Information technologies could facilitate more effective coordination between the various levels of service and therefore could reduce travel time and cost for rural consumers. The technologies could facilitate greater decentralization of services, by electronically connecting local practitioners with necessary specialized support services. The technologies could pave the way for incorporation of more primary-care professionals, such as nurse practitioners, to be more widely dispersed among the population. However, the health-care system's greater utilization of, and dependence on, technology could also contribute to health care becoming more hierarchical and more geographically concentrated in larger centers, which have more of the technological equipment of modern medical care. The tendency toward greater concentration and centralization of services appears to be continuing despite the technological potential for greater decentralization (Clarke & Miller 1990). Meanwhile, traveling substantial distances to specialized health-care services remains a part of the process of obtaining health care for most rural residents.

COMMUNITY RESPONSE

The response of rural communities to health-care issues depends on their size, economy, and strategy for engaging the health-care system. Some nonmetropolitan communities are large enough to attract a sufficient number of physicians, and other practitioners of midlevel specialization, as well as community hospitals with usual secondary level services. Places in the range of 10,000 to 50,000 may be among the most attractive locations for many physicians. In such locations, there may be problems in delivery of services, but they are problems common to the entire health-care system, not unique to rural communities. The maldistribution of physicians and other health services is a more significant problem for smaller communities and those in more isolated areas. Many parts of rural America are at least a two-hour drive from a place of even 10,000 population.

Communities need not be passive in relationships with institutional organizations of the larger society. They can organize and act on their own behalf. Talent and resources exist in rural communities; the goal is to organize and utilize them to provide a high quality of life. Rural communities start with an advantage, because in surveys, both rural and urban respondents report a preference for rural communities as places to live (Zuiches 1982). Stereotypes of rural life must be translated into quality-of-life conditions in order for that preference to be sustained. People should have access to basic services, including health services. This does not mean, however, that the full range of health and medical services needs to be located in every rural community. It does mean that people should have clear and reliable points of access to the health-care system.

In the coming "information era," an approach open to rural people is illness prevention and wellness promotion. Major advances in control of heart disease, for example, have been made through information translated into changed behavior. A wide range of health subjects could be addressed, and different age and occupational groups could be targeted. The National Coalition for Agricultural Safety and Health (1989) emphasized the importance of education in overcoming the safety and health problems of agriculture, the nation's most hazardous occupation.

Public schools are a ready resource in health education initiatives, as is the Cooperative Extension Service associated with each state's land grant university. Education should also provide consumers with information about gaining access to services and judging quality of services, especially for those located outside the community.

Moscovice (1989b) enumerated several principles for a viable rural health-care system. Among them is the need for empowerment in rural communities as they confront the larger health-care system.

It is important that the locus of control for rural health remain in the local community. Aggressive competition from urban-based providers will be particularly harmful if it leads to the one-way flow of patients out of rural communities, the unnecessary closure of rural hospitals, the acceleration of economic problems in rural areas. (Pp. 219–220)

As Moscovice suggests, regaining some degree of local control will be important in devising appropriate and effective responses to rural health-care problems.

Many analysts contend that there is a need today for creativity and innovation in devising methods and approaches for providing essential services to rural areas. Castle (1986), for example, has observed that rural institutions have remained remarkably faithful to the purposes they were created to serve, but the times and problems have changed, and there is a need for new models and new ideas. Many of those initiatives will likely be produced by the rural communities themselves, but only if they are organized to act effectively on their own behalf.

Some power could be gained by organizing available local health-care services into a more comprehensive health center. This would bring together health practitioners and health facilities, both private and public, in a common location. It would be more feasible to provide emergency services from such a location. The center might be the location of some ancillary health-care services such as senior citizens activities, child care, and preventive health education. A more comprehensive center might also provide extended and home health care. Programs from the center might be able to tap the resources of experienced elderly persons in providing health services; a valuable service would be assistance in filing Medicare claims.

The issue of rural health care is one of quality of life. The health-care system represents the technology and organizational forms of the larger society—the second tier. The community represents long-standing and normative relationships among people in local settings as they carry on their daily activities—the first tier. Potentially, communities have the resources to bring a degree of control to the provision of and access to health services. This becomes a vital element in efforts to produce a high quality of rural life in a two-tier society.

Bibliography

Acadian ambulance honored. 1990. *Management Focus* 6:3 (Fall): 3.

Ahmed, Kazi, and Kyle Muus. 1991. Comparison of metro and non-metro nurse practitioner characteristics. *Focus* 8:1 (Spring): 6–7.

Alabama Department of Public Health. 1989. *Survey of state activities*. Montgomery: Task Force on Rural Health.

American Hospital Association. 1989. *Hospital closures 1980–1988: A statistical profile*. Chicago: American Hospital Association.

———. 1990. *The future of rural health*. A draft report: Section for small or rural hospitals. Chicago: American Hospital Association.

American Medical Association. 1986. *Physician characteristics and distribution*. Chicago: American Medical Association.

American Osteopathic Association. 1988. *Yearbook and directory of osteopathic physicians: 1987–1988*. Chicago: American Osteopathic Association.

Amundson, Bruce. 1991. Medical schools responsible for shortages. *Rural Health Care* 13:5 (May): 8–9.

Andersen, Ronald. 1968. *A behavioral model of families' use of health services*. Research Series 25. Chicago: Center for Health Administration Studies, University of Chicago.

Andersen, Ronald A., Allen McCuthcheon, Lu Ann Aday, Grace Chiu, and Ralph Bell. 1983. Exploring dimensions of access to medical care. *Health Services Research* 18:1 (Spring): 50–74.

Anderson, Paul B. 1981. The Idaho statewide EMS communications center. *Emergency Medical Services* 10:4 (July/August): 7–13.

———. 1984. Idaho's statewide communications network. *Fire Chief* (November): 28–30.

———. 1990. *Mobile trauma training unit (MTTU) manual*. Lincoln, Neb.: Rural EMS Institute, Lincoln Medical Education Foundation.

Anderson, Paul B., Richard S. Bennett, Joseph V. Henderson, Jerome A. Hirschfeld, and Michael G. Nichols. 1990. Interactive technology—EMS training goes on line in Idaho. *Journal of Emergency Medical Services* 15:10 (October): 34–38.

Anderson, Paul B., Donald R. Bjornson, and M. Wayne. 1982. Telelecture: providing effective continuing education—an innovative approach to training in rural America. *Journal of Emergency Medical Services* 7:3 (March): 41–44.

Anderson, Paul B., K. J. Neuman, and G. R. Trimble. 1986. Trauma in the country—A statewide approach to trauma skills training for rural EMTs. *Journal of Emergency Medical Services* 11:3 (March): 61–64.

Balanced Budget and Emergency Deficit Control Reaffirmation Act of 1987, P.L. 100–119, 101 Stat. 754.

Banahan, Benjamin F., and Thomas R. Sharpe. 1982. Evaluation of the use of rural health clinics: knowledge, attitudes, and behavior of consumers. *Public Health Reports* 97:3 (May/June): 261–68.

Bateman, Kim. 1991. Technology-driven referrals, a fundamental problem for small rural hospitals. *The Journal of Rural Health* 7:2 (Spring): 95–100.

Bauer, Jeffrey C., and Eileen M. Weis. 1989. Rural America and the revolution in health care. *Rural Development Perspectives* 6:2 (June): 2–6.

Bauer Group. 1991. Survey of rural residents, 1984–1991. Hillsboro, Colo.: The Bauer Group.

Baxt, William, and Peggy Moody. 1983. The impact of rotocraft aeromedical emergency care service on trauma mortality. *Journal of the American Medical Association* 249:22 (June): 3047–51.

Beardsley, E., and G. Davis. 1989. *Interactive videodisc and the teaching–learning process*. Bloomington, Ind.: Phi Delta Kappa Education Foundation.

Bender, Lloyd D., B. L. Green, T. F. Hady, J. A. Kuehn, M. K. Nelson, L. B. Perkinson, and P. J. Ross. 1985. *The diverse social and economic structure of nonmetropolitan America*. Rural development research report, no. 49. Washington, D.C.: USDA, Economic Research Service.

Berk, Marc, Amy Bernstein, and Amy Taylor. 1983. The use and availability of medical care in health shortage areas. *Inquiry* 20:4 (Winter): 369–80.

Berry, Brian J. L. 1967. *Geography of market centers and retail distribution*. Englewood Cliffs, N.J.: Prentice-Hall.

Bishirjian, Terry. 1989. Rural health care in the 1990s: decade of decision and change. *Appalachia* 22:2 (Spring): 31–37.

Blendon, Robert J., Robert Leitman, Ian Morrison, and Karen Donelan. 1990. Satisfaction with health systems in ten nations. *Health Affairs* 9:2 (Summer): 185–92.

Boeder, Syl. 1988. Issues facing rural health care finance. In *Financing rural health care*, edited by LaVonne Straub and Norman Walzer, pp. 25–42. New York: Praeger.

Bronstein, Jane M., and Michael A. Morrisey. 1990. Determinants of rural travel distance for obstetrics care. *Medical Care* 28:9 (September): 853–66.

Bruce, Thomas Allen. 1985. How do we prepare providers: physicians. *The Journal of Rural Health* 1:1 (January): 18–21.

———. 1990. Professional preparation for rural medicine. *The Journal of Rural Health* 6:4 (October): 523–26.

Butler, Patricia A. 1988. *Too poor to be sick: access to health care for the uninsured*. Washington, D.C.: American Public Health Association.

Carr, W. J., and Paul J. Feldstein. 1982. The relationship of cost to hospital size. In *Issues in health economics*, edited by Roger D. Luke and Jeffrey C. Bauer. Rockville, Md.: Aspen Publications.

Castiel, D. 1990. Emergency service via mobile satellite. Paper presented at the Rural EMS Communications Workshop, the National Association of State EMS Directors (NASEMSD), Washington, D.C., May 1990.

Castle, Emery. 1986. Rural institutions for the future. In U.S. Congress. Senate. Joint Economic Committee. Subcommittee on Agriculture and Transportation. 1986. *New directions in rural policy: building upon our heritage*. 99th Cong., pp. 523–28. Washington, D.C.: U.S. Government Printing Office.

Chiu, Grace, Lu Ann Aday, and Ronald A. Andersen. 1981. Examination of the association of "shortage" and "medical access" indicators. *Health Policy Quarterly* 1:2 (Summer): 142–58.

Christaller, Walter. 1933. *Central places in southern Germany*, translated by C. W. Baskin. Englewood Cliffs, N.J.: Prentice-Hall.

Christianson, Jon B., Ira Moscovice, Judy Johnson, John Kralewski, and Colleen Grogan. 1990. Evaluating rural hospital consortia. *Health Affairs* 9:1 (Spring): 135–61.

Chute, Alan G., and James D. Elfrank. 1990. *Teletraining: needs, solutions and benefits*, p. 4550. Washington, D.C.: ITCA Teleconferencing Yearbook.

Cigler, Beverly A. 1991. *Meeting fiscal challenges in the 1990s: innovative approaches for rural local governments*. Harrisburg, Penna.: Center for Rural Pennsylvania.

Clarke, Leslie L., and Michael K. Miller. 1990. The character and prospects of rural community health and medical care. In *American rural communities*, edited by A. E. Luloff and Louis E. Swanson, pp. 74–105. Boulder, Colo.: Westview Press.

Cline, K. A. 1990. Rural trauma and EMS; where we were, where we are, and where we need to be. *Emergency Care Quarterly* 6:1 (May): 11–17.

Cochran, Carole, and Sharon Ericson. 1989. *Innovations in rural health care systems*. Grand Forks, N.D.: University of North Dakota, The Center for Rural Health.

Congressional Record. 1975. 94th Cong., 1st sess. 1975, Vol. 121, pt. 174.

Cordes, Donald. 1991. Personal correspondence with John Williamson, M.D., executive director, Interwest Quality of Care, Inc., Salt Lake City, Utah.

Cordes, Donald L., and LaVonne A. Straub. 1992. Changing the paradigm of rural health care delivery. In *Rural health care: innovation in a changing environment*, edited by LaVonne A. Straub and Norman Walzer. New York: Praeger.

Cordes, Samuel M. 1989. The changing rural environment and the relationship between health services and rural development. *Health Services Research* 23:6 (February): 757–84.

Council on Long Range Planning and Development, American Academy of Family Physicians. 1988. The future of family practice: implications of the changing environment of medicine. *Journal of the American Medical Association* 260:9 (September 2): 1272–79.

Coward, Raymond T. 1987. Poverty and aging in rural America. *Human Services in the Rural Environment* 10:4: 41–47.

Crandall, Lee. A., Jeffrey W. Dwyer, and R. Paul Duncan. 1990. Recruitment and retention of rural physicians: issues for the 1990s. *The Journal of Rural Health* 6:1 (January): 19–38.

Cronson, Robert G. 1991. *Availability of obstetric care in Illinois*. Springfield, Ill.: Office of the Auditor General.

Cummings, Scott, Richard Briggs, and James Mercy. 1977. Preachers vs. teachers: local–cosmopolitan conflict over textbook censorship in an Appalachian community. *Rural Sociology* 42:1 (Spring): 7–21.

Deavers, Kenneth L., and David L. Brown. 1984. A new agenda for rural policy in the 80's. *Rural Development Perspectives* 1:1: 38–41.

Defibrillation by EMTs: concept endorsed by the American College of Emergency Physicians. *ACEP Policy Summaries,* 1991 edition, pp. 26–27. Dallas: American College of Emergency Physicians.

DeFriese, Gordon H., and Thomas C. Ricketts. 1989. Primary health care in rural areas: an agenda for research. *Health Services Research* 23:6 (February): 931–74.

Dettelback, Mark S. 1988. Rural areas still need physicians. *Journal of the American Medical Association* 260:21 (December): 3214–15.

Dewey, Richard. 1960. The rural–urban continuum: real but relatively unimportant. *American Journal of Sociology* 66:1 (July): 60–66.

Dillman, Don A., and Donald M. Beck. 1988. Information technologies and rural development in the 1990s. *Journal of State Governments* 61:1 (January/February): 29–38.

Doekson, Gerald A., and Deborah A. Miller. 1987. Rural physicians make good economic sense. Paper presented to the National Rural Health Association, Nashville, May 1987.

Dunning, Becky. 1989. Interview: Speaking personally with E. Marie Oberle, *The American Journal of Distance Education* 3:1: 75–79.

Emergency Medical Services Systems Act of 1973 (P.L. 93–154), 87 Stat. 594.

Ermann, Dan A. 1990. Rural health care: the future of the hospital. *Medical Care Review* 47:1 (Spring): 33–73.

Eye on Orhion. 1991. *Newsletter* 1:2 (March): 1–3. Oregon Health Sciences University, Biomedical Information Communication Center.

Falk, William W., and Thomas Lyson. 1988. *High tech, low tech, not tech: recent industrial and occupational change in the South*. Albany, N.Y.: State University of New York Press.

Fassbach, Scott. 1990. OBRA '90—the FY 1991 budget and beyond. *Health Care Briefing,* newsletter from the accounting firm of Ernst & Young, 14:2.

Federal Register. 42 CFR 5, 1991. National Archives and Records Administration, Washington, D.C.

Fickenscher, Kevin. 1985. *Rural considerations in Medicare reimbursement policy for physician services*. Grand Forks, N.D.: The Center for Rural Health Services, Policy and Research, University of North Dakota.

Fiedler, John L. 1981. A review of the literature on access and utilization of medical care with special emphasis on rural primary care. *Social Science and Medicine* 15C: 129–42.

Fink, Arlene, Elizabeth M. Yano, Robert H. Brook. 1989. The condition of the literature on differences in hospital mortality. *Medical Care* 2:4 (April): 315–36.

Fisher, John J. 1984. Continuing education when you need it most. *Medical Economics* 61:19 (September): 140–48.

Fisher, Rhona S., Elizabeth Donohoe, Michelle Solloway, and Susan Laudicina. 1989. *Interim report 1989 laws*. Programs of interest to the health resources and services administration. Washington, D.C.: George Washington University, Resources and Services Administration.

Flora, Cornelia, and Jan Flora. 1988. Characteristics of entrepreneurial communities in a time of crisis. *Rural Development News* 12:2 (April). Ames, Iowa: North Central Regional Rural Development Center.

Florida Statute § 395.01465, 1989.

Freeman, Howard E., Robert J. Blendon, and Linda H. Aiken. 1987. Americans report on their access to health care. *Health Affairs* 6:1 (Spring): 6–17.

Frels, Lois, and LaVonne Straub. 1991. The role of education in reducing rural shock. Paper presented to the National Rural Health Association, Seattle, Wash., May 1991.

Gabel, Jon, Howard Cohen, and Stephen Fink. 1989. Americans' view of health care: foolish inconsistencies? *Health Affairs* 8:1 (Spring): 103–18.

Galpin, Charles J. 1915. *The social anatomy of an agricultural community,* Research bulletin, no. 34. Madison, Wis.: University of Wisconsin Agricultural Experiment Station.

Garza, Marion Angell. 1990. Virginia program retrains EMTs by TV satellite. *EMS Insider* 17:7 (July): 2.

Gibbens, Brad. 1991. Rural health legislation of the 101st Congress. *Focus* 8:1 (Spring): 4–5.

Gibbens, Brad, and Daron Olson. 1990. *Rural health professional shortages: legislative strategies*. Grand Forks, N.D.: The University of North Dakota Rural Health Research Center.

Golladay, F. L., and B. H. Liese. 1980. Rural health care looks to the future issues in the institutionalization and management of rural health care: making technology appropriate. *Proceedings of the Royal Society of London.* Series B: *Biological Sciences* 209: 1174: 173–80.

Greenstein, Robert. 1988. Barriers to rural development. Paper presented to Annual National Rural Electric Cooperative Managers' Conference, August, Baltimore, Md.

Ham, K. 1991. Early defibrillation leads to survival increase; goes statewide in Pennsylvania. *American Heart Association and Citizen CPR Foundation Newsletter* 2:1 (Spring): 4.

Hart, Darrell. 1989. Reducing nurse turnover. *Healthcare Forum Journal* (May/June): 37–41.

Hart, Gary, Roger Rosenblatt, and Bruce Amundson. 1989. *Is there still a role for the small rural hospital?* Rural health working paper series, 1:1. Seattle: WAMI Rural Health Research Center, University of Washington School of Medicine.

Hart, L. Gary, Michael Pirani, and Roger Rosenblatt. 1991. Causes and consequences of rural small hospital closures from the perspective of mayors. *The Journal of Rural Health* 7:3 (Summer): 222–45.

Hassinger, Edward W. 1982. *Rural health organizations: social networks and regionalization*. Ames: Iowa State University Press.

Head, Rex E., and Dona L. Harris. 1989. Characteristics of medical school applicants: implications for rural health care. *Family Medicine* 21:3 (May/June): 187–90.

Helmer, F. Theodore, and Patricia McKnight. 1989. Management strategies to minimize nursing turnover. *Health Care Management Review* 14:1 (Winter): 73–80.

Hersh, Alice S., and Robert T. Van Hook. 1989. A research agenda for rural health services. *Health Services Research* 23:6 (February): 1053–64.

Hewitt, Maria. 1989. *Defining "rural" areas: impact on health care policy and research*. Staff paper for Office of Technology Assessment's Rural Health Care study. Washington, D.C.: U.S. Government Printing Office.

Illinois Farm Bureau. 1989. Health care in rural Illinois. In-house report. Bloomington, Ill.: Illinois Farm Bureau, Research and Planning Department.

Illinois Hospital Association. 1988. *Nursing and allied health personnel in Illinois hospitals*. Naperville, Ill.: Illinois Hospital Association.

———. 1989. Small, rural and public hospitals public relations survey. Internal document. Naperville, Ill.: Illinois Hospital Association.

———. 1990. *Small, rural and public hospitals in Illinois, trends 1983–1988*. Naperville, Ill.: Illinois Hospital Association.

———. 1991. Internal briefing paper. Naperville, Ill.: Illinois Hospital Association.

Illinois Institute for Rural Affairs. 1991. Phone survey of state offices providing health care in rural areas (April—June), Macomb, Ill.

Ingersoll, Bruce. 1989. Farming is dangerous, but fatalistic farmers oppose safety laws. *Wall Street Journal,* July 20, p. 1.

Johnson, Lyndon B. 1966. *Message to Congress*. Accompanying the National Traffic and Motor Vehicle Safety Act of 1966 and Highway Safety Act of 1966.

Johnson, Tom. 1989. The three legged stool. Paper presented to the Midwest Great Plains Council of Deans, Omaha, Neb., September 25.

Joint Rural Task Force, of the National Association of Community Health Centers and the National Rural Health Association. 1989. Health care in rural America: the crisis unfolds. *Journal of Public Health Policy* 10:1: 99–116.

Kaiman, Sherry. 1990. 101st Congress rural legislation wrap-up. *Rural Health Care* 12:5 (September/October): 6–7.

———. 1991. 101st Congress improves rural health funding. *Rural Health Care* 13:1 (January): 8–9.

Kennedy, Tom. 1989. Texas in backwoods on Medicaid. *Houston Post,* April 3.

Kindig, David A. 1989. Geographic distribution of physicians: status, policy options, and research issues. Unpublished policy paper prepared for the American Council on Graduate Medical Education, Rockville, Md.

Kindig, David A., and Hormoz Movassaghi. 1989. The adequacy of physician supply in small rural counties. *Health Affairs* 8:2 (Summer): 63–76.

Klebe, Edward R. 1990. *Appropriations for selected health programs FY1980–FY1990*. Washington, D.C.: Congressional Research Service.

Kleinholz, S. B., and G. A. Doeksen. 1991. State legislation for funding of rural emergency medical services. Paper prepared for the Southern Rural Development Center Health Task Force by the Agricultural Extension Service, Oklahoma State University, October 1991.

Kleinman, Joel, and Ronald Wilson. 1977. Are "medically underserved areas" medically underserved. *Health Services Research* 12:2 (Summer): 147–62.

Korczyk, Sophie M. 1989. Health care needs, resources, and access in rural America. A report to the National Rural Electric Cooperative Association and Prudential Insurance Company of America.

Kovner, Anthony R., Denise M. Runde, and Joan M. Kiel. 1990. State health policy and rural hospitals. Unpublished manuscript. New York: National Program Office.

Kraenzel, Carl F. 1953. Sutland and Yonland setting for community organization of the plains. *Rural Sociology* 18:4 (December): 344–58.

Kuhn, Thomas. 1970. *The structure of scientific revolutions,* 2d ed., Chicago: University of Chicago Press.

Landers, Susan. 1991. Financing methods for rural health care. *NATaT Reporter* 108 (January/February): 5–9.

Langwell, Kathryn, Shelly Nelson, Daniel Calvin, and John Drabek. 1985. Characteristics of rural communities and the changing geographic distribution of physicians. *The Journal of Rural Health* 1:2 (July): 42–55.

Lape, Douglas, and Christy Harris. 1989. Keeping rural facilities alive and well. *Health Progress* 70 (Special Section) (April): 44–45.

Legislation focuses on nation's regional trauma care systems. 1991. *ACEP News* 10:1 (January): 11.

Lewis, Irving J., and Cecil G. Sheps. 1983. *The sick citadel: the American academic medical center and the public interest.* Boston: Oelgeschlager Gunn & Hain Publishers, Inc.

Lichty, Richard, Wayne Jesswein, and David McMillan. 1986. Estimating medical industry impacts on a regional economy. *Medical Care* 24:4 (April): 350–62.

Locatis, Craig. 1990. Education and the national library of medicine. *Learning Resources Quarterly,* Spring/Summer: 6–7.

Luft, Harold S., John P. Bunker, and Alain C. Entoven. 1979. Should operations be regionalized? The empirical relation between surgical volume and mortality. *The New England Journal of Medicine* 301:25 (December 20): 1364–69.

Luloff, A. E. 1990. Small town demographics: current patterns of community change. In *American rural communities,* edited by A. E. Luloff and Louis E. Swanson, pp. 7–18. Boulder, Colo.: Westview Press.

MacStravic, Scott. 1989. Market administration in health care delivery. *Health Care Management Review* 14:2 (Winter): 41–48.

Mahar, Maggie. 1990. What's the good news? State taxes are on the rise across the nation. *Barron's,* August 6: 8–23.

May, Joel. 1978. Factors influencing "demand" for health care. *National commission on the cost of medical care,* pp. 117–22. Chicago: American Medical Association.

Mazie, Sara Mills. 1990. Preliminary 1990 census counts confirm drop in nonmetro population growth. *Rural Conditions and Trends* 1:4 (Winter 1990/91): 10–11.

McDermott, Richard E., Gary C. Cornia, and Robert J. Parsons. 1991. The economic impact of hospitals in rural communities. *The Journal of Rural Health* 7:2 (Spring): 117–33.

Mick, Stephen S., and Laura L. Morlock. 1990. America's rural hospitals: a selective review of 1980s research. *The Journal of Rural Health* 6:4 (October): 437–66.

Moscovice, Ira. 1988. The future of rural hospitals. In *Financing rural health care*, edited by LaVonne Straub and Norman Walzer, pp. 65–82. New York: Praeger.

———. 1989a. Rural hospitals: a literature synthesis and health services research agenda. *Health Services Research* 23:6 (February): 891–930.

———. 1989b. Strategies for promoting viable rural health care systems. *The Journal of Rural Health* 5:3 (July): 216–30.

Moscovice, Ira, Jon Christianson, and Judy Johnson. 1988. Evaluation of the Robert Wood Johnson Foundation Hospital-Based Rural Health Care Program: Phase II. St. Paul, Minn.: University of Minnesota, School of Public Health.

Moscovice, Ira, and Roger A. Rosenblatt. 1985a. A prognosis for the rural hospital; Part I: What is the role of the rural hospital. *The Journal of Rural Health* 1:1 (January): 29–40.

———. 1985b. A prognosis for the rural hospital; Part II: Are rural hospitals economically viable? *The Journal of Rural Health* 1:2 (July): 11–33.

Mulhausen, Robert, and Jeanne McGee. 1989. Physician need: an alternative projection from a study of large, prepaid group practices. *Journal of the American Medical Association* 261 (April 7): 1930–34.

National Academy of Sciences. 1966. *Accidental death and disability: the neglected disease of modern society.* 1966. Washington, D.C.: NAS, National Research Council (September).

National Advisory Commission on Rural Poverty. 1967. *The people left behind.* Washington, D.C.: U.S. Government Printing Office.

National Coalition for Agricultural Safety and Health. 1989. *Agriculture at risk: a report to the nation.* Iowa City: Institute of Agricultural Medicine and Occupational Health, University of Iowa.

National Health Planning and Resource Development Act of 1974, P.L. 93–641, January 4, 1975, 88 Stat. 2225.

National Highway Traffic Safety Adminstration. 1990. *Emergency medical services—1990 and beyond.* DOT HS 807–839. Washington, D.C.: National Highway Traffic Safety Administration.

Newhouse, Joseph P., Albert P. Williams, Bruce W. Bennett, and William B. Schwartz. 1982a. *How have location patterns of physicians affected the availability of medical services?* Santa Monica, Calif.: RAND.

Newhouse, Joseph P., Albert P. Williams, William B. Schwartz, and Bruce W. Bennett. 1982b. *The geographic distribution of physicians: is the conventional wisdom correct?* Santa Monica, Calif.: RAND.

Nornhold, Patricia. 1990. 90 predictions for the '90s. *Nursing 90* 20:1 (January): 35–41.

Norton, Catherine H., and Margaret A. McManus. 1989. Background tables on demographic characteristics, health status, and health services utilization. *Health Services Research* 23:6 (February): 725–56.

Nowlan, Janis. 1990. *A process framework relating to changes in rural healthcare delivery.* Denver: The Colorado Trust.

Omnibus Budget Reconciliation Act of 1981, P.L. 97–35, August 13, 1981, 95 Stat. 172.

Omnibus Budget Reconciliation Act of 1986, P.L. 99–509, October 21, 1986, 100 Stat. 1874.

Omnibus Budget Reconciliation Act of 1989, P.L. 101–239, December 19, 1989, 103 Stat. 2106.

Omnibus Budget Reconciliation Act of 1990, P.L. 101–508, November 5, 1990, 104 Stat. 1388.

Ostendorf, Virginia. 1991. *At a distance.* Book 2. Littleton, Colo.: Privately printed.

Owen, J. K. 1971. The effect of ordinances on emergency ambulance service. *Bulletin of the American College of Surgeons* 56:2 (February): 7.

Padfield, Harland. 1980. The expendable rural community and the denial of powerlessness. In *The dying community*, edited by Art Gallaher, Jr., and Harland Padfield, pp. 159–85. Albuquerque: University of New Mexico Press.

Palm, Dave, and LaVonne A. Booton. 1984. An analysis of access to and utilization of primary care services in rural Nebraska. Paper presented to the Mid-Continent Regional Science Association, Chicago, May.

Parker, Albert W. 1974. The dimensions of primary care: blueprint for change. In *Primary care: where medicine fails*, edited by Andreopoulos Seyros, pp. 15–76. New York: John Wiley & Sons.

Parker, Edwin B., Heather E. Hudson, Don A. Dillman, and Andrew D. Roscoe. 1989. *Rural America in the information age: telecommunications policy for rural development.* Lanham, Md.: The Aspen Institute, University Press of America.

Parker, Lorne A. 1990. The revolution is here. *Tel-Cons* 3:6 (December).

Pascal, Anthony, Marilyn Cvitanic, Charles Bennett, Michael Gorman, and Carol Serrato. 1989. State policies and the financing of acquired immunodeficiency syndrome care. *Health Care Financing Review* 11:1 (Fall): 91–104.

Patton, Larry. 1988. *The rural health care challenge.* Staff report to the U.S. Senate, Special Committee on Aging. 100th Cong., 2d sess. Washington, D.C.: U.S. Government Printing Office

———. 1991. Unpublished review of legislation and Health Care Financing Administration fact sheets. Washington, D.C.

Patton, Larry, and Dena Puskin. 1990. Ensuring access to health care services in rural America: a half century of federal policy. In *Alternative models for delivering essential health care services in rural areas*, Appendix C. Rockville, Md.: U.S. Department of Health and Human Services.

Petersdorf, Robert. 1975. Issues in primary care: the academic perspective. *Journal of Medical Education* 50:12 (December): 5–13.

———. 1989. Remodeling the house of academe. *Journal of the American Medical Association* 262:6 (August 11): 826.

Phillips, Stephen, and J. Luehrs. 1989. *Rural hospitals in evolution: state policy issues and initiatives.* Washington, D.C.: National Governors' Association.

Princeton, J., and B. McGrath. 1989. Decentralized nursing education: does it work? *The Journal of Continuing Education in Nursing* 20:2 (March/April): 54–57.

Quittel, Frances. 1988. Healthcare joint venture requires mammoth resources. *Communications* 9:3 (March): 22–24.

Ramzy, A. 1990. Maryland's EMS system. *Emergency Care Quarterly* 6:1 (May): 65–71.

Reczynski, Deborah F. 1987. *Environmental assessment for rural hospitals 1988.* Chicago: American Hospital Association.

Reczynski, Deborah F., and Belva Denmark. 1988. *Profile of small or rural hospitals 1980–1986.* Chicago: American Hospital Association.

Reimer, Marlene, and Claire Mills. 1988. Rural hospital nursing as an elective. *The Journal of Rural Health* 4:2 (July): 5–12.

Rezler, Agnes G., and Summers G. Kalishman. 1989. Who goes into family medicine? *Journal of Family Practice* 29:6 (June): 652–56.

Roback, Gene, Lillian Randolph, Bradley Seidman, and Diane Mead. 1987. *Physician characteristics and distribution in the United States.* Chicago: American Medical Association.

Roberts, S. 1983. Oppressed group behavior: implications for nursing. *Advances in Nursing Science* 5 (July): 21–30.

Robert Wood Johnson Foundation. 1977. *Special report on emergency medical services systems.* Princeton, N.J.: Robert Wood Johnson Foundation.

———. 1987. *Access to health care in the United States: results of a 1986 survey.* Princeton, N.J.: Robert Wood Johnson Foundation.

———. 1988. *The Robert Wood Johnson Hospital-Based Rural Health Care Program management information reports.* Princeton, N.J.: Robert Wood Johnson Foundation.

———. 1989. *The Robert Wood Johnson Hospital-Based Rural Health Care Program management information reports.* Princeton, N.J.: Robert Wood Johnson Foundation.

———. 1990. *The Robert Wood Johnson Hospital-Based Rural Health Care Program management information reports.* Princeton, N.J.: Robert Wood Johnson Foundation.

Rosenberg, Steven. 1989. The changing rural health care delivery system: development of alternative models. Contract report prepared for the National Rural Health Association, Kansas City, Mo., September.

Rosenberg, Steven, and George McNeely. 1989. California alternative rural hospital model. Unpublished final report to the Office of Statewide Health Planning and Development of the State of California, December.

Rosenberg, Steven, and D. Runde. 1988. Restructuring rural hospitals. In *New alliances for rural America.* Washington, D.C.: National Governors' Association, August.

Rosenblatt, Roger, and Ira Moscovice. 1982. *Rural health care.* New York: John Wiley & Sons.

Rowe, Mona J., and Caitlin C. Ryan. 1988. Comparing state-only expenditures for AIDS. *American Journal of Public Health* 78:4 (April): 424–29.

Rowland, Diane, and Barbara Lyons. 1989. Triple jeopardy: rural, poor, and uninsured. *Health Services Research* 23:6 (February): 975–1004.

Rural Health Care. 1986. Newsletter of the National Rural Health Association, Kansas City, Mo., 8:5 (September/October).

Rural Health News. 1991. Newsletter of the Federal Office of Rural Health Policy, Washington, D.C., July.

Rustout Project Report. 1989. *Oregon EMS update*. Portland: Oregon Health Division, Emergency Medical Services Section.

St. Clair, Claire, Myrna R. Pickard, and Karen S. Harlow. 1986. Continuing education for self-actualization: building a plan for rural nurses. *The Journal of Continuing Education in Nursing* 17:1 (January/February): 27–31.

Schroeder, Steven A., Jane S. Zones, and Jonathan A. Showstack. 1989. Academic medicine as a public trust. *Journal of the American Medical Association* 262:6: 803–12.

Schwartz, William, Joseph Newhouse, Bruce Bennett, and Albert Williams. 1980. The changing geographic distribution of board-certified physicians. *New England Journal of Medicine* 303:18 (October): 1032–38.

Sharpe, H. 1987. *Florida's rural hospitals: the prognosis is not good*. Tallahassee, Fla.: Office of Comprehensive Health Planning, Florida Department of Health and Rehabilitative Services.

Sheps, Cecil G., and Miliam Bachar. 1981. Rural areas and personal health services: current strategies. *American Journal of Public Health* 71 (January) (Supplement): 71–82.

6 Colorado Code Regulations § 1011–1, 1991.

Size, Tim. 1990. Cooperative rural health care: encouraging private and public interorganizational relationships. Unpublished manuscript.

Social Security Act, amendment, P.L. 95–210, December 13, 1977, 91 Stat. 1485.

Sokolow, Alvin D. 1982. Small town government: the conflict of administrative styles. *National Civic Review* 71:9 (October): 445–52.

Staab, E. V., J. R. Perry, B. C. Brenton, B. G. Thompson, D. M. Parrish, J. L. Creasy, and B. C. Yankaskas. 1985. Image communications—what is needed and why? *Applied Radiology* 14:3 (May/June): 19–29.

Stein, Leonard, David Watts, and Timothy Howell. 1990. The doctor-nurse game revisited. *New England Journal of Medicine* 322:8 (February 22): 546–49.

Stilwell, Barbara. 1987. Different expectations. *Nursing Times* 83:24 (June 17): 59–61.

Straub, LaVonne, and Lois Frels. 1990. Nursing supply in rural practice. Paper presented to the National Rural Health Association; New Orleans, May.

Straub, LaVonne, and Norman Walzer. 1990. Determinants of consumer mobility in seeking health care. Paper presented at the Southern Economic Association meeting, New Orleans, November.

Szafrom, Alexander J., and Roger Kropf. 1988. Strategic uses of teleradiology. *Radiology Management* 10:2 (Spring): 23–27.

Touger, Gale, and Jimmie Butts. 1989. The workplace: an innovative and cost-effective practice site. *Nurse Practitioner* 14:2 (January): 35–52.

Trauma Care Systems Planning and Development Act of 1990, P.L. 101–590, November 16, 1990, 104 Stat. 2915.

University of Nebraska Medical Center. 1991. UNMC rural health education network. Omaha: University of Nebraska Medical Center, Center for Rural Health Research.

U.S. Bureau of the Census. 1982. *Governmental finances in 1981–82*, Series GF–82–5. Washington, D.C.: U.S. Government Printing Office.

―――. 1983a. *County and city data book, 1983*. Washington, D.C.: U.S. Government Printing Office.

―――. 1983b. *Government organization*. Vol. 1, No. 1: Government organization. GC82:1. Washington, D.C.: U.S. Government Printing Office.

―――. 1986. *Money income and poverty status of families and persons in the United States, 1985*. Current Population Reports, Series P–60. Washington, D.C.: U.S. Government Printing Office.

―――. 1987. *Governmental finances in 1986–87*, Series GF–87–5. Washington, D.C.: U.S. Government Printing Office.

―――. 1988a. *Government organization*. Vol. 1, No. 1: Government organization. GC87(1)–1. Washington, D.C.: U.S. Government Printing Office.

―――. 1988b. *County and city data book, 1988*. Washington, D.C.: U.S. Government Printing Office.

―――. 1989a. *Statistical abstract of the United States 1989*, 109th ed. Washington, D.C.: U.S. Government Printing Office.

―――. 1989b. Current population reports. *Poverty in the United States 1987*. Washington, D.C.: U.S. Government Printing Office.

U.S. Congress. House. 1989. Rural Health Care Coalition of the U.S. House of Representatives. *1989 Legislative Agenda: A Summary*. Unpublished legislative summary. Washington, D.C.: Rural Health Care Coalition of the U.S. House of Representatives.

U.S. Congress. Office of Technology Assessment. 1986a. *Technology, public policy, and the changing structure of American agriculture*. Vol. 2, Background Papers. OTA-F–285. Washington, D.C.: Congress of the U.S., Office of Technology Assessment.

―――. 1986b. *Nurse practitioners, physician assistants, and certified nurse-midwives: a policy analysis*. OTA-HCS–37. Washington, D.C.: Congress of the U.S., Office of Technology Assessment.

―――. 1990. *Health care in rural America*, OTA-H–434. Washington, D.C.: U.S. Government Printing Office.

―――. 1991. *Rural America at the crossroads: networking for the future: summary*. OTA-TCT–472. Washington, D.C.: U.S. Government Printing Office.

U.S. Congress. Senate. Joint Economic Committee. Subcommittee on Education and Health. 1988. *The future of health care in America*. 100th Cong., 2d sess. Washington, D.C.: U.S. Government Printing Office.

U.S. Department of Agriculture. 1984. *Chartbook of nonmetro–metro trends*. Rural Development Research Report, No. 43. Washington, D.C.: U.S. Government Printing Office.

U.S. Department of Commerce. 1982. *Survey of Governments. Annual Finance Statistics* (computer tapes). Washington, D.C.: U.S. Government Printing Office.

―――. 1987. *Survey of Governments. Annual Finance Statistics* (computer tapes). Washington, D.C.: U.S. Government Printing Office.

U.S. Department of Health and Human Services. 1981. Health Resources Administration, Office of Graduate Medical Education. *Report of the Graduate Medical Education National Advisory Committee to the secretary, Depart-*

ment of Health and Human Services. Vol. I: *Summary report*. DHHS Publication; No. (HRA) 81–651. Washington, D.C.: U.S. Government Printing Office.

———. 1987. Centers for Disease Control, National Center for Health Statistics. *Vital and health statistics*, Series 10, No. 162. Washington, D.C.: U.S. Government Printing Office.

———. 1988. Health Resources and Services Administration, Bureau of Health Professions. *Sixth report to the president and Congress on the status of health personnel in the United States*. DHHS Publication No. (HRS) P-OD–88–1. Rockville, Md.: Department of Health and Human Services.

———. 1989. Centers for Disease Control, National Center for Health Statistics. *Current estimates from the national health interview survey, 1988*, Series 10, No. 173. Hyattsville, Md.: National Center for Health Statistics.

———. 1990a. Centers for Disease Control, National Center for Health Statistics. *Health United States, 1989*. Washington, D.C.: U.S. Government Printing Office.

———. 1990b. Health Resources and Services Administration, Office of Rural Health Policy. *Success and failure: a study of rural emergency medical services*. Prepared by the National Rural Health Association.

U.S. General Accounting Office. Report to Congressional Requesters. 1986. *Health care: States assume leadership role in providing emergency medical care*. Washington, D.C.: U.S. General Accounting Office.

———. Report to Congressional requesters. 1991. *Rural hospitals: federal efforts should target areas where closures would threaten access to care*. B–239983. Washington, D.C.: U.S. General Accounting Office.

U.S. National Library of Medicine. 1990. *National library of medicine programs and services*. Bethesda, Md.: U.S. National Library of Medicine.

U.S. Small Business Administration. 1987. *The state of small business: a report of the president*. Washington, D.C.: U.S. Government Printing Office.

Vada, J. 1986. Interactive videodisc for management training in a classroom environment. *The Videodisc Monitor* 4 (October): 16.

Van Hook, Robert. 1989. In *The changing rural health care delivery system: development of alternative models*, edited by Steven Rosenberg. Kansas City, Mo.: National Rural Health Association.

Verby, John E. 1988. The Minnesota rural physician associate program for medical students. *Journal of Medical Education* 63:6 (June): 427–37.

Vidich, Arthur J., and Joseph Bensman. 1968. *Small town in mass society*. Princeton, N.J.: Princeton University Press.

Wakefield, Mary K. 1990. Health care in rural America: a view from the nation's capital. *Nursing Economics* 8:2 (March/April): 83–89.

Warren, Roland. 1978. *The community in America*, 3d ed. Chicago: Rand McNally.

Wellover, A. 1989. A general introduction to medical assistance facilities. Unpublished report. Montana Hospital Research and Education Foundation.

Wiener, Janet Ochs. 1990. Rural help on the way. *Medicine and Health*, October 29, Supplement, Perspectives.

Wilkinson, Kenneth P. 1986. Communities left behind—again. In *New dimensions in rural policy: building upon our heritage*, pp. 341–46. Washington, D.C.: U.S. Government Printing Office.

Williams, Albert P., William B. Schwartz, Joseph P. Newhouse, and Bruce W. Bennett. 1983. How many miles to the doctor? *New England Journal of Medicine* 309:16 (October): 958–63.

Winkenwerder, William, and John R. Ball. 1988. Transformation of American health care: the role of the medical profession. *New England Journal of Medicine* 318:5 (February): 317–19.

Wolfe, Harvey. 1988. *Rural emergency medical services system project study*. In Vol. 1, DOT HS 807–406. Springfield, Va.: National Highway Traffic Safety Administration.

Zuiches, James J. 1982. Residential preferences. In *Rural society in the U.S.: issues for the 1980s*, edited by Don A. Dillman and Daryl Hobbs, pp. 247–55. Boulder, Colo.: Westview Press.

Index

About the Contributors

ROBERT T. VAN HOOK has served, since 1983, as executive director of the National Rural Health Association, a nonprofit health association playing a major role in rural health advocacy. He has been involved in the rural health-care field for more than 17 years at the local, state, and national levels. Mr. Van Hook served as division director of primary care for the West Virginia Department of Health; prior to that he developed and managed a rural medical center in North Carolina. He has taught health administration courses and was project director of a prepaid health project.

LAVONNE A. STRAUB is professor of economics at Western Illinois University. She has consulted on health-care projects for both public and private agencies and is a member of a state rural health task force. Straub's research areas include rural health and nurse market issues; her work appears in *The Journal of Rural Health, Journal of Health Politics, Policy, and Law, Nursing Economic$,* and the *Journal of Human Resources*. With N. Walzer, she is editor of *Financing Rural Health*, published by Praeger in 1988.

NORMAN WALZER is director of the Illinois Institute for Rural Affairs. He was chair of the Economics Department at Western Illinois University from 1980 to 1989. He has authored and edited 7 books on local public finance and economic development and has contributed nearly 200 reports and articles to *Review of Economics and Statistics, Industrial and Labor Relations Review, National Tax Journal, Land Economics, Public Finances,* and *Public Choice*. Walzer consults with state and local governments on local public policy issues. He was an adviser to the Governor's Task Force on the Future of Illinois and the Governor's Task Force on Rural Health.

LANIS L. HICKS is an associate professor with Health Services Management, School of Medicine, at the University of Missouri–Columbia. Hicks also holds an appointment as senior fellow faculty with the National Center for Managed Health Care at the University of Missouri. Her research interests are in rural health-care delivery issues and policies, with special emphasis on physician distribution in rural areas. Her work has appeared in the *American Journal of Public Health*, *The Journal of Rural Health*, *Nursing Economic$*, *Health and Human Resources Administration*, and *The Journal of Health Care Marketing*.

RON DAMASAUSKAS is vice-president, Professional Affairs and Constituencies of the Illinois Hospital Association, and was previously director of Small, Rural, and Public Hospitals and director of marketing for the association. Prior to joining IHA, Mr. Damasauskas spent over 7 years at the American Hospital Association, where he was responsible for publication of AHA's *Guide to the Health Care Field* and *Hospital Statistics*, which are standards for national health-care data.

GEORGE H. MCNEELY is a free-lance consultant specializing in health care. He has worked for Rosenberg Associates, San Francisco, as project director for the California Alternative Rural Hospital Model. His involvement included researching existing rural hospital services and patient statistics, development of alternative models and creation of financial models to test the impact of alternatives on demonstration sites. He has authored several reports and provides technical assistance to rural health-care providers regarding restructuring of hospital and primary-care delivery systems and financial analysis of implementation of the Rural Health Clinics Act.

JEFFREY C. BAUER is head of the Bauer Group, a nationally recognized organization working in rural health care. He is a former professor of health administration at the University of Colorado Health Sciences Center, was executive director of the Institute for Health, and held a full-time faculty appointment in the Schools of Medicine and Dentistry. Bauer has served as a member of the Governor's Science and Technology Advisory Council, and has published numerous journal articles and three books on health-care delivery.

KEVIN M. FICKENSCHER is assistant dean and president of the Kalamazoo Center for Medical Studies, Michigan State University. Fickenscher's experiences include director of the Center for Rural Health Services Policy and Research, University of North Dakota, president of the National Rural Health Association, and active participant at the national level on issues regarding rural health policy.

EILEEN M. WEIS is responsible for rural marketing projects for the Bauer Group. She was an intensive care nurse and has hospital experience in patient education and community relations. Her specialties include assisting communities in attracting and retaining nursing personnel and adapting to hospital closure or conversion.

DONALD L. CORDES is deputy director of the Washington Continuing Education Center for the Department of Veterans Affairs, which is responsible for the design, development, and implementation of national scope training for the Veterans Health Services and Research Administration. His responsibilities include strategic and operational planning and management for the center, as well as involvement in national projects, including oversight for the development and implementation of the VA teleconferencing system. Cordes has held academic positions at the Medical College of Virginia, University of Missouri School of Medicine, and University of Nebraska School of Medicine.

RICHARD L. THORP is presidentof Multi-Media Productions, Rockville, Maryland. Prior to that he was with the Audiology and Speech Pathology Service of the Veterans Affairs Central Office. His specialties include medical informatics systems design, expert systems design, video systems design and analysis, and interactive instructional design. Thorp collaborated on a 1981 textbook, *Scripting for Video and Audio-visual Media*, and is working on a computer-assisted instruction and interactive-video textbook.

PAUL B. ANDERSON is chief of the Idaho Emergency Medical Service System. He has been actively involved in EMS since 1957 and has been instrumental in developing innovative approaches to rural EMS training. He uses a range of technology in training EMS personnel and developing communication linkages. Anderson has written numerous articles related to his work.

ANTHONY R. KOVNER is professor in health policy and management, School of Public Administration at New York University. He is senior program consultant to the Robert Wood Johnson Foundation and directs the foundation's Hospital-Based Program to improve rural health care. He is studying state policy and rural hospitals for the foundation. Kovner is a member of the board of trustees of Lutheran Medical Center in Brooklyn; prior to that he had hospital administrative experience and is the author of *Really Trying: A Career Guide for Health Services Managers* and *Really Managing: The Work of Effective CEOs in Large Health Organizations.*

JOAN M. KIEL is a research consultant with the Mercy Lite Center Corporation in Pittsburgh and professor of business at Robert Morris College, Coraopolis, Pennsylvania. She was a hospital administrator in New York City and research assistant on national demonstration projects funded by the Robert Wood Johnson and W. K. Kellogg foundations. Kiel has published and lectured on rural health policy issues and personnel management.

LARRY T. PATTON is a veteran of Capitol Hill, having worked for 13 years as a legislative assistant for health issues for now retired Sen. William Proxmire (Dem., Wis.). His work includes a study, *The Rural Homeless,* for the Institute of Medicine, *The Rural Health Care Challenge* for the Senate Special Agenda Conference, and *Setting the Rural Health Services Research Agenda: The Congressional Perspective.*

EDWARD W. HASSINGER is professor of rural sociology, University of Missouri–Columbia. His research emphasis is the rural community, rural health, and rural institutions; his published works include *Rural Health Services: Organization, Delivery, and Use* (ed.), and *Rural Health Organization: Social Networks and Regionalization.*

DARYL J. HOBBS is professor of rural sociology and director of the Office of Social and Economic Data Analysis at the University of Missouri–Columbia. He is past president of the Rural Sociological Society; his research emphasis is rural health, rural education, and community development.